# Living at the Water's Edge

## A Heritage Guide to the Outer Banks Byway

*by*

BARBARA GARRITY-BLAKE

*and*

KAREN WILLIS AMSPACHER

THE UNIVERSITY OF NORTH CAROLINA PRESS

*Chapel Hill*

*This book was published with the assistance of the*
*Anniversary Fund of the University of North Carolina Press.*

A SOUTHERN GATEWAYS GUIDE

Designed by Jamison Cockerham
Set in Arno, by Robert Slimbach, and Scala, by Martin Majoor
by Tseng Information Systems, Inc.

Cover photo by Daniel Pullen
Photos on pp. ii–iii, xxiii, xxviii–xxix, and 116–17 by Baxter Miller
Maps created by Breanne Bye

*Manufactured in the United States of America*

The University of North Carolina Press has been a member
of the Green Press Initiative since 2003.

LIBRARY OF CONGRESS CATALOGING-IN-PUBLICATION DATA
Names: Garrity-Blake, Barbara J., 1960– author. | Amspacher, Karen Willis, author.
Title: Living at the water's edge : a heritage guide to the Outer Banks Byway / by Barbara
Garrity-Blake and Karen Willis Amspacher.
Other titles: Heritage guide to the Outer Banks Byway | Southern gateways guide.
Description: Chapel Hill : University of North Carolina Press, [2017] | Series: A southern
gateways guide | Includes index.
Identifiers: LCCN 2016046166| ISBN 9781469628165 (pbk : alk. paper) |
ISBN 9781469628172 (ebook)
Subjects: LCSH: Outer Banks National Scenic Byway (N.C.)—Description and travel. |
Outer Banks (N.C.)—Description and travel. | Outer Banks (N.C.)—History.
Classification: LCC F262.O96 G37 2017 | DDC 975.6/1—dc23
LC record available at https://lccn.loc.gov/2016046166

# Living at the Water's Edge

*I dedicate this book with love and gratitude to the elders of my clan,*

*Donald Garrity and Jean Blake.*

BGB


*My work here is dedicated to the women of these Banks —*
*for their courage and strength that flows generation to generation . . .*
*the tie that binds us to our grandmothers, mothers, and daughters,*
*and to this place — past and present.*
*In all this, I am most thankful for*
*Granny's determination and Mama's sacrifices,*
*and forever hopeful that Katie's deep roots will*
*keep our family tied to this place forever.*

KWA

# Contents

# Crossings

# 7 CROSSING NORTH RIVER: DOWN EAST 205

# Maps

# Sidebars

The edge of the sea is a strange and beautiful place.

*Rachel Carson*

# Welcome to the Water's Edge

The road at the water's edge, like the sounds it crosses and the ocean it parallels, is ever-changing. It runs along sandbanks and thickets of maritime forest, following the contours of the estuaries that bring the region life. A humble two-lane highway provides a way for people to move from place to place within one of the most dynamic environments in America: thin barrier islands of sand known as the Outer Banks of North Carolina, constantly sculpted by the ocean on one side and the sound on the other. Sometimes the road along the way is covered in a veil of sand that swirls and dances in the wake of moving cars. Other times, the pavement glistens like a dark river beneath a slick of rain and tide. After a storm, the road may be cracked and broken, chunks of asphalt scattered on the beach like pieces of shipwreck from long ago.

The road, patched in places and rebuilt again and again, is a lifeline for people living on the edge. Coastal folks know well that the wind and tide can rearrange the landscape, and their lives, overnight. Some people have deep roots in the shifting sand, determined to hold their ground like their ancestors before them, no matter what the risk. Others, new to the coast, may seek paradise but find unexpected challenges, and must quickly learn to adapt. All are dependent on the road that meanders through a world of sand and water, connecting them to the mainland and to one another.

The road is the Outer Banks National Scenic Byway, traversing Hatteras Island, Ocracoke Island, and Down East, linked by two ferry routes and a dozen or so bridges. The byway stitches together twenty-one communities tucked between broad expanses of wild seashore and marshland. It provides access to the pristine beaches and sound-side creeks of Cape Hatteras National Seashore and gets within reach of the barrier islands with *no* roads: Cape Lookout National Seashore, accessible only by boat. The road links the past and the present, the quick-changing and the timeless, and whole communities of people who roll with the elements while maintaining ties to their maritime heritage and sacred places on the banks.

### OUR INVITATION

Much has been written on the natural and social history of the Outer Banks. In this book, we explore the intersection of maritime history, geography, and village life along the banks and sounds, inspired by historian David Stick's 1958 classic *The Outer Banks of North Carolina*. Son of visionary Frank Stick, who was instrumental in the creation of Cape Hatteras National Seashore Park, David Stick laid the groundwork for Outer Banks scholarship with his landmark work that continues to inspire today. Stick did not confine his research to written records but traveled the coast to gather memories and insights directly from the men and women whose ancestors settled the villages. Now, some six decades later, we revisit the twenty-one communities of Down East, Ocracoke, and Hatteras, perhaps tracing some of David Stick's footprints, with a renewed appreciation for his foundational work.

"Do people actually live here?" is a question that has been asked throughout the years by visitors to the Outer Banks. We offer this heritage guide to answer a resounding "yes!" to that question. We strive to convey how folks not only survived but flourished, in a remarkably dynamic place.

Our guide through the villages is not so much a list of places to stop as a collection of voices and stories to deepen your understanding of the people and places along the way. We hope this book can serve as your "porch visit," as you hear from the men and women who have lived through the days of sailboats and sand paths, pony pennings and shipwrecks, land speculation and the creation of parkland. Stories are traded like currency in these parts. Stories about holding on and letting go, about things that last and things that don't. Tales of floating homes, sinking boats, fishing feats and defeats, salty tales told with dry wit and a deep understanding of life on the sandbanks.

The moral of the story is inevitably, "Mother Nature always wins."

By sharing some of these voices, we hope that you, the reader, can feel the energy and electricity of an oncoming storm or the joy of a Down East fisherman making the best haul of his life. We hope you can hear a newborn's cry in a banks village of long ago or catch a glimpse of villagers gathered at the landing in anticipation as the mailboat arrives. May you feel the thrill of teenagers surfing the waves of Cape Hatteras with their longboards or of an angler landing a picture-perfect striped bass.

As authors of this book, we share a love of and appreciation for the people of this region, but from different perspectives. Barbara Garrity-Blake is a cultural anthropologist who has researched fishing communities in the area for thirty years. Much of Barbara's work, particularly her oral history research conducted for the National Park Service, is evident in the guide. Barbara lives in the Down East community of Gloucester, where she and her husband, Bryan, organize the Gloucester Mardi Gras and the Wild Caught Local Seafood and Music Festival.

Karen Willis Amspacher was born and raised on Harkers Island, with roots in the whaling community of Diamond City on Shackleford Banks. She is a true community leader and serves as the founding director of the community-based Core Sound Waterfowl Museum and Heritage Center on Harkers Island. Karen's heart is in this book; her pride is in the history and culture of her people, along with the heartache of witnessing the changes taking place all around. She and her husband, Jimmy, a boatbuilder raised in an Atlantic fish house, live in her grandmother's house in Marshallberg, holding on to the "old ways" in honor of the men and women who taught them what life here means.

We write in celebration of the intangible yet deep connection people have to the water and to their abiding heritage, not easily understood by visitors riding along the sandy road at the water's edge. We weave the past with the present to show how the joys and trials of living on the edge are no less in modern times. The people along the coast continue to express an unbreakable spirit, turning their faces into the winds of change, feet firmly planted in marsh mud along the water's edge. Our hope is that we can guide your journey in a way that builds mutual respect between those who visit and those who live here, remembering those who came before, and mindful to protect this place for those who follow.

I didn't know bow from stern on a boat, much less what a bow line was, until I moved to coastal North Carolina. I quickly learned that "bow" was the front of a boat and "stern" was the back; "starboard" was the right side and "port" the left. When a captain barks the order to tie off the bow line or move to the starboard, one is wise to know which end is what.

The uninitiated "greenhorn" on a boat is almost always in the way. Coming aboard a fishing vessel with its swinging gear and moving parts is a crash course in how not to get injured or killed. Getting invited in the first place is a tremendous act of generosity on behalf of the captain.

I am from "off," as they say, and have had my share of being underfoot and in the way. But I have gradually become part of the community, blessed to have been invited aboard in the first place and gladly adding to the mix of people and personalities that hold small places together.

Unlike my coauthor, Karen Amspacher (you will hear from her at the "stern" of this book), I am not from this place but "adopted." I count myself lucky to bear witness to the ways of this region and to be within earshot of one compelling story after another. We are happy to share what we know, and what we've learned, with you. Let the journey begin!

# The Road

## THE OUTER BANKS NATIONAL SCENIC BYWAY

### SHARING THE HERITAGE OF PEOPLE AND PLACES

Amish Country. The Northwest Passage. Historic Route 66. Only 150 roads in the United States are designated as National Scenic Byways, a program created by Congress in 1991 to protect and preserve the country's most scenic, historically significant, and often less-traveled roads. The reason for the byway program, according to *The Journal for America's Byways*, is to identify "the best routes to the most interesting scenic, natural, recreational, historical, cultural and archaeological wonders . . . [that] adventurous people have always sought to discover."

North Carolina's Outer Banks National Scenic Byway is indeed an experience. The northern end of the byway, anchored in the sand-swept flats of Whalebone Junction, is gateway to the thinnest of barrier islands that arc thirty miles offshore into the Atlantic. Just offshore, the cold Labrador Current and the warm Gulf Stream clash and roil, helping generate conditions that led to the coast's nickname, Graveyard of the Atlantic. Westward of the sand banks, across the Pamlico Sound, is what writer Bland Simpson calls Sound Country, mainland communities like Elizabeth City, Engelhard, and "The Original" Washington, lifelines in the days of freight boats and maritime trade. Across Hatteras Inlet to the south lies Ocracoke, the centerpiece of this strand of community gems. The southern sweep of the byway bends westward toward the mainland, anchored in the pine hammocks and salt marshes of rural Down East Carteret County.

The entire length of the Outer Banks National Scenic Byway is only 138 driving miles. But it is a long, adventuresome 138 miles, broken up by ferry rides across two inlets and Pamlico Sound. The byway winds through mapped communities, such as Rodanthe, Ocracoke, and Cedar Island, as well as places not found on maps, like Down East, Kinnakeet, and Chicamacomico.

The byway bisects Cape Hatteras National Seashore, parallels Cape Lookout National Seashore, and traverses two National Wildlife Refuges: Pea Island and Cedar Island. The road takes travelers to the steps of three lighthouses: Bodie Island, Cape Hatteras, and Ocracoke. It gets visitors within sight of Cape Lookout across Core Sound, reachable by passenger ferries from the mainland. Along the way are numerous U.S. Lifesaving Service and Coast Guard Station sites, as well as churches, graveyards, and home-places that give a sense of the generations of islanders who have carved out a life here. The byway passes fish houses and markets where fresh North Carolina seafood is iced and sold, as well as numerous other businesses that help make today's coastal economy viable.

Older folks have witnessed everything from German U-boat attacks just offshore to talk of wind farms and sea level rise. Whole villages have been swept off parts of the banks by hurricanes, while others found new prosperity from a storm-cut inlet and easier access to fish. Creeks and harbors full of wooden workboats now share anchorage with sport boats for hire and private yachts. Ocean beaches, once the domain of free-range livestock and shipwreck salvagers, are now managed and zoned according to national park policy.

The Outer Banks National Scenic Byway is a journey across vast waters and a barrier island landscape relentlessly shaped by wind and tide. It's also a journey through time, as lived by people whose entire world has been shaped by life on a sandbar, on a marshy peninsula, at the water's edge. A different way of life is honored here, one of hard work, adaptation, and determination, qualities that have long defined, and continue to form, the character of banks communities at the water's edge.

## HOW TO USE THIS GUIDE

Our guide is divided into two main sections. The first part describes qualities that bind all the communities together, organized around the themes of water, land, people, and change. The second section of the book, organized around specific crossings to different parts of the byway, takes the reader

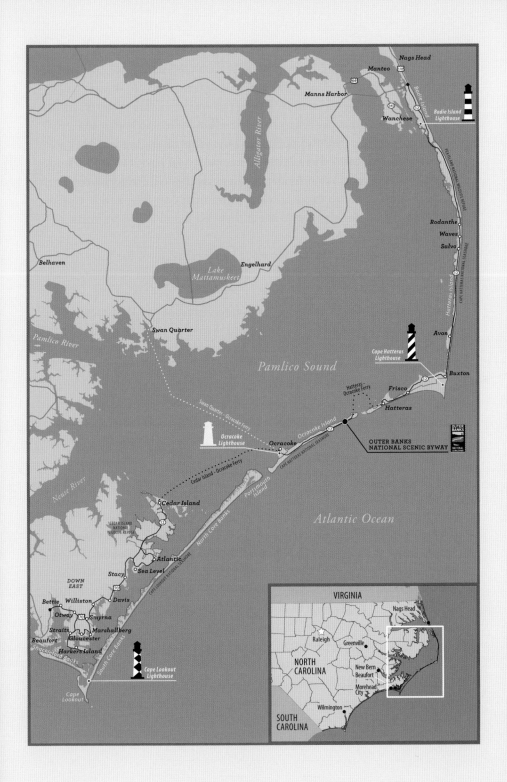

OUTER BANKS NATIONAL SCENIC BYWAY

on a visit to each of the twenty-one villages, each unique in its own right. Although volumes could be written about each community, we offer just a glimpse, hoping to encourage travelers to visit these folks for themselves.

The communities are humble places, but inhabitants are proud of where they live and who they are. Many have mixed emotions and honest concerns about tourism, but they also understand the value of sharing who they are and what they do with others. Fishermen in particular have learned the hard way that stereotypes and misunderstandings can translate into policies that cut into their ability to make a living. More than ever they have a vested interest in educating the public about their work and their role in the regional economy.

The Crossings section of this guide is organized from the gateways to the byway. The first sections, "Crossing Oregon Inlet" and "Crossing Hatteras Inlet," run north to south, from the northern gateway of Whalebone Junction down through Hatteras and over to Ocracoke and Portsmouth Villages. The Down East part, "Crossing North River," runs southwest to northeast, from the southern gateway east of Beaufort at North River through Down East to Cedar Island.

All roads, or ferries, we should say, lead to Ocracoke, a popular destination along the byway. Ocracoke is our guide's midway point, the banks crossroads, as travelers can reach it from the northern gateway, the southern gateway, or directly from the west through mainland Hyde County and the ferry terminal at Swan Quarter. From Ocracoke, adventurers can take a passenger ferry to Portsmouth Island to visit historic, uninhabited Portsmouth Village.

The journey from the northern gateway to Ocracoke follows Highway 12 South, a linear route that bisects all the villages, including the Hatteras Island communities of Rodanthe, Waves, Salvo, Avon, Buxton, Frisco, and Hatteras Village. The journey from the southern gateway to Ocracoke through Down East is less linear, as US 70 east of Beaufort bisects Bettie, Otway, Smyrna, Williston, Davis, Stacy, Sea Level, and Atlantic, and Highway 12 branches off at Stacy to Cedar Island and the ferry terminal to Ocracoke. A scenic loop off US 70 at Otway leads to Straits and Harkers Island, where adventurers can take a passenger ferry to Cape Lookout. Passenger ferries are also located in Davis and Atlantic for day trips or rustic camping on Core Banks. A scenic drive from Straits meanders through Gloucester and Marshallberg, rejoining US 70 at Smyrna. All routes are marked by Outer Banks National Scenic Byway wayfinding signs.

### TAKE YOUR TIME

As you travel the byway, we encourage you to linger not only on the sights you'll see but on the sounds you'll hear—the rumble and swish of ocean surf, the wind-tossed cries of gulls, the blast of the ferry horn that marks time for islanders and cuts through everything. Keep your ears tuned to local voices and dialects that bring to life the history and culture of the coast. The journey you will take is one linked as much through time and community as by road. You'll find some of the voices in the welcoming words at the start of each crossing, some woven into each chapter, and others in our sidebars throughout the book. So slow down as you travel, find a rocking chair, and enjoy the tales told along the byway.

This book differs from visitor's guides that provide information on local motels, restaurants, and beach attractions. Our belief is that "people make the place," and our mission in writing a heritage guide is to help you get to know the communities and people along the byway, past and present. The key to enjoying a trip along the Outer Banks National Scenic Byway is flexibility. As the families who have lived in this environment for generations have done, "going with the flow" and preparing for the unexpected will enhance the traveler's experience.

By vehicle, the total route from Whalebone Junction at the northern end of the Outer Banks Scenic Byway to Bettie at the southern end can be driven in as little as eight hours. The "quick tour," however, is contingent upon good luck, perfect weather, and careful time management to catch the desired ferry departures. Hurrying along sacrifices roadside stops and side lane explorations. To rush through the byway with its stretches of wild beach, winding roads, vast stretches of salt marsh, and interesting people is to miss the heart of the journey.

As coauthors of this book, we have traveled up and down the banks many times in all kinds of weather. We've barely caught ferries and missed ferries. We have traveled in the early morning light and the darkest, foggiest times imaginable. We have napped on the placid route across Pamlico Sound and held on as waves broke across the bow of the ferry, washing our cars in saltwater. We have taken chances and side roads and met wonderful people in unexpected places, such as the Ocracoker who pulled us out of an overflowing ditch on a dark night. Believe us when we say that sometimes the unplanned delay proves to be the best experience with the finest people to be found anywhere. Those who live here have seen it all and are prepared to help make your journey safe and memorable. Enjoy the road!

# Timeline of the Outer Banks

1524    *Italian explorer Verrazzano encounters indigenous inhabitants of coastal North Carolina*

1587    *John White's expedition lands on Roanoke Island; first English child born in America*

1590    *John White's last contact with colonists*

1663    *Beginning of land grants issued by lord proprietors*

1700    *English explorer John Lawson arrives*

1711    *The start of the Tuscarora Indian Wars*

1718    *The end of the age of piracy in North Carolina; death of Blackbeard at Ocracoke*

1726    *First permit granted to establish shore-based whaling operation off Cape Lookout*

1743    *Ocracoke settled as Pilot Town*

1753    *Portsmouth officially settled as lightering port*

1794    *Shell Castle Lighthouse authorized*

1803    *First Cape Hatteras Lighthouse*

1808    *Ocracoke opens its first school*

1812    *First Cape Lookout Lighthouse*

1823    *Ocracoke Lighthouse built*

1840s    *First post offices established on banks*

| 1846 | Oregon and Hatteras Inlets cut by storm |
|------|------------------------------------------|
| 1861 | Battle of Hatteras Inlet; first Union victory in Civil War |
| 1868 | Congress appropriates funds for new beacon at Cape Hatteras |
| 1871 | Congress creates U.S. Lifesaving Service |
| 1880 | First all–African American lifesaving crew, Pea Island Station |
| 1883 | Federal legislation adds three lifesaving stations along the Outer Banks |
| 1885 | Lifesaving stations receive the first telephone service on Hatteras Island |
| 1899 | Diamond City families begin off-island exodus in wake of storms |
| 1903 | Wright Brothers "first in flight" at Kitty Hawk |
| 1915 | Lifesaving Service combines with the U.S. Cutter Service to become U.S. Coast Guard |
| 1918 | Migratory Bird Treaty Act signed into law, ends market hunting |
| 1922 | North River Bridge built |
| 1924 | Toby Tillett's ferry service established across Oregon Inlet |
| 1933 | Storm opens inlet at Cape Lookout, later dredged and named Barden's Inlet |
| 1935 | North Carolina General Assembly bans free-range livestock on Hatteras |
| 1936 | Cedar Island Bridge built |
| 1937 | Manteo-Hatteras bus line begins |
| 1937 | Cape Hatteras National Seashore signed into law by President Franklin D. Roosevelt |
| 1938 | Pea Island National Wildlife Refuge established |
| 1941 | Harkers Island bridge opens |
| 1944 | Great Atlantic Hurricane; extensive damage on Portsmouth and Ocracoke |

| 1953 | State ferry system and road paving projects begin |
| 1954 | Hurricane Hazel takes out North River Bridge |
| 1957 | State-owned Hatteras-Ocracoke ferry established |
| 1961 | State-owned Cedar Island–Ocracoke ferry established |
| 1963 | Herbert C. Bonner Bridge opens |
| 1964 | Cedar Island Wildlife Refuge established |
| 1966 | Cape Lookout National Seashore signed into law by President Lyndon B. Johnson |
| 1971 | Last two residents leave Portsmouth Village |
| 1978 | Portsmouth Village placed on the National Register of Historic Places |
| 1999 | Cape Hatteras Lighthouse moved to safer ground |
| 2000 | Cape Lookout Historic Village added to the National Register of Historic Places |
| 2003 | Hurricane Isabel cuts new inlet north of Hatteras Village, floods Down East |
| 2004 | Hatteras holds Blessing of the Fleet on anniversary of Hurricane Isabel |
| 2009 | Outer Banks National Scenic Byway designated |
| 2011 | Hurricane Irene floods Hatteras Island, damages houses in tri-village region |
| 2016 | 100th anniversary of the National Park Service |
| 2018 | Bonner Bridge replacement over Oregon Inlet scheduled to open in autumn |

# Living at the Water's Edge

# 1

# *Water*

*Every morning I get up and see my kingdom here—the water.*
—Irvin Guthrie, Harkers Island

For centuries, men and women along these shores have sustained their families with everything found in and near the sea. They have fished, tilled gardens, and hunted. They have traveled good distances to work in the sturgeon, river shad, and mullet fisheries and fished for shrimp and scallops up and down the Atlantic Coast. To this day, they leave their families for months at a time to work in the menhaden fishery off Virginia or the Gulf of Mexico or in the sea scallop ports up north.

People living on the coast have made use of everything washed up on their beaches and offered by the surf. They have invented and reinvented tools. They've built houses from salvaged timbers, and boats without blueprints, perfectly adapted to the environment. They've made a living patrolling the coast and saving lives and maintaining the vital beam of a lighthouse. They've guided sportsmen and shared secrets to ensure them a successful day's fishing or waterfowl hunting. In the old days, folks left nothing off their menu, from shorebirds to sea turtles. Mothers, wives, and children have headed shrimp, opened scallops, picked crabmeat, and raked clams. The narrative of their daily lives has been defined by the waters around them.

The waters here are everything. The sea is useful, vital, destructive, productive, unpredictable, spiritual, and constant.

Saltwater heals what ails you, as anyone will attest to who has spent time watching the shorebirds dip and sway in the surf at sunrise. It has long served as good medicine for summer cuts on bare feet and mosquito bites. A cool dip in the ocean cures oppressive summer heat and hot, sticky

Young Cameron Smith, aboard his father's shrimp boat, *Miss Gina* (named for his grandmother), watches his grandfather's boat, *Cameron T*, working the waters off Marshallberg. Shrimping on Core Sound is a family legacy. (Photo by Cathy Rose, "Core Sound Living")

sou'westers. Water is a balm for the soul. Congregations sing about lighthouses and storm-tossed seas, while photographers and writers, painters, and poets try to capture the power of this landscape. The sun rises and sets over sounds and ocean, changing position and colors from season to season, giving us a daily reminder of God's gifts to the people here. Poet Gretchen Guthrie Guthrie, daughter of Shackleford Banks whalers, wrote in *Carteret Love Song*, "Quickly now the sun slides from the sky into a waiting sea, and in its wake a crimson afterglow softens into deep tones, erasing the rim of the horizon."

Saltwater gives, but it also takes. The tide enriches marshes and estuaries yet has been known to destroy trees, farmers' crops, and freshwater wells when unleashed by storms. Salt can preserve food yet corrode equipment. Waves rob sand from one place and build beaches in another. For people living in the midst of endless water, the ocean and sounds both separate and bind the communities along the byway. The sea is the lifeblood and sometimes the cruel end, its power and beauty a consistent force in coastal people's lives.

Isabel Inlet, September 2003, cutting off Hatteras Village.
(Photo by Michael Halminski)

## STORMS

*We just look after one other. Always have.* —Nathaniel Jackson, Ocracoke

Water has its way. When picked up and delivered by winds clocking more than 100 miles per hour, saltwater is a force like no other. A single storm can knock Outer Banks communities back in time to utter self-sufficiency, a lesson Hatteras Village learned again in 2003 when Hurricane Isabel punched a new inlet through the banks just north of the community and cut residents off from the rest of the banks. Although downgraded to a category 2 storm after making landfall near Old Drum Inlet, Isabel's front quadrant—the powerful shoulder of the storm—delivered a wall of water over the banks, flattening dunes, obliterating beachfront mansions and motels, and moving houses across the road into Pamlico Sound. Many families lost photo albums, Bibles, quilts, marriage licenses, and birth certificates to floodwaters. Some lost it all.

It took two months before the inlet was filled and the road repaired. Neighbors from villages to the north and south stepped up and helped with day-to-day survival. They ferried children to school across the new channel to Buxton. They hauled dirty clothes north across the new inlet and returned them clean and folded to their neighbors to the south. Local restaurants provided meals. They joined the disaster relief agencies and helped rebuild the community. One year later, Hatteras Village held a heartfelt Blessing of the Fleet ceremony, now repeated annually at the Day at the Docks festival in September, inspired by overwhelming community spirit in the wake of disaster.

Only five homes in the Down East community of Stacy were spared the devastating floods from Isabel. School officials counted more than a hundred Down East students who were homeless for the first time in their lives, farmed out to families, crammed in temporary campers, or commuting from the homes of relatives who lived inland. Volunteers with the North Carolina Baptist Men and Women Disaster Relief Ministry and other relief agencies were on the ground when the tide receded and got to work helping communities rebuild.

"We put out a call for help," said Tabbie Nance of the Carteret County school system, who worked with the Core Sound Waterfowl Museum to rally members, friends, and family from across the state. Caring people from near and far helped put students' families back together, buying hot water heaters, sheetrock, and refrigerators. They helped provide "Santa" for distraught children that Christmas of 2003. More than two years would pass before families were back home and FEMA trailers out of sight.

When a hurricane hits, the effects are awesome and violent. Bent and cracking trees and a howling wind remind residents just how close to nature they are living. But people along the Outer Banks know to watch for what comes next. The rain subsides. Gale-force winds die down. The sun comes out. It's the eye of the storm, signaling that the front wall of the counterclockwise circulation has passed and the winds will soon shift. On the front side of the storm, ocean and sound waters have blown westward, pushed up the sounds and rivers by the approaching hurricane. When the eye passes and the winds shift from the southeast to the northwest, all that water comes roaring back toward the ocean, washing over marshes, islands, dunes, and roads. Waters can rise to biblical proportions within just an hour or two, as the vast estuary system acts like a giant bathtub during storms, water sloshing from one side to the other.

Hurricanes are talked about like troublesome ancestors: Hazel, Donna, Connie, Gloria, Emily, Floyd, Bertha, and Fran. These storms mark time, dividing life into "before" and "after." Fishermen say, "The blue crabs have never been the same since Floyd." A resident of Rodanthe was heard saying,

## CEDAR ISLAND: PICTURE OF RUIN

The *Beaufort News* reported on September 21, 1933, "Grim death and devastation strode across Carteret County Friday night in the form of the worst hurricane that has hit this section in more than three quarters of a century." A few days later, this story followed the headline, "Cedar Island Is the Picture of Ruin."

> The people were dressed in whatever clothing they had been able to salvage from the wreckage. . . . With all worldly goods wholly or partially destroyed and their means of livelihood swept from them, the people were still bewildered in the plight that the hurricane and destiny had cast them. They were undoubtedly the most pitiful folks, the entire 350 of them, that the writer has ever seen anywhere. . . .
>
> Not only have they lost their homes, their clothing and other property, but their livings are gone. Only four skiffs and three motorboats—and two of these were small—had been found by Monday afternoon. . . . The water rose ten feet above the average high-water mark and the waves rolled several feet higher. Both wind and the tide carried on their destructive work for more than fifteen hours on the island.
>
> Source: "Cedar Island Is the Picture of Ruin," *Beaufort News*, September 21, 1933

"We cared for the old home-place until Irene took it away." A realtor might shake her head and say, "Those were pre-Isabel prices." Life on the coast is not only affected but transformed by the weather.

Before storms were officially named and the word "hurricane" came into fashion, people referred to them by the year or season: the '44 Storm, the Ash Wednesday Storm, and the Halloween Storm. Some folks Down East call the Storm of '33 the Jimmy Hamilton Storm. Jimmy Hamilton was a fisherman from Sea Level who was swept away with his three sons. Their sharpie was found days later, capsized near Turnagain Bay. Mr. Hamilton had been warned of the approaching storm by fellow fishermen. They say he replied, "You can't eat bad weather."

# SIGNS AND WONDERS

*The ocean makes a completely different sound when a storm is coming.*
*It crackles and talks to you.* — Ellen Fulcher Cloud, Ocracoke

Long before NOAA (National Oceanic and Atmospheric Administration) weather alerts and storm tracking, people on the coast paid attention to natural signs, such as reading the sky and listening to the ocean. They noted subtle or not-so-subtle shifts in the wind and changes in the color and formation of clouds. They watched the behavior of animals. Some claimed they could smell a storm coming, and others could feel the drop in atmospheric pressure. Douglas "Chubby" Dorris of Frisco recalled that his grandfather routinely walked by the barometer, tapping it gently to make sure it wasn't "hung up or nothing."

Chopping a hole in the floor with an ax might seem odd, but for people living on the flood-prone sandbanks, it was a practical method of storm preparation. Even today some of the older houses have removable plugs in the floor, just in case. Letting the floodwaters inside, creeping along the halls, swirling into the living room, and inching up the staircase, helped keep the house from floating off the blocks.

"My brother and I would slide down the banister into the water and have the best time," said Ellen Cloud, recalling the day her family home filled with tide during a storm. Some people went as far as opening windows and doors, anything to keep their home from washing away as the floodwaters would rush in and out quickly. Once the waters began to recede, the weather-ready old salts would get ahead of the cleanup by stirring the floodwaters with a mop, hoping that most of the mud would flow out of the house with the tide.

"In the '44 Hurricane the sound and ocean met, I think, on this corner!" said Elizabeth Howard of Ocracoke. She waded through rushing water so fierce that it tore the straps off her shoes. Herds of livestock that roamed the banks — cattle, sheep, and horses — drowned. An Ocracoke fisherman noted that the cows floated "head up."

Some storms are so fierce that all the preparation in the world could not prevent houses from getting swept off their foundations and damaged beyond repair. The Red Cross calculated that 98 percent of the houses were washed off the blocks in Avon during the '44 Storm. A dyke built around the village after the '33 Storm offered little protection. A section of Carrie Gray's house was pushed across the road, over the sandhills. She remembered spying unearthed graves and skeletons wearing shirts with the but-

"Rodanthe P.O. after August storm, 1899." San Ciriaco hurricane destroyed communities all along North Carolina's Outer Banks from Shackleford Banks to Rodanthe. (Photo by unnamed photographer, Carol Cronk Cole Collection; courtesy of the Outer Banks History Center, State Archives of North Carolina)

tons rotted off. Men from the community gathered them up and reburied them on higher ground, and life went on.

## SHIPWRECKS AND RESCUES

*I've seen right many boats hit the shores of this island. Some of them they got off, and some of them busted up. —Anderson Midgett, Hatteras Island*

"Graveyard of the Atlantic" is a well-earned moniker for North Carolina's coastal waters. Hundreds of vessels have sunk or broken apart in the deadly combination of quick-changing weather, dynamic currents, and hidden shoals along what was once a key shipping route between New York and Charleston. The Diamond Shoals off Cape Hatteras are especially notorious for dooming ship after ship in their attempts to round the cape en route to northern or southern ports.

Shipwrecks were once so frequent that the state appointed commis-

April 8, 1942: Hatteras village's Maurice "Dick" Burrus meets with the
wreck commissioner to discuss beached lifeboats from ships torpedoed
by German submarines during World War II off Cape Hatteras.
(Photo by Sara Burrus Shoemaker, part of Maurice L. Burrus Collection)

sioners to manage wreck auctions called "vendues." Well into the twentieth
century, banks dwellers and mainlanders alike gathered on the beach to bid
on sails, turnbuckles, barrels, lanterns, ropes, and cargo. Lumber wasn't easy
to come by; planking was coveted as building material. The Salvo Assembly of God Church was built from the timbers of the *G. A. Kohler,* a grand
four-masted schooner wrecked on the beach between Avon and Salvo during the '33 Storm. Many old houses have beams, joists, and other materials
salvaged from a wreck.

One of the worst wrecks in American history occurred off North Carolina in 1837. The steam packet *Home,* en route from New York to Charleston, encountered the Racer's Storm and broke apart off Ocracoke. Ninety
of the 135 people aboard—many of them women and children—drowned.
The vessel was equipped with only two life jackets. The dead were buried
by Ocracoke villagers, as a lifesaving station wasn't established on the island
until 1905. The tragedy of the *Home* received national press coverage and led
to the federal requirement that all vessels carry life preservers for each passenger. Shipwrecks like the *Home* brought to light the need for the establishment of lifesaving stations up and down the nation's coasts.

The village of Portsmouth, made up of 150 souls in 1900, once cared for
shipwreck victims whose numbers far exceeded the population of the small
community. The 605-ton brig *Vera Cruz VII* wrecked offshore in 1903, bringing forth 421 Cape Verde Islanders needing food, clothes, and a dry bed.
Every villager was enlisted to help. A Portsmouth Islander recalled, "Some

# WRECK-BUSTING: A TIME-HONORED TRADITION

Shipwreck salvaging, or wreck-busting, is a time-honored tradition. It was the largest cash industry on the coast during the 1700s, 1800s, and early 1900s. On Hatteras and Ocracoke, islanders would often pull down as much as $800 a pop, or a group of men would split several thousand dollars.

Years ago, David Stick underscored the intensity of wreck-busting in an interview with an insurance agent on Ocracoke for his book *Graveyard of the Atlantic*. "The Ocracokers," the man said, "would drop a body while carrying it to the grave, and leave it on the road, or leave Sunday services, if someone yelled, 'Ship ashore!'"

On our beaches there were shipwrecks, and in the case of major storms, several at once. With shipwrecks, the international maritime salvage laws came into play; that is still recognized today, but with some exceptions. Essentially, the first on board took possession, providing they "raced" to the notary public to register their claim.

Wreck busters were not pirates because they acted within the law. The original ship owners, with the captain as representative, possessed priority rights. Charles Williams II wrote in *The Kinnakeeter* that the governor appointed a respected community leader as wreck commissioner who acted on the recommendation of the township's representative to state government.

At news of a wreck, the commissioner went to the scene. He was the authority figure that kept order and prevented the ship from being plundered. He was there mainly to protect the rights of the ship's owners and their insurers and, secondly, to allow the salvagers to unload the ship. The commissioner was also responsible for the vendue, a loose English translation and pronunciation of the French verb *vendre*, or "to sell." At the vendue, the commissioner presided over an auction sale of the ship and its contents at the scene of the wreck. His fee was set by law at 5 percent.

In most cases, the ship's owners and wreck busters split the remaining balance 50–50. Though sometimes, certain factors would cause disagreements. If the captain or owners could not prove total ownership, whether by loss of papers or questionable dealings, the wreck commissioner would call in an arbitrator. If there was a cloud on the vessel's ownership or bad faith dealings on part of the owners, it was not unusual for the arbitrator to award wreck busters as much as 75 percent.

Source: Danny Couch, "Shipwreck Salvaging Is a Time-Honored Tradition on Hatteras and Ocracoke," *Island Free Press*, July 28, 2008

Bodie Island Light.
(Photo by Baxter Miller)

of the foreigners ran away from the station crew and crawled through the marshes to beg for food at the homes. We fed them when they came." The villagers used up all the flour in the community to feed these weary victims of the sea.

## TOWERS OF LIGHT

*No matter how hard the winds blow around her, she will stand,*
*wrapped in diamonds, giving us strength every time we see her*
*light come around.* —*Madge Guthrie, Harkers Island*

A light piercing the darkness gives hope and helps orient the lost. No wonder the lighthouse has become a symbol for strength and guidance. Outer Banks lighthouses have long provided an essential navigational aid to ship's captains, whether the steady burning, fixed light on Ocracoke or the flashing beacons of Bodie Island, Cape Hatteras, or Cape Lookout towers. Not only do the lights alert mariners as to how close they are to shore and shoals, but the timing of the beam is specific to its location along the shore. If the flash occurs every fifteen seconds, the crew knows they are near Cape Lookout, no matter how dark or foggy it may be. If it flashes every seven and a half seconds, the Cape Hatteras light is their guide.

The U.S. Congress, alarmed at the growing number of shipwrecks, au-

Cape Hatteras Light. (Photo by Michael Halminski)

Ocracoke Light. (Photo by Kerry W. Willis)

Cape Lookout Light. (Photo by Sarah Katelyn Amspacher)

thorized the first North Carolina lighthouse in 1794. It was to be built on Cape Hatteras, the most treacherous part of the coastline. Vessel captains declared the light to be faint and sorry. The 90-foot tower was raised to 150 feet in 1854 and fitted with a powerful Fresnel lens. Today's black-and-white spiral tower was built in 1870 and was moved to higher ground in 1999. At 208 feet Cape Hatteras is the tallest lighthouse in America.

Another lighthouse was built on Shell Castle Island in 1798 to serve ships carrying cargo through Ocracoke Inlet. Today's 65-foot-high, solid-white structure was built on Ocracoke in 1823, emitting a nonflashing, steady light. The first Cape Lookout light was lit in 1812, and today's 163-foot, diamond-painted tower went into operation in 1859. The black-and-white pattern was the inspiration for the name Diamond City, Shackleford Banks's whaling community.

## THE SURFMEN

*The Blue Book says we've got to go out and it doesn't say a damn thing about having to come back. —Keeper Patrick Etheridge, Cape Hatteras Lifesaving Station*

Lighthouses could not protect against all dangers. The winter that spanned 1877 and 1878 was fierce, causing numerous wrecks along the North Caro-

Lifesaving drill (Durants Station), ca. 1920.
(Photo by unnamed photographer, Carol Cronk Cole Collection; courtesy
of the Outer Banks History Center, State Archives of North Carolina)

Little Kinnakeet station and crew, ca. 1880s.
(Photo by H. H. Brimley, H. H. Brimley Collection; courtesy of the
Outer Banks History Center, State Archives of North Carolina)

Cape Lookout station, ca. 1900. (Photo by H. H. Brimley, H. H. Brimley Collection; courtesy of the Outer Banks History Center, State Archives of North Carolina)

lina coast. Congress had created the U.S. Lifesaving Service before the Civil War, and after the war several manned stations were built up and down the heavily traveled Atlantic Coast. The loss of 200 souls within a thirty-mile stretch of beach in one season, however, compelled Congress to fund more lifesaving stations along the Outer Banks.

These new lifesaving stations meant a federal paycheck for a growing number of coastal families, at least during the fall and winter months, when the stations were manned and active. Ruby Williams of Avon said that her father, a surfman, was considered a "good liver" for receiving a steady paycheck, as opposed to the majority of Hatterasmen, who were fishermen with no guaranteed income from season to season.

The men took nightly shifts, making beach patrols on foot or on horseback from dusk to dawn in search of wrecks. Patrolmen were required to punch a patrol clock with a key hanging from a post located at the end of their patrol area. There they would meet a surfman from a neighboring station, as every inch of beach was watched over. Lionel Gilgo, who served in the Portsmouth Island Lifesaving Station, explained that a surfman "couldn't get rid of going" on a beach patrol and was required to set out in all kinds of weather.

*Water*

## FROM SLAVE TO CAPTAIN: RICHARD ETHERIDGE
## OF THE PEA ISLAND LIFESAVING SERVICE

The U.S. Lifesaving Service was formalized in 1871 to assure the safe passage of Americans and international shipping and to save lives and salvage cargo. Station 17, located on the desolate beaches of Pea Island, North Carolina, and manned by a crew of seven, bore the brunt of this dangerous but vital duty.

A former slave and Civil War veteran, Richard Etheridge, the only black man to lead a lifesaving crew, was its captain. He recruited and trained a crew of African Americans to man Station 17. Benjamin Bowser, Louis Wescott, William Irving, George Pruden, Maxie Berry, and Herbert Collins made up part of this team and formed the only all-black station in the nation. Although civilian attitudes toward Etheridge and his men ranged from curiosity to outrage, they figured among the most courageous surfmen in the service, performing many daring rescues from 1880 to the closing of the station in 1947.

In 1896, when the three-masted schooner *E. S. Newman* breached dur-

Richard Etheridge and the Pea Island station crew, ca. 1890.
(Photo by unnamed photographer, National Park Service Collection; courtesy of the Outer Banks History Center, State Archives of North Carolina)

ing a hurricane, Etheridge and his men accomplished one of the most daring rescues in the annals of the Lifesaving Service. The violent conditions had rendered their equipment useless. Undaunted, the surfmen swam out to the wreck, making nine trips in all, and saved the entire crew. This incredible feat went unrecognized for a full century until 1996, when the U.S. Coast Guard posthumously awarded the crew the Gold Lifesaving Medal.

Source: David Wright and David Zoby, *Fire on the Beach: Recovering the Lost Story of Richard Etheridge and the Pea Island Lifesavers* (Oxford University Press, 2002)

If a ship was spotted in distress, the crew had to cart a surfboat to the water. This was no easy job, since the ship could be miles down the beach from the station. Large "government horses" were employed to help with this task. The boat would then be launched through the breakers, six men rowing with long oars. If the ship was close to shore, the lifesaving station crew set up a shore-based mechanism to transport passengers to safety. First, they would shoot a line out to the vessel with a cannon-like Lyle gun. A heavy hawser was attached to the line with a note instructing the victims where to attach it. The lifesaving station crew, in the meantime, would set an A-frame to raise the line as high as possible. They attached the breeches buoy, which was a harness with a canvas bottom and leg holes, via block and tackle and sent it out to the ship. One by one, passengers would step inside the breeches buoy and get pulled across the surf to safety.

The U.S. Lifesaving Service merged with the Revenue Cutter Service and became the U.S. Coast Guard in 1915. After World War II, many stations became decommissioned. Merchant ship traffic had been declining with the expansion of railroads, paved roads, and trucking. The need for this service has not disappeared, however, as the Coast Guard performs daring rescues to this day. One rescue was captured in song. On January 1, 1948, the Coast Guard crew at Ocracoke Island answered the call of the *Charlie Mason*, a menhaden fishing boat from Beaufort, and rescued all but one crewmember. Ocracoke native Roy Parsons recalled that the fishermen were brought ashore in the breeches buoy, and all lived save one. The wreck became legendary, as factory owner Harvey Smith offered a hefty reward for the ship's rescue and return to Beaufort. The crew itself rose to the challenge, and the whole event was chronicled in a folk song called "The *Charlie Mason* Pogie Boat."

## THE *CHARLIE MASON* POGIE BOAT

It was the first of January in the new year '48
While fishing off the Loop Shack, *Charlie Mason* met her fate.
It was a pretty day that morning, with a light southerly wind
In the evening it looked different, the cap thought he should come in.

He gave orders to pick up port boat and the starboard, too.
When the falls broke on the starboard side, the net went in the screw
Now, Wiley called the Coast Guard, "Nan Mike Nan 2–9
Send your 83 footer and your best piece of line."

The crew they man the patrol boat immediately left the station
Proceeded through the inlet, up to the *Charlie Mason*
They got the line made fast when the bit broke like a match
Then Wiley knew he lost his boat, and all of his catch.

I'm coming ashore Coast Guard, you better make a start
Then the crew of the Coast Guard station broke out the old beach cart
They backed up the bomb service for the beach cart to hook
There was nothing but Core Sounders anywhere you might look.

And then Van Henry said, "Stanley hear my plan
Harvey Smith says he'll pay us thirty grand
He'll pay that sum if we can float,
That *Charlie Mason* pogie boat."

Now Lum he said to William, "You load the old Lyle gun,"
When he went to pull the lanyard you could see the fellows run
The Lyle gun she wouldn't fire, it was an awful disgrace
Lum couldn't see a blessed thing his hat blew in his face.

They finally got the hawser out and tied it to the mast
They stepped the crotch and fixed the buoy the thing was rigged at last
First man crawled in the buoy, the crew they heaved around
He was so heavy the hawser sagged, poor Devil nearly drowned.

Now all the men were saved that night all except'n one
This man he had a heart attack his name was Peyton Young

Ansley O'Neal brought him over to the Coast Guard station
The crew they worked him over on artificial respiration

But Van Henry said, "Stanley hear my plan
Harvey Smith says he'll pay us thirty grand
He'll pay that sum if we can float,
That *Charlie Mason* pogie boat."

Up at Travis Williams's you could hear this conversation,
"If I had the equipment, I'd float that *Charlie Mason!*"
But Stanley Wahab told his men, "You float that craft for me!"
And Sunday the 4th of April, she was in Beaufort, NC.

Source: Lyrics and music by Charles Stowe, *Between the Sound
and the Sea: Music of the North Carolina Outer Banks* (Smithsonian
Folkways Recordings, 2004 / Folkways Records, 1977)

## WORLD WAR II

*We lost our innocence during World War II. — Earl O'Neal, Ocracoke*

As David Stick wrote in his classic *Graveyard of the Atlantic*, for the first six months of 1942, people living along the coast of North Carolina were "closer to the war than were most of our troops . . . on overseas duty." Ships navigating along the Atlantic Coast of North Carolina were sitting ducks for German submarines, which surfaced at night to target vessels silhouetted against the lights on the mainland. The Germans sank as many as five ships in one night, destroying some fifty large ships in ninety days in what came to be known as the Battle of Torpedo Junction. In all, according to Stick, eighty-seven vessels were lost along the coast during the war, plus four German U-boats.

The bombings were not widely publicized at the time, given the U.S. government's concern that "loose lips sink ships," but the people of Down East, Ocracoke, and Hatteras witnessed firsthand the horrors unfolding in their own backyard. Oral histories record memories of bodies washed ashore, flaming ocean waters from destroyed oil tankers, and china falling out of cupboards due to the percussive explosions off the coast. The local hospital in Carteret County quietly dedicated its basement to treating Ger-

In April 8, 1942, these lifeboats were washed up on the beach between Hatteras Village and Frisco during World War II. This area was called the Atlantic Turkey Shoot because of German submarines torpedoing Allied ships off Cape Hatteras almost daily. (Photo by Sara Burrus Shoemaker, part of Maurice L. Burrus Collection)

man soldiers, and sounded a whistle calling for extra help for wounded U.S. soldiers and allies.

The requirement to blacken headlights and keep curtains drawn was strict. A soldier in an Army jeep patrolled communities to make sure no lights seeped through windows. The Coast Guard patrolled the beaches and waters in search of spies. They reported oil slicks so thick from downed tankers that waves rolling up on the beach could not break, and gobs of oil snared jeeps in the sand. Local fishing boats from Hatteras to Salter Path along Bogue Banks joined the ranks of civilian "mosquito fleets" that patrolled the Atlantic Coast during the war.

The U.S. Navy built bases on Ocracoke and Hatteras during World War II. The Ocracoke Lighthouse was shaded and then put out entirely. The American freighter *Caribsea* was destroyed off Ocracoke Island by a German U-boat on March 11, 1942. The ship's engineer, James Baugham Gaskill, happened to be from Ocracoke. Gaskill's cousin found wreckage along the shore on Ocracoke, including a panel off the ship with the twenty-year-old's mate's license attached. He had, in effect, come home. An islander made a cross using the panel, which hangs in the Ocracoke Methodist Church today.

Cape Lookout had strategic importance in this era, as it was the only anchorage between Cape Hatteras and Charleston. An Army outpost was built on Cape Lookout during World War II to protect military convoys anchoring in the bight. The 193rd Field Artillery personnel built a dock and cement road to receive supplies and ammunition. They also built barracks and attempted to install gun mounts along the tops of the sandhills. But with all their trucks and tractors, they could not move heavy guns through the loose sand until local house-mover Denard Davis showed them how it was done with rollers, horse, and capstan.

World War II changed life on the banks forever. Wartime had created widows and veterans and brought "new blood" to communities with soldiers marrying local girls. The newly established Marine Corps Air Station Cherry Point in Havelock became a significant employer. More homes were built when residents had the security of a steady job. Bridges replaced ferries, paving the way for a future burgeoning tourism economy. Plans resumed for the establishment of Cape Hatteras National Seashore, private ferry services became state-run, and motels, restaurants, and new jobs became available in formerly sleepy fishing villages.

## IN THE BLOOD

*I don't fish with a pole, this so-called sport fishing. . . . Why wait for a fish to come along and get on the end of a line?* — Gak Austin, Salvo

Commercial fishing became one of the enterprises that picked up after the war, and new fisheries emerged. Shrimp, called "bugs" by locals and long considered a nuisance that clogged nets, became a valuable commodity in the 1950s. The crab fishery improved as well, as old-fashioned trot-lines gave way to more efficient pots. Better highways paved the way for fish companies to transport more product to lucrative markets, such as Fulton's Fish Market in New York. Congress passed a set of economic incentives in the late 1970s designed to expand domestic seafood markets and companies. Wooden skiffs shared the waters with expanding fleets of oceangoing trawlers and steel vessels.

The ecology of North Carolina's fisheries is diverse, encompassing features from southern creeks to northern cypress swamps, rivers and vast estuaries inland, and the cold Labrador Current and the warm Gulf Stream meeting just off the coast. Cape Hatteras serves as the meeting point of species from the north and south. This rich and varied ecology gives rise to an incredible diversity of fisheries, from the deepwater bluefin tuna to the humble but tasty Core Sound clam. North Carolina is a world-class fishing area for both commercial and recreational anglers.

Commercial fisherman Chris Hickman in Hatteras, 2012. (Photo by B. Garrity-Blake)

Commercial fishermen—those who make a living selling the fish they catch—are known as watermen for a reason. They live and breathe the marine environment. They say saltwater runs in their veins; fishing is in their blood. They weather the elements, the ups and downs of market prices and fuel prices, and a barrage of regulations. Yet fishermen, last of the hunter-gatherers, hang in there to provide seafood lovers with a taste of wild-caught fish, the only wild animal sold in the grocery store.

Fishermen have adapted and held on, modifying their practice from age-old methods to more environmentally friendly gears and habits. Escape panels, fish excluder devices, and cull rings are a sample of devices they employ to help conserve juvenile fish and crabs. Trawl nets, pulled behind the boat to sift shrimp from the water, are now fitted with turtle excluder devices, oval grates allowing sea turtles to escape the net. Fishermen have made many changes in the name of sea turtle conservation, including yielding a huge swath of fishing area in Pamlico Sound to gill netting. Some find these measures hard to swallow, considering that sea turtles were once eaten in coastal communities.

Nowadays regulations and market prices determine what fishermen catch as much as what's in season. Nonetheless, North Carolina fishermen work with the seasons, shedding soft crabs in the spring, fishing crab pots in the early summer, trawling for shrimp in the summer and fall, and fishing pound nets and gill nets as the weather turns colder.

"Nobody understands the habitat ecology of an animal better than its

Uriah and Sullivan working the reef off Ocracoke. (Photo by Ann Ehringhaus)

### THE ART OF MULLETING

Several fishermen remained faithful to the occupation. To them fishing was a way of life; the pursuing, catching, and selling of fish was so much a part of their lives that they kept at it and they wouldn't have thought of doing anything else. Two such fishermen were Uriah and Sullivan Garrish, brothers, who fished the waters off Ocracoke from their youth until they were well into their eighties.

Of all the different kinds of fish to be caught and the various methods of catching them, the favorite for Uriah and Sullivan was catching mullets. Found all over the world, the striped jumping mullet is bluish gray or greenish on top—greenish, according to Sullivan, if they have just come from the cleaner ocean waters—silvery gray on the sides, and white underneath. The stripes are formed by scales with dark centers. Although mullets average one to two feet long, Uriah once caught thirteen mullets that weighed as much as fifteen pounds each and were approximately two feet long.

Mullets are caught with gill nets. The diamond-shaped netting acts as a fence, which prevents fish from swimming through. If the size of the netting, or "meshes," isn't too large or small, the fish will become entangled, or "meshed" by the gills as they try to free themselves.

At the top and bottom, the netting is tied to ropes. Corks spaced approximately a yard apart along the top line float the net, while the bottom line is spaced with leads that sink the netting toward the bottom. At the two ends of the net the cork and lead lines are fastened to a staff, which keeps the net spread open and provides a means of pulling the net through the water.

At Ocracoke, mullets are caught along the many sand reefs and sloughs of Pamlico Sound that run the length of the island within a mile of shore. When a school of mullets is spotted, a staff from each net is tied together and pitched overboard. Since most mullets are caught in shallow water, the fishermen then pole their skiffs in semicircles, eventually meeting to close the circle after all the nets have been set. The nets are then pulled together, forcing the fish to mesh.

The whole process is really quite simple — simple, that is, when there are plenty of mullets and you don't have to look over every grass lump and into every slough to find them. When you're out there on those other days, though, scouring the reefs, and even the whirl of a stingray seems promising, then it takes a real mullet man to catch them. "There's an art to this mulleting," explains Sullivan. "A lot of ones that go out don't know this. They think you can just set a net and catch 'em. They don't know the art of it."

Source: Alton Ballance, *Ocracokers* (University of North Carolina Press, 1989)

predator," said a fisheries biologist, explaining why he liked to work with fishermen.

### FISHING FOR FUN

*Trout fishing is the thing I'm most sneaky about, and it's hard to*
*keep anything secret around here. — George Pratt, Buxton*

There is nothing like the sight of a child with a fish on the end of her line. Rod bent over, parents cheering her on, passersby pausing to see what she caught. So much excitement in such a simple act.

Recreational fishing is an extremely popular sport in North Carolina, as people cast hooks and lines from beaches, bridges, piers, charter boats,

This image, "Gals with Grey Trout," marks the early years of surf fishing off Hatteras Island and the active role women have played in this sport from the beginning. (Photo by Ray Couch, Aycock Brown Collection; courtesy of the Outer Banks History Center, State Archives of North Carolina)

head boats, and private boats. Fishing is fun, it's relaxing, and it is also big business, from mom-and-pop tackle shops to high-dollar events like the Big Rock Blue Marlin Tournament of Morehead City and its million-dollar purse.

Sportfishing has its own history along these banks. Thurston Gaskill, who, at eighty-four, was the oldest guide on Ocracoke in 1986, described the evolution of sportfishing technology. He recalled seeing his first rod and reel around 1915, when a man showed up in Ocracoke with a simple reel and thumb leather for a drag. Gaskill recalled using loon bones when trolling for bluefish or mackerel. Store-bought lures emerged in the 1920s. At that time, tourist season ran from June through August, compared to today's almost year-round season. Gaskill said his goal was to teach weekend anglers true sportsmanship, not "how many fish you can catch."

In the late 1960s, Hatteras women formed one of the first female surf-

Anglers at Cape Hatteras, 2012. (Photo by B. Garrity-Blake)

fishing teams, known as the Hatteras Gulls. They competed as far away as New Jersey, winning several tournaments. Hatteras is home to the Marlin Club Marina, a private club that sponsors an annual fishing tournament. Today Cape Hatteras Anglers Club sponsors a tournament, as does the Hatteras Village Civic Association. Proceeds from the tournaments serve community needs, such as scholarships, food pantry donations, and hurricane relief.

Today some half-million saltwater fishing licenses are sold in North Carolina each year. Anglers have access to a diverse array of fish from an ecological paradise. No spot is more coveted than Cape Point on Hatteras Island, known for having the best surf fishing on the East Coast. Mother Nature's power is palpable at Cape Point, as clashing currents attract fish of all sorts, migrating or congregating just off the beach.

Anglers and their "beach buggies," four-wheel-drive trucks equipped with PVC-pipe rod holders, line up at the shore in pursuit of trout, flounder, cobia, mackerel, red drum, blue fish, and striped bass. The currents are not the only things that clash at Cape Point. Anglers and local business owners recently battled environmental groups who sued the National Park Service for not managing beach driving in areas important to endangered shorebirds. The conflict resulted in a beach driving plan that the public must heed, including a required driving permit and periodic closures of the cape and other areas during nesting season.

"It's not just about the fishing," Buxton angler George Pratt explained, stressing the social aspect of meeting friends at the shore, not to mention the thrill of the wild. He described the first time he fished at Cape Point. "My first experience was walking over the dune into the fog, and seeing birds coming out of the fog and disappearing back into the fog in a circular pattern. . . . I caught fifteen- to twenty-pound bluefish that day."

## WATERFOWL HUNTING

*As long as I can get out here in this duck blind I think I'll be alright.*
—*Fowler O'Neal, Ocracoke*

Waterfowl hunting is a time-honored tradition in North Carolina, which is situated on the Mid-Atlantic Flyway. Subsistence hunters took full advantage of the wide range of waterfowl available along the banks. Expansive marshes and open water drew rafts of ducks and geese so thick they would darken the sky at times. Stewed redheads and baked goose, along with many other kinds of ducks, were part of the diet of those early settlers, who depended on the birds to feed their families in the long winter months.

Things began to change in the early 1900s as market hunting became popular and ducks were hunted en masse, packed in ice, and shipped in barrels to high-end restaurants in the North. Other species such as egrets, herons, and swan provided plumage for the millinery trade so popular in the early 1920s. Market hunting was outlawed with the passage of the 1918 Migratory Bird Treaty Act, but waterfowl hunting for recreation was beginning to grow. Hunt clubs, some lavish, were built by Yankee industrialists on Hatteras, Ocracoke, Portsmouth, and Core Banks in the early twentieth century.

Today waterfowling lives on. Descendants of those who hunted, guided, and carved decoys decades ago follow their memories to many of the same duck blinds and hunting creeks their fathers showed them. Hunters still come from inland to share in the excitement of "the hunt," knowing they are keeping the tradition alive. "Duck hunting is about sharing the marshes and bays and places that I know with my friends, family, and fowl," explains Corey Lawrence, the son of David Lawrence, a cofounder of the Core Sound Decoy Carvers Guild. "Each trip provides an opportunity to find balance, to

Young David Lawrence and his father, David Corey Lawrence, carve decoys at the Core Sound Waterfowl Museum and Heritage Center's "David's Room," dedicated to the legacy of their father and grandfather, David A. Lawrence. David A. Lawrence, along with his best friend and fellow carver, Wayne Davis, cofounded the Core Sound Decoy Carvers Guild on Harkers Island in 1986.

teach and to learn, and most of all, to remember all those great hunters and carvers who came before me. I never regret a day spent doing these things with the crowd who share my love for these old ways."

## BOATS MADE BY HAND

*We come from a long line of wood butchers.*
*— James Allen Rose, Harkers Island*

Boatbuilding was a necessity in every community of the Outer Banks. George Washington Creef of Roanoke Island designed the shad boat in the late nineteenth century, a widely used vessel in the Albemarle and northern Pamlico waters. With its distinctive hourglass-shaped hull, the shad boat was recognized by the North Carolina General Assembly as the official "state boat" of historic significance. Avon was known for building large vessels in the early years, and in the 1940s and 1950s Willie Austin was a lead builder. Boatbuilders in Buxton included Bill Quidley, who built sail skiffs and shove

## HISTORY OF THE OLD CLUB HOUSE:
### CARTERET GUN AND ROD CLUB

This information has been given to me by my father, Mr. Francis Murphy, Mrs. Leroy Davis, and Mr. Florence Paul Davis, whose father was the first caretaker. My father said that Mr. Paul was paid one dollar a day and everyone, including Mr. Paul, thought he had a good job.

The "Club House" was built in 1902 and burned down on May 25, 1970. The first caretaker was Ammie L. Paul from 1902 to 1905. A man from Morehead was the second one, but I can't remember his name. Walter Moore was the third caretaker, followed by George Willis from Hatteras, [and] Leroy Davis, who was the caretaker from May 1915 to December 1945.

When Mr. Leroy Davis took over the job of caretaker, there were 60 members, mostly from up north. When he left in 1945, there were only two members left: brothers, Charlie and Johnnie Geiger from New Jersey. A lot of the members left the club after the hurricane of 1933. Mr. Leon Dermaneous from New Jersey was the last member of the original Club House and came back to Davis for visits for many years.

My precious memories of the Club House go back to the days when the people from Davis used to go over in boats to the Banks for church picnics. The children were free to run up and down the big sand hills, which were destroyed by the hurricane of '33. People would go by buggy ride down to the Cape to a square dance led by a Mr. Hunter who lived at Harkers Island, but he was from up north. He was a big man, but he danced smoothly and gracefully.

The running water and telephone were exciting, but I don't remember about the radio. I have heard Mrs. Davis say that people came from far and near to put on the earphone to hear a word from far away. Most of the time static was the only thing they heard. A great landmark has gone from our view.

Source: Mabel Murphy Piner, *Once Upon a Time: Stories of Davis, North Carolina* (Carteret County Historical Society, 2002)

The Carteret Gun and Rod Club was built on Core Banks in 1902 by Raymond Paul of Davis. Known by locals as the "Club House," the structure was home to two other clubs, the Cedar Banks Club and the Core Banks Club. (Photo from the Richard Gillikin and Sue Buck Collection, Core Sound Waterfowl Museum and Heritage Center)

skiffs, and Rocky Rollinson, who "hewed ribs from trees and steamed them," according to a banks native.

Builders who lived along the shallow waters of Core Sound were known for designing the shallow-draft pole skiff that was later modified to sail. The Core Sound sail skiff or sharpie, with either a spritsail or gaff rig, depending on what a fisherman could get, was a modification of the New Haven sharpie of Connecticut. The Core Sound sharpie was a flat-bottomed sailboat with a centerboard. Thurston Gaskill of Ocracoke said a sharpie could sail in a foot of water, perfect for "sloughs and channels and big enormous mud flats that go from two or three feet of water to bare at low water."

These hand-built wooden skiffs with worn canvas sails were the lifeblood of the people who lived along the shallow waters. Coastal families sailed from Portsmouth to Atlantic, Avon to Hatteras, Ocracoke to Belhaven, and Harkers Island to Beaufort. Boats carried supplies and transported people to tend business in town and to visit family in other com-

Ambrose Fulcher of Atlantic built the *Linda* (*left*) in 1939 for John Weston Smith, who named it for his daughter. The *Linda* was constructed as a runboat to fetch fish caught by long-haulers, but in this photo it was rigged out as a shrimp boat. The *Wasted Wood* was built in 1933 by Will Mason, also from Atlantic, for the long-haul fishing trade. In the 1950s Atlantic's Charles Smith acquired the boat, rebuilt it, and renamed the vessel the *David M.* for his son. In 1979 John "Buster" Salter purchased the boat and fished it until the late 1990s, when it was abandoned in the marsh. (Photo by Lawrence Earley)

munities. Often men spent more time in their boats than in their homes because that was where they made their living. On the west end of Harkers Island, Blind Joe Willis would manage to sail his skiff across Back Sound for a "mess" of clams or oysters, just to feed his family that day. Guided by the wind and currents and a mental picture of the lay of the land, Blind Joe did what he had to do for his family's survival, and it took a boat to do it.

One morning around 1915, a group of Portsmouth Island fishermen were oystering in Pamlico Sound near the shore. They heard an unfamiliar sound, a steady "thump, thump, thump," according to Lionel Gilgo, and looked up to see where such a noise was coming from. Around a point came a skiff moving without aid of sail, pole, or oar. The fishermen were witnessing, for the first time, a boat propelled by a gas engine. "Everybody laid their oyster tongs down," said Gilgo, "and just gazed at that boat coming." Bill Gaskill, who ran a hunting lodge on Ocracoke, was one of the first to try the new propulsion, with the financial assistance of his Yankee clientele. "After that, everyone wanted one," added Gilgo.

Once gas engines became available, sail skiffs were converted to "putt-putts," often making use of any motor that could still turn. It was not un-

Ray Davis stands in front of his marine railways and boathouse, preparing for the launching of the *Nansea*, Marshallberg, ca. 1970. (Photo from the Donald Boone Collection, Core Sound Waterfowl Museum and Heritage Center)

usual for a washing machine motor or an old car engine to be used in a boat. Most of these were straight-drive with no transmissions. Once it was started, there was no stopping until the motor was turned off; tying up to a dock was a process of cutting the motor and drifting with the tide, hoping for a gentle return.

Once engines were more accessible, the Core Sound V-bottom became popular up and down the banks. Its design with rounded stern for working the nets proved to be an effective adaptation for fishing and was eventually rigged with engines for ocean fishing and shrimp trawling. Today this "Core Sounder" style of boat is a symbol of the time-honored adaptability of local craftsmen. Harkers Island builder Calvin Rose explained, "If she ain't purty, she won't work right."

Beginning as early as the 1920s, every community in Down East Carteret County had their own master boatbuilders. From Ambrose Fulcher and Marvin Robinson in Atlantic to Elmo Wade in Williston, the foundations for boatbuilding traditions of North Carolina were being skillfully laid. Smyrna and Williston were known for turning out freight boats and men-

Sea trials for Lewis Brothers's *Bobby D*, near Harkers Island bridge, 2015. (Photo by Billy Merkley)

haden vessels in the late nineteenth century. Marshallberg emerged as a focal point of boatbuilding in the late 1930s–40s, with M. W. Willis and sons, Myron Harris, and the Davis family. Gloucester's Nathaniel Smith earned himself the job of building a boat for the state Division of Marine Fisheries.

Still today, no region of the East Coast is more recognized for wooden boatbuilding than Harkers Island, a legacy captured in documentaries, books, and museum exhibitions. Countless boats have been built under live oak trees in side yards, while others were launched from grand old sheds on the water, such as Rose Brothers Boatworks and the Lewis Brothers. Harkers Island's signature "flare bow" design, developed by Brady Lewis as a way to deflect water from the hull as gas engine–propelled boats sped through the sound, is perfectly suited for shallow waters and prevailing sou'west winds of the Cape Lookout region. Builders, famous for using the "rack of the eye" instead of blueprints, are masterful in combining the art of boatbuilding with their deep knowledge of the environment. "Pretty work," the locals say.

## LOOKING OFFSHORE: LAND OF WATER

Along the shores of North Carolina, there's more water than land.

Water is a vital element of life everywhere, but nowhere is it more important than along these Outer Banks. The sea has defined the landscape and the culture, the past and the future. Today is no different. It is why people come, why they stay, and why they leave. Water, glistening on a sunny day or roaring on a stormy night, is the tangible force that holds this place and our people together, a shared gift, a common bond. Water is a gift to be treasured and protected.

Along these shores, everything begins and ultimately ends with water. It is the force that binds the people together and the element that separates this culture from the mainland. Water provides isolation and protection from the larger world yet gives our people a shared inheritance with other islanders, no matter how far away they are. Water defines the "islandness" of the people here and our acceptance of the relentless forces of nature at the edge of the sea.

Water continues to be the call to these sandbanks for long-time residents and first-time visitors. The ocean sustains this economy in the production of fresh local seafood; it is the determining factor in real estate values and is the sought-after view from a hotel window. It is the "why and how" we come to this place at the edge, the reason we return, and the force that holds us if we decide to stay. The people here are more of the water than of the land. It gives, they take, and as everyone here knows, nothing stays the same.

Visitors to the Outer Banks Byway will come to look at the water, splash in it, fish from it, and enjoy its bounty and its beauty. Water beckons those who come to the edge to experience the beauty and power of the ocean for a week, a season, or a lifetime, drawn to be part of the give and take, finding their place in this fragile, ever-changing land of water.

# 2

# *Land*

*I love where I come from; I love where I live.* — Tilman Gray, Avon

Land in coastal North Carolina ebbs and flows with the sea. Constantly sculpted and changed by tide and ocean wind, what counts as land consists of ephemeral sands, wetlands, and scrub pine hummocks that barely lend relief to vast expanses of flat horizon. The waterline can move subtly, ripple by ripple, with the rise and fall of tides. It can also move abruptly, swallowing roads and gardens ahead of a storm.

"The mullets are eatin' the collards," people say with straight-faced delivery.

Land has no choice but to yield to the ocean forces, and it is that vulnerability that gives this region its wildness and uncertainty. Land shifts and breathes, rises and subsides. In the wake of a storm, the imprint of ancient tree stumps emerges along the wash of the beach, as barrier islands continue their slow roll westward and reveal remnants of old sound-side forest. "Sand don't melt or run off," reflected Thurston Gaskill of Ocracoke. "It just shifts slowly around over the centuries." He added, "That's the beauty of sand—it don't disappear."

A nor'easter storm can bury or break apart sections of coastal highway, rendering asphalt as vulnerable as candle wax dripped on sand. Beach erosion has caused many an ocean-side mansion to slump helplessly into the surf, inevitably prompting someone to quote the Bible verse about the foolishness of building on sand. "And the rain fell, and the floods came, and the winds blew and beat against that house, and it fell, and great was the fall of it," Matthew 7:27 reads.

Descendants gather at Wade's Shore Cemetery for the Diamond City Homecoming in 2014, the 115th anniversary of the storm of 1899 that drove its residents to higher ground, settling at Salter Path, the Promise Land, and Harkers Island. (Photo by Dylan Ray)

Ferry captains and fishermen are forever altering their courses as channels shoal up in dynamic areas such as Hatteras Inlet. Hurricanes punch new inlets open to let the water out and choke existing inlets with sand. The prosperity of communities has increased or dwindled depending on the depth of inlets and trade routes abandoned, revised, or newly formed. Mother Nature, in the form of wind and weather, has written the history and geography of settlements along the coast of North Carolina.

Along the banks and throughout Down East are stands of longleaf and loblolly pines, red cedar, and wind-twisted live oaks, their canopy pointing in the direction of prevailing southwest winds. Miles of thicket, such as the lush and diverse Buxton Woods, must still resemble what Arthur Barlowe saw in 1584 as the "most plentifull, sweete, fruitfull, and wholesome of all the world." Maritime forests rooted in sandy but productive soils hover between the dunes and the sound. Scrub oaks, holly, wax myrtle, and the ubiquitous yaupon provide habitat for wildlife and a buffer for communities on the sound side, natural protection from ocean wind and tide.

# HUNKERING DOWN

*Villages are always nestled back on the sound side.*
—*Ellen Fulcher Cloud, Atlantic*

Early settlers on the banks hunkered down. From the "whalers hutts" tucked behind the sandhills of Shackleford Banks to the modest bungalows in wooded clusters of Chicamacomico, houses were built on the more sheltered nooks along the banks where sound waters gave people safe haven and creeks provided easy access to their workboats. They worked from the sound side most of the year, fishing, oystering, and clamming as the seasons dictated. The beach was left to free-roaming livestock, lifesaving and beach seining crews, and villagers combing the shore for lumber and other treasures after a blow.

Old folks of the coast are resourceful, making do with what washes ashore, saving whatever they find that they might need later. Harkers Islanders call this talent "progging" and declare themselves "proggers," an Old English term for foraging. Houses were built of cedar and pine with timber salvaged from shipwrecks. Homes were moveable, as the shifting sands and rising seas made it necessary to move houses, section by section, to safer ground.

Harkers Islander Annette Willis, whose ancestors lived on Shackleford Banks, heard tales of axe-hewn cedar posts, rafters fastened with wooden pegs, and sharkskin door hinges. People filled mattresses with seaweed and tracked the passing days with a calendar made of corks on a string. Early settlers filled conch shells or wooden skiff bailers with whale oil to use for lanterns. Nothing went to waste.

"Smart old codgers!" Edna Gray of Hatteras Island said of her in-laws, who took apart their house, put it on a freight boat, and sailed it to higher ground in Buxton. The house had "seen some storms," she reflected. "Could tell some tales."

Elsie Hooper's house was moved from Rodanthe to Salvo by "bedways and rollers," or a block-and-tackle system long used to launch boats. Inch by inch, the structure was rolled on logs on a track made of boards in the sand. A horse and capstan literally provided the horsepower. Hooper's 200-year-old house was typical for its time, built with lumber from ships and wooden pegs instead of nails. Only a few houses remain today of the many that were originally built on Shackleford Banks, dismantled and floated across the sound on skiffs as people sought a more sheltered place to live in the wake of horrendous 1890s storms.

Residence of W. H. Rollison, Hatteras, N.C., after August storm, 1899.
(Photo by unnamed photographer, Carol Cronk Cole Collection; courtesy of
the Outer Banks History Center, State Archives of North Carolina)

Older folks, who referred to "sandhills" instead of "dunes," remember hills that formed around the carcasses of shipwrecks, or giant mounds used as lookout points for whales off Cape Lookout or porpoises off Hatteras. Sand rose up and flattened; hills shifted and walked. Outer Banks old-timers recall when the beach was "flat as a shield," which allowed people on the sound side to see across to the ocean and read the water for signs of changing weather. "We used to stand on the front porch," said L. P. O'Neal of Avon. "And you could watch breakers roll up on the beach."

The dune line seen today along Hatteras and Ocracoke Islands is a matter not of nature but of human engineering in the wake of storms. Bulldozers clear the road of sand and rebuild a barrier, a project first begun in the 1930s by the Civilian Conservation Corps and the National Park Service. Some islanders noticed that erosion seemed to accelerate with the building of dunes, and flooding worsened in villages. A flat beach, people reasoned, allowed the ocean to wash over to the sound and back with minimal damage, while the slope of the dunes both trapped water from escaping back into the ocean and caused worse erosion on the beach. The dunes, many islanders surmised, increased flooding in the villages.

"The dunes was a sad mistake," said Ben Spencer of Ocracoke. "In a storm, the water eats the foot of the dune out."

## THE DAY OLD MA LEFT THE BANKS

At dawn the day was bright and clear. It was on a Monday in April of 1890. If everything went well, it was also moving day for Ma and her brood of four little girls and baby boy. They were going to the mainland across the sound.

Old Ma rose earlier than usual. As was her custom, she went to the door, opened it, and scanned the skies and water. Had it not been so calm and peaceful, she would rather wait. Sudden clouds and squalls could make the sound mighty rough and, in a small sharpie, awfully dangerous. So she decided this was the day.

"Uncle" Kib (her brother-in-law) would soon come in his sailboat after her, the children, and their meager belongings. He was moving his family and had offered her this opportunity to go live with them in their new home. She had recently lost her husband, and there was no way to make a living on the Banks. He had died while serving in the lifesaving station at Cape Lookout.

There were many thoughts going through her mind as she turned toward the part of the house where she cooked their meals in the fireplace. She walked over by the hearth, gathered a few sticks of wood that were nearby, and started a fire, put fresh coffee in the pot and hung it over the fire to boil,

Sand dunes on North Carolina coast, Shackleford Banks, formerly known as Diamond City. (Photo from the North Carolina Collection, University of North Carolina Library at Chapel Hill)

and put the iron spider close to the fire and placed dough she had made the night before in it to bake. "Now," she thought, "I'll go call the young'uns and by the time they have their clothes on, breakfast will be almost ready." Just as she was going to get the children, a loud jolly voice called through the doorway, "Julia, honey, are you about ready?" It was Uncle Kib. He had come in time to eat breakfast with them.

Hurriedly, she managed to help the smaller children with their clothes while the larger girls helped each other and soon came running to the kitchen to see their dear old Uncle. Making himself useful, he watched the bread, turned it over, and smelled the coffee to see it had brewed enough. The girls set the table, and when all of them sat down for the meal, Old Ma came in with the young baby and took her place at the head of the table.

This was the last meal they would have in this small home they loved so well, and because she could hardly speak, with sadness she asked Uncle Kib to ask God's blessings on all of them, the few things they possessed, and to ask that they would have a good life in their new home.

Soon afterwards, several women who lived nearby came in to help. They packed the dishes, pots, and pans in tubs. They folded all the bed quilts, sheets, and pillowcases and tied them together with a piece of rope. Uncle Kib took the beds apart and stood them outside the door so the women could take them down to the shore. It wasn't long before all the household items and their belongings were in the boat. Most of the children were eager to get started and began calling, "Come on, come on."

However, Old Ma was not very anxious to hurry away from the home and people she loved so well. Her heart was heavy as she called Uncle Kib to one side and whispered something in his ear. He took her by the hand, and they walked slowly toward the old family cemetery where both of them had mothers, fathers, brothers, sisters, and where old Ma's husband was buried. For a while they stood silent, just looking at the graves. I think they must have wept.

The children's calling and yelling aroused them from their thoughts, and so they began walking towards Uncle Kib's boat; a long trip on the water — a new beginning for all of them, and nobody looked back at the place they had left and loved.

Source: essay written by David Murrill for Rosalie Dowty's English class, Morehead City High School, 1960; reprinted from *Our Shared Past: Diamond City and Ca'e Bankers Reunion — Remembering 100 years* (Core Sound Waterfowl Museum and Heritage Center, 1999)

Cape Hatteras State Park grass planting, 1937.
(Photo by unnamed photographer, National Park Service Collection; courtesy
of the Outer Banks History Center, State Archives of North Carolina)

## LANDINGS

*A Harkers Islander never gets too old or too far away that he doesn't want to return
to the landing and just look offshore. —Elbert Lee Davis Sr., Harkers Island*

The "landing" has traditionally been a gathering place, a place of work and
play, a focal point for commerce and transportation. Along the landing, skiffs
were pulled up each spring and turned over for the barnacles to be scraped
off and the bottom painted. Nets were draped over frames called "spreads"
for drying and mending. In the summer, barefooted children swung and balanced on net spreads like acrobats or helped load net needles with cotton
twine in exchange for a penny or a nickel. Out of the way of fishermen, children played among the piles of net bunt and corks, tools, and engine parts.
Pieces of broken dishes made good pretend china, and fish boxes became
stately Windsor chairs. The children made sand pies with pokeberries that
would stain their hands and clothes and dye their doll clothes purple.

Net sheds, camps, or "little houses" were found at landings, serving as
much-needed places for fishermen's gear: nets, decoys, wire baskets, corks,

*Land*

## EVERYWHERE THE WIND

The moment you turn right onto Highway 12 South at Whalebone Junction, one of the world's most scenic byways, you enter a world blanketed in generations of cultural heritage, a place imputed with unreined and exceptional beauty. The breeze gently tugs at your car and egrets flank the pristine marshlands to your right. At golden hour, Bodie Island Lighthouse pierces through a radiant sunset. One last curve of Highway 12 South, and she appears: the criticized, condemned, celebrated and soon-to-be-replaced Bonner Bridge, your ticket across one of the most tumultuous and dynamic inlets on the east coast, Oregon Inlet. At the bridge's crest, the curve of the earth extends in all directions. The world ahead, Hatteras Island, seems boundless, filled with freedom and possibility.

Stretching 48 miles from Oregon Inlet to Hatteras Inlet, Hatteras Island makes up almost the entire southern half of North Carolina's Outer Banks; it's the heart of the Cape Hatteras National Seashore and home to seven villages: Rodanthe, Waves, Salvo, Avon, Buxton, Frisco, and Hatteras. It is miraculous, really: a simple sandbar, 3 miles across at its widest point, poised between two mighty bodies of water: the Atlantic Ocean and the

"You can see the wind. . . ." (Photo by Baxter Miller, great-granddaughter of lifesaving station keeper Baxter Benjamin Miller [Cape Hatteras and Little Kinnakeet]; originally published in *Bit & Grain*, October 14, 2015)

Pamlico Sound. This thin sliver of sand stands sentry to the mainland against an often destructive and angry sea. Resolute, yet adaptive, the island is ever-shifting with the wind and tide, breaching periodically to cut new inlets that can close just as quickly as they open.

Hatteras Island is home to, arguably, North Carolina's most recognizable feature on a map: the protruding elbow that reaches far east into the Atlantic. David Stick, the premier Outer Banks historian, describes beautifully that at the Cape, known locally as The Point, "the Banks jut out so far into the Atlantic that the Gulf Stream currents caress the shoals, warming the atmosphere. . . . Here the northbound Gulf Stream swerves out to sea as it encounters the cold waters coming down from the Labrador Current, and at the junction of the two is Diamond Shoals, the Graveyard of the Atlantic, a point of constant turbulence and of countless shipwrecks."

This convergence creates an ecosystem of marine life from southern and northern latitudes that forms one of the few places in the world where such different species, like warm-water dolphin and cold-water tuna, cohabitate. Unpredictable and often underestimated wind patterns emerge from this convergence and challenge the expertise of U.S. Navy forecasters who are responsible for routing ships safely through the Atlantic. Jan De-Blieu, native Outer Banker and author of *Wind: How the Flow of Air Has Shaped Life, Myth, and the Land*, reports, "'Something happens out there, some local phenomenon that we're just missing,' one meteorologist told me. 'The wind speeds we predict will be off by ten or fifteen miles per hour, sometimes more. It's got to have something to do with the temperature difference between the Gulf Stream and the cooler water along the coast. But in terms of sea conditions, it makes a huge difference.'"

You can see the wind everywhere here. You can see it in the intensity of the weather: in the storm that moves in from miles offshore in minutes, engulfing you in its rapture. You can read it on people's faces: a light breeze has the ability to heal, while a strong northeast blow is a humbling reminder of mankind's insignificance. And when you can't see it, you can feel it in the sand biting at your ankles, and you can hear it in the rustling yaupon trees hugging the sound, themselves bent and shaped by a powerful, persistent force. This island was formed by and revolves around the wind—its direction, its strength, its mood, its relationship with the ocean determines life here.

Source: Baxter Miller, great-granddaughter of lifesaving station keeper Baxter Benjamin Miller (Cape Hatteras and Little Kinnakeet); originally published in *Bit & Grain*, October 14, 2015

Harkers Island waterfront, Stacy W. Davis and Garland Porter. Stacy Davis fish house and net spreads are seen along the shore, the original home of the Captain Stacy fleet, 1944. (Photo courtesy of the State Archives of North Carolina)

and net needles and palm saddles for mending sails and leatherwork. Net camps smelled of tar, dried seaweed, and fish. "These guys' whole lives were in there," said Dwight Burrus of Hatteras.

Landings were sacred, providing a Sunday afternoon place for baptisms. During the summer, landings served as the sites of camp meetings and revivals and as the meeting place for visitors sailing in from other communities to join in worship.

People gathered at landings every day waiting for the mailboat. Few events brought more excitement than the daily mail call at the post office, which often doubled as a store. The mailboat route from Beaufort included stops at Harkers Island, Cape Lookout, Marshallberg, Davis, and Atlantic. These mailboat routes were run by private contractors who converted their workboats to accommodate travelers and cargo. Captains Elmo Fulcher and George O'Neal took turns running the *Aleta*, a forty-five-foot mailboat with cabin and canvas awning. For seventeen years the *Aleta* ran faithfully from Atlantic to Ocracoke, seven days a week. "You'd get to Ocracoke in the evening about 5 o'clock," said Julian Brown. "And everybody in the neighborhood would meet the mailboat—the old folks, the children—everybody'd be there to the dock of Little Ike's store."

Community baptism service, Davis Shore. (Photo from the Anne Bobbitt Murphy Collection, Core Sound Waterfowl Museum and Heritage Center)

A mailboat route also ran from Manteo to the Hatteras Island villages. Tom Meekins of Avon "had an old horse named Charlie and an old cart, and if the tide was low he would just take his old horse and wade out in the water and back the cart up to the skiff," recalled Manson Meekins. Children would jump up and down at the landing, excited that the day's mail was getting "overhauled." Susan West, who worked at the modern post office in Avon, where mail has long been delivered by truck, said that some residents still asked, "Is the mail overhauled yet?"

Mailboats carried more than letters. They carried passengers, such as "drummers" (salesmen), visiting preachers, teachers, and visitors, all squeezed among the parcels. Before a ferry service was established in the early 1950s, folks en route to Ocracoke from Down East, or vice versa, would board the mailboat and spend several hours crossing the Pamlico amid parcels, produce, fish, and other items. The waterway was quite often the only way to transport people and products from village to village, and the sole means of communication. Just a few telephones could be found at the community stores in the years after World War II and were used for only emergencies.

The mailboat ran no matter what the weather; it was the lifeline to and from the mainland. From the last part of December 1917 to January 1918, however, Pamlico Sound froze over, and the mailboat was stuck for days. "The little mailboat from Atlantic froze outside of Portsmouth Island," re-

Island boys bringing in supplies from the *Dolphin*, the daily mailboat from Atlantic, 1955. (Photo by Martha McMillan Roberts, Standard Oil [New Jersey] Collection, SONJ 80665, Archives and Special Collections, University of Louisville, http://louisville.edu/library/archives)

The *Aleta* leaving Clayton Fulcher's dock at Atlantic, headed for Ocracoke, late 1940s. (Photo from the Katherine Steger Collection, Core Sound Waterfowl Museum and Heritage Center)

Passengers coming across on the mailboat included not only locals going back and forth or family and friends traveling from community to community, but strangers too. Doctors, revenu'ers, salesmen, and politicians, along with preachers and missionaries and, once a year, the new schoolteachers. While most everyone else "came and went" the schoolteachers stayed, some for longer than they bargained. They became "mailboat brides," marrying into the families of these islands and villages along the shore and becoming a vital part of each community.

My Aunt Ruby came from New Bern on the mailboat to teach and found her a room at Mr. Charlie's boardinghouse. It was there that Uncle Willie saw her first and told her immediately that he was going to marry her.

Henry Davis's store served as community gathering place, general store, post office, and mailboat dock on Harkers Island. (Photo from the Madge Guthrie Collection, Core Sound Waterfowl Museum and Heritage Center)

*Land*

And he did! She came in September and they were married in December of the same year: 1923.

Earl Davis married Joel's Aunt Lillian on the mailboat in 1924. Earl was afraid she might change her mind if he waited until they reached the shore. He recounted that story with pride, and in great detail, for the next sixty years.

Mr. Fred tells about seeing "Miss Mabel" for the first time, getting off the mailboat at Cleveland Davis's dock with her trunk. He went to the dock to help them get the teachers ashore. "The most beautiful woman I ever saw!" he says, even now [1990], and that was in 1926. Mr. Fred married "Miss Mabel" in 1927 and she taught second grade to every young'un on the Island.

"Mailboat Brides" I guess you could call them. When they came to these small and isolated settings little did they suspect that their lives, as well as the many they would touch, would be forever changed and enriched.

Source: Karen Willis Amspacher, *The Mailboat*, Fall 1990

called Roy Parsons of Ocracoke. "She froze all around her, and the captain got out and walked to Portsmouth Island on the ice." He said the fish froze in the ice with their tails sticking up "just like lily sprouts."

## FOOD TO LIVE BY

*Our family meals featured fish and shellfish pulled from the sea, poultry from our backyard pens, waterfowl from the Pamlico Sound, and vegetables from our home garden.* — Sharon Peele Kennedy, Hatteras

"Everybody would take a hoe and hill potatoes up after the wind blowed them down," said Nathaniel Jackson of Ocracoke. Collards, onions, potatoes, and beets; people on sandy barrier islands managed to keep gardens in the harshest environments. Surfmen at the lifesaving stations kept gardens too, like a keeper of the Little Kinnakeet Lifesaving Station who raised peanuts and strawberries.

Like the indigenous tribes before them, islanders grew gourds to use as bailing scoops in boats and dippers for water barrels. Crab scraps and seaweed have long been strewn on gardens as fertilizer. Wild grapes and berries were more plentiful than they are now and were used in preserves and homemade wines. On Harkers Island, wild huckleberries covered the

## ALL ABOARD THE MANTEO-HATTERAS BUS LINE

In 1938 T. Stockton Midgett of Rodanthe began the Manteo-Hatteras Bus Line, which amounted to a Ford station wagon that ran daily from Hatteras Village to Manteo. The bus stopped at all the villages and boarded Toby Tillet's ferry to cross Oregon Inlet. But Mr. Midgett died of a heart attack just two months after starting his line, leaving eighteen-year-old Harold, fourteen-year-old Anderson, and ten-year-old Stockton "Stocky" Midgett to carry on. For the next thirty-five years, the brothers continued the Manteo-Hatteras Bus Line, upgrading to small buses that frequently rusted out.

"We must have used over a hundred buses," reflected Anderson Midgett.

Sand ruts and hard beach formed the only routes. "We used to call our route the 101—one hundred and one roads because there was no designated road. . . . If the tide was out, you drove the surf. If the tide was in, you drove the bank of the beach or inside roads," said Anderson. They drove across shallow inlets cut by storms and avoided aquatic potholes by driving out into the sound. They maneuvered around shipwrecks and across sandy beaches. They routinely got stuck in the sand, requiring passengers to get out and push.

"One day we found a lifeboat that (was) bullet-ridden, with two bodies in it," said Anderson, recalling the World War II period on Hatteras Island. The paving of a road in the early 1960s spelled the end of the business, as people were able to provide their own transportation. The brothers simply moved on to a new business venture, which would prove lucrative for them as well as their children and grandchildren: Midgett Realty. "We've been in real estate for right good while," reflected Anderson Midgett. "But I still enjoy driving the beach."

interior, and women and children spent days picking, cooking, and preserving them.

Several varieties of fig trees grow like gangbusters along the coastal banks. Locals put oyster shells around the bases of fig trees to lend calcium to the growing process. Figs are eaten raw, stewed, or canned. Fig preserves are delectable, as are traditional fig cakes. Today, Ocracoke hosts a fig cake contest, and the local fish market sells the homemade dessert. Local

Harkers Island fishnet garden fence, 1943.
(Photo courtesy of the State Archives of North Carolina)

food classes in Down East and Hatteras are teaching traditional recipes, including fig preserves. A family's fig tree is a treasured gift, often rooted and shared with the next generation.

"The old folks liked the yaupon tea," said Douglas "Chubby" Dorris of Frisco. Yaupon bushes are everywhere along the coastal plain, and people used to cure the leaves for the tea trade, from Harkers Island to Avon. Ocracokers sold yaupon tea at the turn of the twentieth century for 50 cents a bushel, and in the 1930s yaupon was processed in Frisco and sold to traders in Elizabeth City for $1 a bushel. A certain stigma was attached to consumers of yaupon, once considered a "poor person's" substitute for "China tea." Children in Avon were taunted by the phrases "Kinnakeeter, yaupon eater," and "Kinnakeeters, highly fed, yaupon tea and crackling bread." Likewise, Harkers Islanders were once called "choppers" due to their processing yaupon tea. Ira Lewis, a descendant of Shackleford Banks whalers, continues to seek out the best yaupon bushes along the southern shore of Harkers Island for roasting, chopping, and brewing tea to share with family and friends.

Ira Lewis of Harkers Island still picks, chops, and brews his own yaupon tea.
(Photo by Neal Hutcheson, *Coresounders*)

In addition to limitless fish, banks families had cows as a source of protein. They would butcher a "beef" in the cold months and make butter and "clabber biscuits" from cow's milk. Miss Elma Dixon of Portsmouth said they would "make butter" by shaking a mason jar full of cream. If the butter was slow to separate from the cream, they would put a fig leaf in the jar. The tiny hairs on the leaves would "grab" the butter from out of the cream, and voilà, there was a lump of butter.

Coastal families were not inclined to waste resources and usually consumed, traded, saved, or sold everything they caught, found, and harvested. They enjoyed hogfish, mullet, and spot. The spots, a locally favored fish, were cleaned, salted, and preserved for winter meals. Gak Austin recalled smoking shad and hanging them on the clothesline to air dry on Hatteras, much like David Yeomans did with salt mullet on Cape Lookout. Fish was also canned for the winter before refrigeration became available.

"Old drum" has long been a favorite traditional dish on the Outer Banks. The largest of the red drum fish was sought after for this meal. Some red drum were taller than a man and so big they needed to be scaled with a garden hoe. Today smaller drum are harvested, as the largest are illegal to catch. To make the traditional dish, red drum is boiled, flaked, and served over potatoes, onions, and hard-boiled eggs. Cracklings and fatback grease are poured over the top with black pepper. Served with biscuits or cornbread, according to Edna Gray of Buxton, it is "a real down homer."

Though it would be hard to imagine today, the occasional sea turtle made its way to island kitchens. Women cleaned it and stewed it with potatoes and onions, and it was considered yet another food source for islanders. Julian Brown of Marshallberg spent summers in Hatteras Village and recalls that islanders ate sea turtle on Wednesday. "Every fish house had three or four turtles turned over flapping and flopping." They'd be killed, butchered, and distributed throughout the community, providing the only midweek source of fresh red meat until the freight boat arrived that weekend. "Grandma would make turtle hash that evening," he recalled.

On Harkers Island, "turkle" has been a treasured experience along with loon, stewed robins, and shorebirds, the meat meticulously picked from their tiny bones to feed hungry men, women and children. Today recipes for these species can be found in the Harkers Island United Methodist Cookbook, with the disclaimer that these were traditional dishes that have, under federal law, become "forbidden fruit." Even though the consumption of these species is now appalling to most, locals understand that they are symbols of the past generation's ability to survive on what nature provided.

Shackleford Banks descendants on Salter Path and Harkers Island are still called "loon eaters" for a hunting tradition passed down through the generations. History records a fateful day when fifty-some islanders were arrested for shooting loons by game wardens who had been hiding out in the sandhills of Shackleford Banks. Over the years, the idea of loon eating has evolved from a negative to a self-proclaimed "badge of honor," reinforcing the community's deep cultural ties to the past and to their ancestors of Shackleford Banks.

The idea of harnessing the wind for energy seems new to some, but old-timers recalled the days when windmills marked various points and promontories all along the coast. These post mills were versatile and could be rotated into the wind. Like the sails of a boat, canvas on the windmill's arms caught the wind. People would trade salted fish to mainland plantations for corn and then have their neighborhood miller grind it into cornmeal. Grand old grist stones can still be found decorating yards, and place names, such as Mill Point in Sea Level, bear witness to this heritage.

Everyone had a few chickens and ate the meat and eggs year-round. Chickens had to be penned up at least a week in advance for the best-tasting eggs; otherwise they would range freely, and their eggs would taste "fishy" or "marshy." Some islanders ate seagull eggs, sailing to nearby shoals frequented by shorebirds, and some gathered and ate sea turtle eggs.

## ROAMING FREE

*That was a beautiful sight to me, manes and tails a'flying and they just going wide open, sand behind them. Here come them cowboys from Cedar Island!* —*Margaret Daniels*

The Outer Banks were settled during the colonial period by yeoman farmers and stockmen from mainland Virginia and north. They packed their meager belongings, including cattle, sheep, hogs, goats, and chickens, onto wooden vessels and set sail to the distant banks, enticed by the prospect of new opportunity and an island life that made fencing for livestock completely unnecessary.

"All the sea banks (are) covered with cattle, sheep, and hogs," a colonial officer observed in 1776, concerned that British vessels would find ample supplies of fresh meat. The settlers built "paling" fences, not to keep animals enclosed but to keep the free-roaming livestock out of their yard gardens and off their porches. Steer scraped their horns on scrub oaks and outhouses, and clouds of flies and mosquitoes followed herds into the shade of maritime forests. Cows and horses waded into salt creeks or onto shoals to stay cool, and they kept a wary eye on the occasional human passerby. Their grazing kept the bushes and grass trimmed and eventually led to defoliation.

From Shackleford Banks to Hatteras Island, the days of livestock roaming free on the beach were a dream come true for children. Anderson Midgett of Hatteras grew up catching wild horses for a breakneck gallop along the surf. They thought nothing of riding "banker ponies" on "moonshiney nights up and down these roads." Boys also played a game called "tailing the cattle," where a child would grab a cow's tail and "let him sling you up and down the beach." Today, some old folks find it quite ironic that on Ocracoke the horses are penned and the people run free. It wasn't long ago that people fenced in their yards to keep the animals out.

Annual spring sheep drives were big events on the banks. Fathers and sons would gather at the outer edges of villages and fan out, walking or riding while hooting and hollering. They'd meet another group of livestock drivers coming from the opposite direction and pen hundreds of animals. The men built a platform on which the sheep were sheared. The sheep herders camped out on the beach, making tents out of the sails of their boat. They built campfires, sang, and "carried on" deep into the night. Wool was shipped to mainland ports of commerce, and some was used by local

Livestock and banker ponies grazing, late 1800s.
(Photo by unnamed photographer, Carol Cronk Cole Collection; courtesy
of the Outer Banks History Center, State Archives of North Carolina)

woman for spinning. "We'd go out in the woods and pick the wool off bushes
and briars where the sheep had been," said Lettie Guthrie. "Wash it and
clean it good and nice."

Frank Moore of Harkers Island said that his family slaughtered about
thirty rams three times a year, providing meat to the stores in Beaufort and
wool for military uniforms during World War II. He recalled transporting
live sheep on a thirty-two-foot boat called the *Ram* to an island near Middle
Marsh for slaughter. His father would cut the throats of the sheep and hang
them on scaffolding to skin them, three at a time.

Local men were hired as "range riders" in the 1920s to round up livestock twice a month, running the animals into a concrete "dipping vat" filled
with a creosote mixture. Government inspectors charged with managing
the "tick wars" oversaw the process as men from the community led the
roundup. A man painted the rump of each freshly dipped animal with a
dab of green paint, and a range rider patrolled the whole island in search of
any animal without the green mark. If livestock was discovered without the
green mark, the owner could be called into court.

"[My father] had not dipped his cattle," said Ben Spencer of Ocracoke.
"The judge said if you can't dip them, kill them." He recalled that the island
men found the wildest, rangiest "gang" of cattle and shot them all. "They
were just slaughtered." Cows and bulls can be seen today on the outlying
beaches of Cedar Island, and pigs, cattle, and horses wander the shores of
Browns Island near Harkers Island.

From Hatteras to Down East, roundups and pony pennings took place two or three times a year to brand the flanks of horses and cows or notch the ears of sheep. Family brands and notch patterns were recorded in county courthouses on the mainland, as livestock was valuable property. After calves were born in the spring, two teams of men on horseback would work from opposite ends of barrier islands to drive cattle into a pen, and ownership of the newborn livestock was determined by observing how mothers and babies paired up in the corral.

These pennings were huge events for Down East families, as parents and children traveled to the outlying beaches of Cedar Island, Core Banks, and Shackleford. Many people have vivid memories of the annual Fourth of July rite, complete with the smell of burning horsehair from branding irons, the buzz of flies in the midsummer heat, and the taste of cold Pepsi or lemonade as they sat on the fence rail watching the local men rope wild-eyed horses raised on wire grass and salt marsh. Any horses auctioned off would be transported to the mainland on skiffs, yet another source of excitement.

In 1935, the North Carolina General Assembly outlawed free-roaming livestock on the banks to shore up the grass-planting and dune-building programs, but horses roamed free on Ocracoke until 1953. Cattle, sheep, and goats weren't removed from Shackleford Banks until the mid-1980s, and horses, thanks to the political action of local advocates, remain there today. "These horses have been here longer than we have," Carolyn Mason told legislators, newspaper reporters, scientists, and anyone who would listen. She and an unlikely band of locals, scientists, newspaper reporters, and politicians from across the country worked diligently to save the wild herd on Shackleford. Thanks to them these horses continue to roam freely but are managed carefully on Shackleford Banks.

## AMERICA'S FIRST NATIONAL SEASHORE PARK

"A coastal park for North Carolina" was proposed in 1933 by naturalist and illustrator Frank Stick, calling for the protection of vast beach areas south of Nags Head with erosion control, sand reclamation, and dune grass plantings. Stick argued that the establishment of a park would provide Depression-era jobs for banks villagers and enable visitors to enjoy the seashore by way of a coastal highway from Nags Head all the way to Beaufort.

Stick's proposal got a boost when four nonresident hunters donated almost 1,000 acres surrounding Cape Hatteras Lighthouse to the government that same year. The devastation wrought by the 1933 storm in September brought the Civilian Conservation Corps to the coast for dune building and grass planting, jump-starting beach protection efforts.

Congress formally authorized the establishment of Cape Hatteras National Seashore in 1937, the country's first national seashore park. But plans were put on hold during World War II. In 1952, according to David Stick, two Mellon family foundations donated over a half-million dollars toward buying parkland, which the state matched, putting the national seashore project back on track. Free-roaming livestock had been outlawed, so some banks residents were glad to sell what had become useless grazing land to the government. Others had hard feelings about what they considered a "land grab" by the U.S. government.

Farther south, plans for Cape Lookout were under way by the 1960s. President Lyndon Johnson signed a bill in 1966 authorizing the park service to establish Cape Lookout National Seashore on 30,000 acres of Core and Shackleford banks. A group of non-local property owners with the Core Banks Gun Club refused to sell, as did a businessman from Sanford who planned to develop land next to Cape Lookout Lighthouse. This compelled the government to make them a more lucrative deal, planting resentment among those who had sold their land for little to nothing.

In 1974, the state officially transferred Core Banks lands to the federal government, and Shackleford Banks—after lengthy property disputes— was added to the seashore park in 1985. Unlike Core Banks, which retained limited beach driving and fishing privileges, Shackleford was designated a "wilderness area," and notice was given that all livestock and personal property, including camps, had to be removed by midnight of December 31, 1985.

Islanders stood on the shores of Harkers Island on a cold night in December of 1985 and watched with tears as their beloved camps on Shackleford went up in flames. Locals set fire to their own cabins in an act of spite against the park's directive. With those flames went the last tangible connection to the banks for Shackleford descendants, with the exception of the community graveyards. The park's visitor center on Harkers Island mysteriously burned to the ground soon afterward. After years of investigation, no one has ever known for sure who lit the match.

The relationship between locals and the National Park Service continues to be a "work in progress" throughout the byway. Indeed tensions have run high over the years as the park service's mission of protecting nature, preserving culture, and promoting fun can be contradictory and result in angry fishermen, beachgoers, and residents who feel hemmed in by rules.

In 1966, Cape Lookout National Seashore was created, incorporating all of Core Banks. Twenty years later, Shackleford Banks was added to the national seashore, and all signs of human existence—cottages, fishing shacks, livestock—were removed from the interior of the island. Unclaimed ponies gained their freedom, and Shackleford Banks became a sanctuary for wild horses.

With cattle, sheep, and goats gone, the ponies had no competition for grazing land. Over the next decade, they multiplied quickly, and the herd expanded to about 200 individuals—too many for the island to support, according to biologists. Something had to be done.

Coming together for horses in the mid-1990s, dissent rose on the mainland and Harkers Island over the National Park Service's plans for the Shackleford Banks horses. The park service proposed removing most of the horses on the island and maintaining a herd of fifty to sixty. Equine geneticist Gus Cothran of the University of Kentucky warned the park service that their number was too small to sustain a genetically viable population. Local horse lovers became convinced that the ponies' days would be numbered if the plan were implemented.

A group of Carteret County citizens formed the nonprofit Foundation for Shackleford Horses and appealed to U.S. Representative Walter Jones for help. Meanwhile, disease testing found that some of the ponies were carriers of equine infectious anemia, a horse illness similar to AIDS in that it has an inapparent carrier stage. State law requires that any horse, wild or domestic, found to have equine infectious anemia be quarantined for life or destroyed.

Seventy-six of the Shackleford horses tested positive—41 percent of the herd. Because no quarantine site was available for that many horses, they were all euthanized. Shocked into action, Jones drafted legislation in 1998 titled "The Shackleford Banks Protection Act," which mandated that a herd of at least 100 free-roaming horses be co-managed on the island by the park service and the foundation.

About that time, the park service hired equine biologist Sue Stuska to work with the herd and the foundation. For the last five years, the unique arrangement appears to have functioned efficiently, with the co-managers working together well. The Shackleford population has been certified free

Grazing on Shackleford, protected and safe. (Photo by Lillie Miller)

of equine infectious anemia, with no danger that it will return. The ponies are safe on their island home, away from any other infected horses that could spread the disease. Stuska handles surveys, censuses, and constant assessments of herd health. She and the foundation act as liaisons to other scientists who have studied the Shackleford ponies for years. The group also facilitates the adoption of any horse that must be removed from the island.

"We make sure they're healthy and well taken care of," said Carolyn Mason, president of the Foundation for Shackleford Horses. "We have vets brought down if need be, and we look for some really good homes for them. Our main interest is the long-term security and safety of the horses." Stuska agrees that the foundation has proven its worth. "We're handling things that would be labor intensive for them, and vice versa," she said.

"It has taken a long time to find a happy balance between the ecology of the island and the viability of the horses," she said. "It has also taken a lot of time to build the cooperation that now exists between the local population and the park service." That kind of cooperation is of historic importance.

Source: Greg Jenkins, "Unbridled Alliance," *NC Wildlife*, February 4, 2005

"Say what you will," said Sandra Gaskill of Harkers Island. "If it weren't for the park, we'd be looking at another Myrtle Beach."

## LOOKING ASHORE: HOLDING ON

Land—it's a relative term on the coast, a mix of marsh and sand, a lot of mud, and a few high ridges. Land is home, yet it's not easy to hold on to. Generations ago, storms moved communities of people to higher ground. Today a new sort of storm has altered where people live, as coastal development, rising property values, loss of working waterfront, and higher taxes collude to compel some to leave their home communities for more affordable areas. These forces of change are different but no less powerful than storms that sweep houses off their foundations.

The land, always at the mercy of the rising sea, is what we fight to hold on to so that we can pass it reverently to our children and their children. We depend on land to mark our place and to provide the space to raise families and build lives. Land is where we live and where we die, sacred, holding in its sandy soil a deep history. Land cradles our ancestors, marked by a picket fence under a wind-sheared oak, old names etched on a stone.

Still, land here is temporary, ours for a while, threatened by forces greater than ourselves. Yet we hold firm, marking our place with stakes and handwritten deeds, caretakers for our family's legacy and the next generation's inheritance. The beauty of this landscape, in all its magnificence, pales in comparison to the meaning of this place and all that was, is, and will be. This is home, here at the water's edge, fragile and uncertain; this is our place, not purchased but given, ours—with a value that cannot be bought or sold, its true significance known only in the heart of its people.

# 3

# *People*

When I was a girl people up Norfolk way would say,
*"There ain't nothing across Oregon Inlet." I'm sorry but there*
*sure is and I live there.* —Mildred Midgett, Rodanthe

Families along the banks of North Carolina have thrived, struggled, worked, and adjusted as the tide and wind come and go. Today, northern banks communities are booming in the midst of federal parkland. The southern banks, Portsmouth, Core, and Shackleford, once thriving, were abandoned long ago. Diamond City and Shell Castle Island have since washed away. If not for the National Park Service's preservation efforts, little would remain of Portsmouth. Cape Lookout village continues to wait, its historic structures to be restored and opened for descendants to cherish and the public to appreciate. One thing is for sure: life on the edge has few certainties.

Banks families who scratched a living from the sea and gave thanks for what they had passed along hard-earned lessons of self-sufficiency. As Josiah Bailey, once captain of the *Diamond City*, noted, for Shackleford Banks descendants, "memories remaining only in the blood" hold natives to the narrow strip of sand that was once their home. Today, the "Core Sounders" of Down East, Ocracokers, and folks up the banks still carry forth that same deep-seeded spirit that sustained their ancestors.

Ferries, bridges, and roads connect people at the end of these roads to the world, and the world to them. Today, some communities have exploded with growth, and others have faded, the result of multiple factors and sometimes despite great odds. Both newcomers and a remnant of those long-time residents "whose ancestors came by boat" are here to stay—some for a while, some forever.

Portsmouth Methodist Church stands quietly, reverently, in
Portsmouth Village, a testament to the faith of bankers past and present.
(Photo by Michael Halminski)

Whether living on the banks or in the low-lying communities on the mainland, the people of the Outer Banks have been somewhat of a mystery to the mainstream world. "Who are those people?" and "How can they live there?" are common questions. More than one visitor to the Core Sound Museum on Harkers Island has confessed an unfounded fear of traveling east of the North River Bridge. "I don't know," said a teacher visiting Down East for the first time. "I just grew up hearing stories of Down East being a rough place!"

Years of oral histories provide a glimpse into the world of coastal people—past and present. Old voices evoke a sense of the C'ae Bankers who lived on Shackleford Banks before storms drove them to the mainland, or of the loss of Portsmouth Village's youth to the siren call of a world beyond its quiet, provincial shores. The old folks remember Ocracoke and Hatteras illuminated by kerosene lanterns, the daily news passed along on porches by neighbors. Their voices crack and tremble with deep emotion, rich in a lyrical dialect that continues to echo today at corner stores, schools, and fire stations.

*People*

# THE WAY WE TALK

*If I'm around someone, and I hear an islander accent, I gravitate*
*toward that, to tap into something. —Ernie Foster, Hatteras*

The notion that "this place is different" usually strikes newcomers first by ear when they hear the distinctive coastal dialect. A visitor Down East, standing at the counter of a convenience store, might realize that the fishermen behind him are deep in conversation lost to an unfamiliar ear. Some call this the "Hoi Toider" dialect due to a trademark *oi* pronunciation of the *eye* sound, as in "It's hoi toid (high tide) at the Cape!" Others refer to the coastal dialect as a carryover of Elizabethan English brought to the coast by English settlers. North Carolina State University linguist Walt Wolfram considers that theory a simplification that ignores other influences, such as Scots-Irish settlers who came from the mainland. Most agree that the dialect has persisted thanks to the relative isolation of island living.

Some young folks, particularly in Down East communities, have a remarkably strong dialect in spite of the influence of popular culture and the media. Walt Wolfram suggests that the brogue on Ocracoke has gotten stronger among middle-aged fishermen who are pushing back against the change all around them. Young folks growing up in the era of school consolidation were often teased for their brogue by students from larger mainland communities, causing the island children to realize for the first time they did talk different. Today the local dialect is considered a proud birthright— a badge of honor—that cannot be learned, a gift of kinship with other truly isolated communities like Smith and Tangier Islands in the Chesapeake Bay.

The coastal dialect is sprinkled with words heard few other places, such as "pizer" for porch, and "mommicked" for tired or aggravated. Down Easters have colorful terms for people who are "from off" that are sometimes endearing and sometimes not, depending on the situation. Folks often say the opposite of what they mean, as in "He's got a lot of sense" directed at someone who forgot to untie his boat before trying to leave the dock. "You're purty" might be said to a fisherman covered in engine grease. A compliment might consist of "She ain't ugly" for a little girl in an Easter dress. The old vocabulary has clear maritime influences, such as when someone pushes back from the Thanksgiving table, groans, and says, "I've run aground!" Or "her oars don't hit the water" in reference to someone who doesn't think things through. Children rattle these phrases off without a thought, giving hope that this "way of talking" will last another generation.

Various terms have been used to describe the dialect of the Outer Banks, including "Banker Speech" and "Hoi Toider speech," though the most common term used by native islanders is the brogue.

Residents of the Outer Banks are accustomed to outsiders' recognition and some are even prepared to perform the brogue on command. Rex O'Neal, one of eleven boys born to Essie and Harry O'Neal on Ocracoke Island, can "perform" the dialect. He said to a dialect researcher in 1993, "Well, it's *hoi toid* on the sound *soid*. Last night the water *far*, tonight the moon shine. No *feesh*, what you supposed the matter, Uncle Woods?"

O'Neal performs several dialect traits of Outer Banks speech, including the iconic *oi* for long *i* in *toid* for *tide* and *soid* for *side*, the pronunciation of *–ire* as *ar* in *far* for *fire* and the pronunciation of the vowel of *fish* as *feesh*. This performance phrase, first recorded in 1993, has continued to serve as a marker of island identity.

The Outer Banks brogue is arguably one of the United States' most distinctive dialects. It is also one of the few dialects spoken in the nation that is commonly misidentified as British or Australian or Irish. Islanders commonly recount stories of tourists asking them what country they're from and acting confused when they respond "right here." The brogue elicits a wide range of comments from people trying to guess where it comes from, but most first-time listeners think it is from Australia or England, usually in the southwest of England, where they pronounce their *r*'s in words like *ear* for *far*.

The other part of the story about Outer Banks English is the way in which it's receding, including the commodified status it now has even for natives. Though the brogue was once spoken by the majority of residents born and raised on the Outer Banks, this is certainly no longer the case. In some areas, particularly the northern islands of the Outer Banks, the vast majority of property is now owned by outsiders and beach development has made ancestral islanders an endangered species. In places like Corolla, Kitty Hawk, and Nags Head, it is hard to find representative traditional brogue speakers. In concentrated communities that retain a community base of ancestral islanders and a few traditional marine-based occupations, brogue speakers can be found if you know where older locals hang out.

Source: Walt Wolfram and Jeffrey Reaser, *Talkin' Tar Heel: How Our Voices Tell the Story of North Carolina* (University of North Carolina Press, 2014)

# WHAT'S IN A NAME?

*My family is who I am. —Mary Fulford Green, Down East descendant*

"Who's your crowd?" is the question among natives when trying to figure out who someone is and where they come from. Folks connect themselves in terms of kinship and family history, a trait common in the South. "I knew your grandfather's brother; are you part of that Willis crowd from down sound? Who is your grandmother?" Styrons and Goodwins in Cedar Island, Midgetts and Grays in Rodanthe, O'Neals and Austins on Ocracoke—family names remain rooted in the fabric of particular communities, as revealed by reading church rolls or wandering through community cemeteries. Back in the day, the only "foreign" names were those of the families of preachers or servicemen marrying into the community.

When almost everyone shares a last name, and often a first name too, nicknames become a necessity. If a community is home to five John Styrons, they could be called Big John, Little John, Nellie's John, Uncle John, and Old Man John. Nicknames can be creative and have a story behind them. Little Pie, Mossy Cat, Snowball, and Bump are just a few Down East examples.

Ocracoker Nathaniel Jackson explained how his boyhood buddy Ronald "Conch" O'Neal got his nickname. As young boys they were helping an older fisherman set a long-haul net. When the fishermen yelled, "Set away!" Nathaniel jumped overboard to set the net but Ronald ignored the call, sitting on the bow "singing and having the biggest time." So the fisherman reached over and hit him upside the head with a gourd and knocked him overboard, hollering, "Conch!" Local folks know that a conch is synonymous with deafness, as in "He's deafer'n a conch!" Ronald O'Neal lived a long and adventurous life and remained Conch to all who knew him.

The old folks tell of a creative way to keep women's names straight. A woman was sometimes identified by her first name plus her husband's first name. If three women in the community were named Annie Willis, for example, but one was married to Ben Willis, one to Joe Willis, and the third to Jim Willis, their nicknames would be Annie Ben, Annie Joe, and Annie Jim. Children often referred to adults as "aunt" or "uncle" no matter what their actual kin ties, and kids were sometimes identified with a parent's name as a prefix to their own. "Sal's Mart," for example, lived on Shackleford Banks with his mother, Sal.

Boats are named as well. From little skiffs to large trawlers, boats carry the names of family members (*Justin T, Lucy B*), places (*Cape Point, Bay Rambler*), or sometimes afterthoughts (*Big Mistake, Wasted Wood*). Boats—

Harkers Island harbor, holding on to the old way.

and anything on wheels, including lawn mowers, cars, and trucks—are decidedly female. "I got her running this morning," could refer to a lawn mower, a car, or a chainsaw. When a student from the Duke Marine Lab asked a fisherman why boats are gendered female, he replied, "Because boats, like women, are unpredictable!"

Places receive nicknames as well. The southern portion of Hatteras Village is known as "Sticky Bottom" for its wet, marshy land before drainage ditches and canals were dug. Ocracokers were either "Pointers" or "Creekers," depending on what side of Cockle Creek they lived on (unless one lived "up Trent" in the woods). Even today, if someone is going to "the Pur," they are going to the Down East community of Atlantic, known also as Purlantic—as in "She's a Purlanticer." Some believe this is from an old directional phrase, as in "Sail northward per Atlantic." Pejoratives such as "Loon Eaters" for Harkers Islanders, "Onion Eaters" for Davis shoremen, and "Frisco Ticks" for dwellers of the once heavily wooded Frisco community are remembered by the natives, but with the passing of time they seem to carry less sting.

Neighborhoods too had their names. On Harkers Island, Hancock Landing, was exactly that, a nest of kin, all Hancocks one way or the other

## THE LAST DAUGHTER OF DAVIS RIDGE

When Nannie Davis Ward was a child, Davis Ridge was an all-black community on a wooded knoll, or small island, on the eastern shore of Jarrett Bay, not far from Core Sound and Cape Lookout. A great salt marsh separated the Ridge from the mainland to the north, which was known as Davis Shore. Davis Island was just to the south. A hurricane cut a channel between Davis Ridge and Davis Island in 1899, but in her grandparents' day, it had been possible to walk from one to the other.

The founders of Davis Ridge had been among many slave watermen at Core Sound before the Civil War. Ward's family was in many ways typical of the African American families along the Lower Banks. They were skilled maritime laborers with a seafaring heritage. They had eighteenth-century family roots in the West Indies and had black, white, and Native American ancestry. They moved seasonally from fishery to fishery, working on inshore waters, rarely the open sea. They also had a history of slave resistance. Nannie Davis Ward's mother, who identified herself as Native American, had grown up on Bogue Banks, a 26-mile-long barrier island west of Beaufort, and her mother's grandfather had evidently been a slave aboard a French sailing vessel. According to Ward, the great-grandfather had escaped from his French master while in port at New Bern and had been raised free in the family of a white waterman at Harkers Island, ten miles west of Davis Ridge.

It was Sutton Davis, Ward's paternal grandfather, who first settled Davis Ridge. As a slave, Sutton Davis had belonged to a small planter and shipbuilder named Nathan Davis at Davis Island. Sutton had been a master boatbuilder and carpenter. According to his granddaughter, he had learned the boatbuilding trade at a Wilmington shipyard owned by a member of the white Davis family and then moved back to Davis Island.

When Union troops captured Beaufort and New Bern in 1862, Sutton Davis led the Davis Island slaves to freedom. They rowed a small boat across Jarrett Bay to the fishing village of Smyrna, from where they fled to Union-occupied territory on the outskirts of New Bern. After the war, some of those former slaves founded the North River community, a few miles out of Beaufort, but Sutton Davis bought 4 acres at Davis Ridge in 1865. Nathan Davis sold him the property for the sort of low price usually reserved for family. Sutton Davis and his children eventually acquired 220 more acres at Davis Ridge.

Sutton Davis and his thirteen children operated one of the first successful menhaden factories in North Carolina, long before the industry's boom in Beaufort. Sutton built two fishing schooners, the *Mary E. Reeves* and the *Shamrock*. His sons worked the boats while his daughters dried and pressed the menhaden—known locally as "shad" or "pogie"—to sell as fertilizer and oil. "Men should have been doing it," Ward explained, "but he didn't have them there, so the girls had to fill in for them." In fact, Ward pointed out, at Davis Ridge, "the girls did a lot of farm work, factory work too."

The black families at Davis Ridge were what local historian Norman Gillikin in Smyrna calls "saltwater farmers," the old-time Downeasters who lived by both fishing and farming. They hawked oysters across Jarrett Bay and raised hogs, sheep, and cattle. They grew corn for the animals and sweet "roasting ears" for themselves. At night they spun homegrown cotton into cloth. Their gardens were full of collard greens and, as Ward recalled vividly, "sweet potatoes as big as your head." They worked hard and prospered.

Davis Ridge was a proud, independent community . . . a remote hammock, but Ward could not remember a day of loneliness or boredom. . . . "We enjoyed ourselves on the island," Ward said. "There wasn't a whole lot of things to do, but we enjoyed people. We visited each other."

Source: David Cecelski, "The Last Daughter of Davis Ridge," in *A Historian's Coast: Adventures into the Tidewater Past* (John F. Blair, 2000)

as described by Charlie William's youngest son, Joel. "Growing up in a compound of numerous families related in every direction by blood or marriage allowed me to walk into anyone's house without knocking," he explained. "I knew someone would feed me, and mother knew someone was keeping watch on me and all the other children of the neighborhood. The Hancock Landing area was our own world."

Neighborhoods had meaning and purpose as well. Families settled in "compounds" of sorts, with a tract of land divided as the family grew. Generations of Guthries, Roses, Austins, O'Neals, Midgetts, and Burruses would spend their entire lives within walking distance of their birthplace. Here brothers, sisters, cousins, aunts, and uncles would share not only the land but the adjoining shoreline, docks, and storage sheds. From these family hamlets, men and women would make their living, side by side, fishing, farming, and making a life together.

# DAY BY DAY

*We were dirt poor, but I didn't know that until later years. — Gaskill Austin, Salvo*

Connie Farrow described the quiet, natural world of growing up in Frisco during the 1920s. "You could listen to the ocean's roar and tell pretty well what direction the wind would be the next day, and you could tell by the sunset whether it would be rainy or clear." Students interviewing him for the *Sea Chest*, Hatteras Island's answer to the *Foxfire* journal of mountain lore, took notes. "You could walk down the road in the early morning and hear people grinding their coffee beans," he continued. "You could smell such a sweet aroma from the fresh boiling coffee." He talked about missing the sound of chopping wood. "Everyone burned wood in those days and even the smoke from a wood fire smelled good."

Drinking water was collected from the sky via a cistern attached to every house. Rainwater, according to Gaskill Austin, "purified itself every seven days" and improved in taste. Water collected in May tended to "rot or stink," he claimed, and water collected in a cistern would get a shot of bleach or a couple of drops of kerosene to keep mosquito larvae, or "wigglers," out of the drinking water.

To keep the mosquitoes at bay, people set up "mosquito smokes," pails with kerosene-soaked rags that smoldered and smoked. Islanders also swabbed their window screens with kerosene to keep the gnats out. They swatted biting insects with a myrtle bush branch and, in later years, used a mixture of kerosene and DDT called "Flit."

Before refrigeration, families had "dairy houses," "milk houses," or "cool houses," screened enclosures designed to keep food cool and off-limits to insects. Chickens were killed on Saturdays and hung in the cool house in preparation for Sunday dinner. Some folks filled a pan with ice from a "buy boat" to keep the dairy house cool; buy boats were sent from the fish house to fishing grounds to collect or "buy" fish from netters. "We were dirt poor," observed Gaskill Austin, "but I didn't know that until later years because everyone was the same." Sandra K. Willis remembered, "They would get their living from the sea and sound. . . . They worked hard. You could tell it by their hands and faces, but they always found a way to survive."

Women's work knew no end. Everyday tasks were done with materials salvaged and saved. Sand was once used to scrub floors and clean the smut off irons, and floors were swept with palmetto fronds from the mainland. A woman recalled that her mother tied rags to a hoe to mop the floors. Ashes

Arriving back home on the *Dolphin*, the daily mailboat from Atlantic, are a mother with her children and day's shopping and another mother with her child and her new baby carried by the grandmother, 1955. There is neither doctor nor hospital in Ocracoke. (Photo by Martha McMillan Roberts, Standard Oil [New Jersey] Collection, SONJ 80697, Archives and Special Collections, University of Louisville, http://louisville.edu/library/archives)

from the woodstove were used to clean iron pots and pans. Nothing was wasted or thrown away, including time.

During the winter, nets were hung inside the house to prepare for the spring fishing season, and in the warmer months, they were hung on the porch or in the yard for repairs in preparation for the fall fishing season. Everyone big enough to stand and work a needle helped. Laundry was done by heating water in lard cans and using a scrub board. Some women washed clothes for Coast Guard personnel for pay. Ikie Willis recalled his mother, Miss Addie, "taking in" washing from the Cape Lookout Coast Guardsmen who sent tow sacks of dirty uniforms by mailboat to Harkers Island, where

*J. E. Sterling*, one of the small, fifty-foot, shallow-draft freight boats that supply Hatteras, 1945. (Photo by Sol Libsohn, Standard Oil [New Jersey] Collection, SONJ 26652, Archives and Special Collections, University of Louisville, http://louisville.edu/library/archives)

she would wash and iron the uniforms. "The work helped keep us fed after my father died," he added.

Just about every landing and neighborhood had a store. Most were small, with a few shelves and irregular hours, while others—particularly those larger establishments that were accessible to freight boats—were central hubs where men and women could find or order almost everything. Canned goods, flour, sugar, coffee, and lumber all came by boat. Ice was delivered in 300-pound blocks. Many stores had a big barrel where customers could fish out a pickle for a nickel. "[Some children] would take a pickle and put it up their bloomer leg," recalled Ruby Williams of Avon. "Get a free one, y'know?"

One of the sail-operated freight boats that ran from the Outer Banks to Elizabeth City was the *Missouri*, owned and operated by Avon resident Loran O'Neal. The *Missouri* was a fifty-six-foot-long, shallow-drafted, two-

Lucy Maurice holds her baby, Sandra Carol, as she receives an injection of
anti–whooping cough serum at the improvised clinic in the A. Burrus Store
on Hatteras, 1945. Miss Bessie Draper is the health department nurse.
(Photo by Sol Libsohn, Standard Oil [New Jersey] Collection, SONJ 26775, Archives
and Special Collections, University of Louisville, http://louisville.edu/library/archives)

masted sailing sharpie. The juniper vessel was built Down East in Smyrna.
The *Missouri* was rigged with a large block and tackle for heavy cargo. The
vessel "weren't beautiful [but] it done its job," said L. P. O'Neal, the captain's
son. "It fed people, hauled freight, tombstones, and lumber—whatever anybody wanted."

"You can put this on a bag," folks would say to storekeepers, as some
used a paper sack to record transactions. Credit was extended in fishing
communities in hopes that fishing would improve and the bill would be
paid. Little stores such as Willis Oddie Guthrie's business, located on Red
Hill on Harkers Island, was called the "Jot 'em Down" because he "jotted

down" what people got. People worked out their debts by the week, month, or season, the best way they could.

Community stores were the first to have telephones and electricity. Hatteras Villagers had access to the phone in Lee Robinson's store in the event of emergencies. Stores and fish houses got electricity by the 1930s, years before most houses were equipped. When electricity came to Harkers Island in 1939, homes were wired for one light bulb to hang from the center of the room. That changed everything. "The whole world lit up," recalled an islander. Luther Yeomans soon opened an appliance store on Harkers Island, much to the delight of the women, as families could buy Kelvinator iceboxes and washing machines.

## LIVING BY FAITH

*Their faith in God is what kept them strong.* — Sandra K. Willis, Harkers Island

The highest point in almost all of the low-lying coastal hamlets was the church steeple reaching above the oaks. Church has long been at the center of community life. In the early days, church and school often took place in the same building. On Harkers Island, the first school was Jenny Bell's Academy, a mission school of the Northern Methodist Church in Boston that sent "shoes by the barrel" to the barefooted children of Harkers Island.

Even before churches built permanent structures, camp or "protracted" meetings were held on Shackleford in the late 1800s for several days, maybe weeks, at a time, beckoning villagers from the mainland and other communities Down East. They often slept in their boats, sometimes when the weather (too much wind or not enough) caused them to stay for another day of visiting and the next night's service. The revivals were called "protracted" because the meetings would last "as long as the Holy Spirit was working."

The earliest denominations were Southern Methodist, Northern Methodist, Primitive Baptist, Freewill Baptist, and Southern Baptist, although communities differed as to which denominations took hold. The charismatic Pentecostal faith found a home on Hatteras Island during the turbulent unification period for Southern and Northern Methodists in the late 1930s. Not all Methodists were happy about uniting under the same steeple, and several joined the Assembly of God church instead. The Pentecostal faith took hold in Salvo, and the timbers of the *Kohler* shipwreck were used to construct "The Little Church with the Big God." This church is now called the Salvo Assembly of God.

Harkers Island has a history of congregations that splinter into new

Square dancing at "The Beach" Night Club, Hatteras, 1945.
(Photo by Sol Libsohn, Standard Oil [New Jersey] Collection, SONJ 27032, Archives
and Special Collections, University of Louisville, http://louisville.edu/library/archives)

churches over the years. Today there are eight houses of worship on the island. In the wake of terrible storms and dislocation that uprooted Diamond City in the early 1900s, the Mormon Church sent elders to Shackleford Banks and Harkers Island. Joel Hancock's book *Strengthened by the Storm* is a gripping account of the challenges the Mormon Church faced in trying to find a church home. The Church of Jesus Christ of Latter-day Saints of Harkers Island now maintains the largest congregation in the Down East region.

No matter what community, church was pretty much mandatory for children growing up along the Outer Banks. "Mom would tell us, you go to one or you go to the other, that's your choice," said Margaret Willis of Frisco. "But if you don't go to Sunday school, you don't leave home all day."

Some recall spending all day at church, between the morning's sermon and an afternoon and evening Bible study session.

Music played a central role in social and religious gatherings, and Harkers Island in particular developed a reputation for outstanding music that persists today. Church groups from the island continue to travel the country to sing for camp meetings and revivals. "We sing by let'er," Paul Lewis, a member of the Methodist choir, explained with a smile. "We open our mouths and let'er fly." Just like the Harkers Island boatbuilders who have little use for blueprints, musicians and singers share a natural God-given talent and have little need for sheet music or formal training to be able to sing full harmonies and play almost any instrument available, as islanders sing and play "by ear."

Ocracoke has a long musical history that is ever-evolving with the creative spirit that permeates the island. New genres mix with bluegrass and old-time fiddle-and-dance tunes. Summer visitors get a touch of this talent at the Ocrafolk Opry and the live music found on docks and porches throughout the village. The island has a lively history of performance art in music, drama, storytelling, and dance. Folks traveled far and wide to attend Ocracoke square dances in the 1940s and 1950s.

Square dances were popular all along the banks. String bands made up of fiddles, guitars, harmonicas, and sometimes the triangle played for dances. Folks came down from Hatteras Island or sailed from "Little" Washington to Ocracoke. Fiddle legend Ivey Scott of Harkers Island played for dances from Ocracoke to Cape Lookout. He was best known for "The Booze Yacht" ballad, a true account of a shipwrecked rumrunner that supplied islanders with "good spirits" for more than a year.

## EDUCATION AND INNOVATION

*Reading was an adventure, my gateway to the vast world*
*beyond the bridge. —Joel G. Hancock, Harkers Island*

One-room schoolhouses were built during the latter part of the nineteenth century, and the number of grades (and combinations of grades) changed depending on the number of students. Lance Midgett of Waves, born in 1935, recalled graduating with five students in his class. Their school had an old woodstove that the children would stoke in the morning and a cistern with a conch shell that the students shared as a cup.

Small village schools of Hatteras Island began consolidating after the roads came, often quieting years of community rivalries. "All of that clan-

Ocracoke classroom, 1955.
(Photo by Sol Libsohn, Standard Oil [New Jersey] Collection, SONJ 80712, Archives and Special Collections, University of Louisville, http://louisville.edu/library/archives)

nish thing started to change when all the schools come together at Buxton," said Jimmy Austin, referring to the opening of Cape Hatteras School in the early 1960s. "It was the greatest thing that ever happened [because] they made a community out of the island; instead of seven communities you had one." What had been community ball teams became Cape Hatteras School teams, allowing community allegiances to expand and fostering a sense of Outer Banks identity.

The expansion of communications brought almost as much change as roads and bridges. The role of the military before, during, and after World War II provided much of the infrastructure (radio towers, generators, elec-

Outer Banks Bookmobile, Dare County, visits Hatteras Village, 1952.
(Photo courtesy of the State Archives of North Carolina)

tricity, telephones) that transitioned these communities from the days of written letters, storm flags, and mailboat call-outs to radio and telegraph access for the people here. The isolation of the Outer Banks was a draw for pioneers in new inventions, such as the Wright brothers' "first flight" in Kitty Hawk. But that was not the only history being made on the Outer Banks.

Learning was definitely an "applied science" along the banks. Davis Shore legend William Luther "Mr. Fixit" Paul's experimental helicopter project was under way about the same time air travel was being tested farther north at Kitty Hawk. Paul was barely able to obtain an engine with enough power to lift his invention, but the locals believe that Igor Sikorsky, inventor of the helicopter, benefited from Paul's work. General Billy Mitchell famously proved that vessels could be effectively destroyed by aerial bombings, a theory that he tested off Cape Hatteras in 1923.

"Thomas Edison, Jr., who spent weeks with Mr. Theissin and worked with him," wrote Margaret Davis of Hatteras, "stayed at our house as no motels were available. I have forgotten how long they were there, but they came home all excited they had 'dots and dashes' from Manteo." She was referring to the early experiments at Cape Hatteras in wireless, also conducted by Reginald Fessenden on radio transmissions. The unoccupied sandbanks and the unobstructed sky and sea provided the perfect testing grounds for all sorts of inventions.

Native bankers, with inborn ingenuity and an aptitude for engineering, science, and math, often ventured from their island homes to establish distinguished careers around the country. Their successes can often be traced back to their capacity to "make do" with limited resources and to create, repair, and develop equipment out of necessity. Islanders are confident when trying new ways and modifying old ways. People are born knowing how to make things work because they've had to "make do with what they had" all their lives.

## MAKING THINGS HAPPEN

*Fishermen were the ones who built the courthouses, the schools, the churches along the coast. — Jonathan Robinson, Atlantic*

"I packed shrimp right in the trunk of the governor's car and rounded it off with ice while the highway patrolman just watched," a fish house worker from Atlantic explained. "That's how things got done around here." The "fish barons" of Down East had political clout and knew how to maintain it with frequent visits to Raleigh or Washington, D.C. They also hosted high-ranking politicians, taking them hunting and fishing and plying them with seafood. "We used to get things done by picking up the phone and talking to the right person," said Clayton Fulcher Jr. of Atlantic. "Times have changed."

Politicking has deep roots on the coast, which was predominantly ruled by Southern Democrats until recent history. Sonny Williamson wrote about people jockeying for Lifesaving Service positions when being a Democrat was a job requirement.

In an essay called "Folks I Met on the Road Down East," writer Bill Ginn recalled stumbling on a small enclave of Republicans while making a sales call to Davis. He entered a little store and encountered men "whittling duck heads out of cedar." When the salesman inquired about the store-owner, he was asked, "Are you a Democrat or Republican?" When he re-

Elmer Willis Clam House at Williston entertained governors and congressmen for years, garnering political support for local roads, schools, and economic opportunities for Down East. This image is titled "Clam Bake for Conservation and Development Board members—Carteret County, July 1945." (Photo courtesy of the State Archives of North Carolina)

sponded "Democrat," the storeowner responded dryly, "We used to have a Democrat down here on Davis Shore, but he hung himself on the church bell rope."

## BEING THERE

*The best part about growing up on Harkers Island was just being there.*
  *—Bertie Clyde Willis, Harkers Island*

Growing up on the sandbanks was a matter of "making your own fun." Hard-packed sand flats along the barrier islands made a perfect site for pony races, old car races, and ball games. Children played a game called "Cat," which was like baseball except with a tight ball of yarn. The batter was tagged "out"

## DANNY STYRON: THEY DECIDED TO MOVE THE FERRY

The ferry was actually located in Atlantic, North Carolina, at D. Mason's store. . . . Uncle Leffield wanted the ferry to come to Cedar Island. Well, Uncle Monroe wanted it to come to Cedar Island and old man Clayton Fulcher had the motel. . . . They had eight rooms and a restaurant. . . . Buck Dean came down here, keep in mind he's the Secretary of Department of Transportation in Raleigh, so, he started talking to them and he said, "What do you want?" They said we want the ferry to move to Cedar Island. This was done around a card table on Hog Island. They decided that night that the ferry was actually going to move to Cedar Island.

You know back then, there were very few people who had influence. Uncle Monroe had a lot of influence in Raleigh. Billy Smith had a lot of influence in Raleigh and Clayton Fulcher Jr. Later in life, Eugene Willis when Bob Scott was Governor had a lot of influence in Raleigh. There was people Down East that could touch people and Governors and people like that that would come down to see them. . . .

I remember one time they weren't going to open shrimping and Uncle Monroe went to Raleigh and when he come back that evening, he told everybody to get right to go shrimping. They were shrimping at midnight that night. That's how things were done back then but you ain't going to get nobody to do nothing like that now.

Source: from an interview with Danny Styron, National Park Service
Oral History Collection, Core Sound Waterfowl Museum and
Heritage Center; interview by Connie Mason, February 2011

by getting physically hit with the ball. Boys and girls played "Cat" together. Young men formed community baseball teams, tremendously popular from Down East to Hatteras.

"We even had a Polar Bear Club on Cedar Island back in the sixties," Danny Styron remembered. "Eric Todd Smith started it and each person had to pay fifteen cent." The kids would meet at the old fishing pier and plunge into Pamlico Sound every morning as the fall gave way to winter and the temperature dropped. "We young boys were not real smart," he added. "Whoever the last person was to plunge got 50 percent of the money that was involved, so Eric was getting 50 percent of it and he wasn't even plunging!"

Children still ride their bikes to school, just like they did in 1955.
(Photo by Sol Libsohn, Standard Oil [New Jersey] Collection, SONJ 80752, Archives
and Special Collections, University of Louisville, http://louisville.edu/library/archives)

## IN LOVE, SICKNESS, AND DEATH

*They didn't have weddings back then. They just got married.*
*— Mrs. Ernal Foster, Hatteras*

Whether the bride arrived on the mailboat or happened to be the girl just down the road, traditional coastal weddings were simple affairs and usually occurred in someone's house. The usual plan was to have a social gathering with homemade wedding cake after the ceremony. Decorations, like everything else in these communities, were made from what was available. An account of a 1911 wedding in the Portsmouth Methodist Church described

## THE MOUNTED SCOUTS OF OCRACOKE

The name Pony Island brings to mind vivid images of wild, ocean-grown ponies, fierce and free in their isolated barrier-island environment. Ocracoke's association with banker ponies is based on historical fact and is as old as recorded knowledge of the island itself.

In 1585, a ship . . . was stranded on the shoals inside Ocracoke Inlet. The crew forced livestock—including horses—overboard at high tide to lighten

Village Boy Scouts on a training ride in 1955. Each Boy Scout in the Ocracoke troop has tamed one of the wild ponies that roam the island. Caring for the pony and learning to ride it well was part of the scout training. (Photo by Martha McMillan Roberts, Standard Oil [New Jersey] Collection, SONJ 80763, Archives and Special Collections, University of Louisville, http://louisville.edu/library/archives)

the load and refloat the vessel. They never returned for the animals. And for the next 150 years, undisturbed by the Indians who weren't exactly sure what to do with them, they survived.

In 1737, a ship bound for Virginia, *The Prince of India*, shipwrecked near Styron's Hill (on the north end of Ocracoke) with perhaps 20 or more horses from Hispaniola aboard. As local lore has it, the horses swam ashore and enough survived and adapted to the salt environment.

By 1755, additional horses were brought in from Carteret County and the islanders used them to control the ever-increasing number of cattle. So began the legacy of Ocracoke's wild banker ponies.

It would be 200 years before a group of young boys, ages 10 to 14, harnessed this legacy and fortified Ocracoke's reputation as "Pony Island." These fearless young men were the mounted Boy Scout Troop 290 of Ocracoke, who captured, penned, and tamed their own wild ponies. Troop 290 received national recognition as the only mounted Scout Troop in the country (so far as anyone knows) in a feature article in *Boys Life* magazine in March 1956.

"Every boy on the island in our age group was involved," says David Esham, one of the original mounted scouts and now the owner of the Pony Island Motel in Ocracoke. On isolated Ocracoke, the banker ponies gave the youth an outlet to direct their energies into. There was no state ferry system yet, and it was four and a half hours to the mainland by mailboat. The only phone was at the Coast Guard Station. It would be another four years before the first paved road was built.

Source: Daniel C. Couch, "The Mounted Scouts Harnessed
the History of Ocracoke Island," *Island Breeze*, July 1993

an archway "of cedar and evergreens sprinkled with fall flowers from Portsmouth yards" and white ribbon bows. The wedding feast was often at the bride's parents' home.

"If you lived on Ocracoke back when I come up, you married your kin," recalled an islander. "Who else was there?" Cousin or second-cousin marriage was not unusual, but the Coast Guard, Navy, or Civilian Conservation Corps brought in potential new marriage partners for islanders. The strong military presence in the central coastal area brought people from all over to Marine Corps Base Camp Lejeune in Jacksonville and Marine Corps

Air Station Cherry Point in Havelock, both near the coast. Sometimes they married local girls and added "fresh blood" to communities.

Almost every community had a midwife to attend to births. These "aunties" would often stay with the new mother for days while she recovered. The lack of doctors in remote places made home remedies a necessity, although Hatteras Island had access to a Navy doctor beginning in the 1940s and Portsmouth Island was the site of the first marine hospital in North Carolina. Down East had easier access to doctors after roads and bridges were built. Dr. Moore was a Marshallberg native and loved by all. He left for medical school with hand-cut cardboard soles in his shoes and one suit of clothes. He returned a doctor, content with a light bread biscuit in his pocket or a mess of fish for payment.

Tuberculosis, pneumonia, typhoid fever, colitis, and the flu were just some of the afflictions. Before vaccines were developed, children died of diphtheria. "Back in the old days they used to say these old women were floating around the road on Laudanum," recalled L. P. O'Neal of Avon. Paregoric was also common. "Chill Tonic" was taken in the fall to prevent colds. Asafetida was purchased as well. People chewed willow bark for pain and wrapped a sprain in mullein leaves.

"Ollie's salve" was known to cure just about anything on Harkers Island. Ollie Moore was especially gifted at dealing with skin problems such as ground itch and ever-present boils. Islanders trusted her healing "black salve" that could "draw an iron nail out of a piece of heart pine." This was handy with barefooted children playing amid rusty nails, oyster rocks, and fishing gear along the shore.

Folks in Avon called on Omi Meekins, who had some training in nursing from St. Vincent's hospital in Norfolk. She delivered more than 100 babies during the course of her career on Hatteras Island. She charged $10 or $15 for several days of care. Ocracoke midwife Charlotte O'Neal delivered 523 babies on Ocracoke and Portsmouth Island during her tenure as an island midwife.

In small communities, the death of a community member brought everyone together, and still does. Funerals involved having a "watch" to "sit up with the dead." Folks spent the night with the deceased, still in his or her bed or laid out in the parlor. A woman, usually a midwife, was often called in to wash and dress the dead person. The body was typically buried three days after death. A local carpenter, usually a boatbuilder, made the coffin.

"An older person's coffin would be covered in black material [and] if the person was younger it would be covered in white," said Fanny Fulcher of Ocracoke, describing how women sewed padding for the coffin. She said that local stores sold embroidery material, and the women "used this to make a ruffle around the coffin." A recent quilt history day at the Core Sound Museum brought a "coffin quilt" from the community of Stacy, symbol of a little-known tradition from generations past when women would make a quilt to wrap the deceased person before placing him or her in the wooden handmade coffin. It became an honored tradition, a "last gift" for a special loved one.

## LOOKING CLOSELY:
## STRONG, PROUD, DETERMINED

Bankers are "a people set apart," proud of who and whose they are, born standing firm on the land with their eye cast toward the water, and a part of both. Men and women raised on shifting sand learn quickly that change is a constant and survival is dependent on a person's (and a community's) ability to hold on while letting go, their willingness to accept what is to come by remaining steadfast and strong yet powerless against the elements.

Growing up in this paradox requires innate resilience, instills determination, and strengthens resolve. Whether facing the storms of the late 1800s or the fear of World War II, these communities have held together, self-sufficient but dependent on one another and their faith that He will calm the stormy sea and restore the spirit needed to face hardships unimaginable. For generations our people have adapted, moving to higher ground, working where and when the fish were running, always seeking new opportunities for their families.

People have survived, not unchanged but holding on to the unspoken, mostly unseen, connection to their past. The character of the people continues to be shaped by the fact that our forebears could not rely on anything but their own hands and minds to meet the needs of their families. They were forced, by sheer geography, to be self-determined, to adapt and survive, on their own terms.

Resourcefulness is both learned and inherited. Today's parents and grandparents still live with the understanding that with independence comes self-sufficiency, a truth that remains vital as mainland conveniences come and go with the wind and tide along these banks. Taking care of one another, saving what might be needed tomorrow, and borrowing and bartering still prevail among the year-round residents of these villages.

People here don't forget. They, and now we, remember the stories of their childhood in vivid detail; they can quote sayings with the exact same inflection their grandmother or aunt once taught them, and they know how to take care of one another, no matter what the challenge.

Young islanders face their own "storms" in much the same way, determined to hold to the edge of what was while reaching for the future, proud and strong. Even those bankers at Portsmouth and Diamond City who moved, adapted, and built new lives on safer shores faced their changes without sacrificing who they were. Today that same character — those same roots of determination, ingenuity, and adaptation — continues as the next generation makes its way, carrying-on with the same salt in their voices their grandfathers and grandmothers had 100 years ago.

Living here together on the tideline means preparing for the changes from season to season, taking care of one another, sharing joys and sorrows, working through the differences, celebrating the commonalities, realizing the risks and understanding the challenges, yet hoping for a good season and working to make sure it comes. That's the way it's always been on the edge.

# 4

# *Change*

*You don't want to mistake a change for progress. Your house*
*burning down is change.* — *Ernie Foster, Hatteras Village*

The Outer Banks, Ocracoke, and Down East have been destinations for travelers since the days of market hunting in the early 1900s. Hunters were drawn, as they are today, by the intimate connection of land and water and the abundant variety of waterfowl found along the sounds, lakes, rivers, and seashore. They came to this sliver of land through places like Lake Mattamuskeet, the largest freshwater stopping point for migrating waterfowl this side of the Chesapeake. They came to the vast marshlands between Pamlico and Core Sounds, bringing jobs to hunting guides, decoy carvers, innkeepers, and caretakers. Early visitors cracked opened the door to a new twentieth-century economy in addition to fishing, trading, and subsistence living.

World War II brought twentieth-century advances to war-weary banks neighborhoods and opened lines of communication and transportation never before realized. Like the rest of America, this region's "greatest generation" saw even more change taking place around them after the war. It was an exciting time of opportunity. From telephone service, television, and newspapers to paved roads and state ferries, the 1940s and 1950s opened doors that did not exist before the war. Federal government jobs in civil service and careers with the military helped improve the economic futures of many families, while the GI Bill and Federal Housing Administration home loans provided fishermen choices they had never known before. It was a new day.

But the tipping point of change was the building of the Bonner Bridge in

On the approach to Hatteras Island from the south, change is evident all around, with ferry lines overflowing with out-of-state cars waiting to load, large rental homes, shopping centers, and traffic lights. (Photo by Lillie Miller)

1963, ushering in visitors to the Cape Hatteras National Seashore and connecting islanders with the wider world. In 1969, an article was published in the *National Geographic* describing Cape Hatteras as a wonderland for families on vacation and a paradise for fishermen. The author described walking on the beach in the morning. "The offerings of the sea . . . lay all around; the shells . . . charred wood and pieces of splayed rope; empty applesauce cans and a wrinkled tube of facial cream bearing the label of a pharmacy in Marseilles." The world had arrived, and things haven't been the same since.

For local people, the postwar period was an exciting time of opportunity. Not only was tourism growing, but more civil service and military jobs became available after the war. Markets for seafood, especially crabs and shrimp, began to boom in the 1950s. So did charter boat fishing, with sportsmen seeking the majestic blue marlin after an angler on the *Albatross* hooked a world-record 810-pound giant off Cape Hatteras in 1962.

Real estate development was growing as well all along coastal North Carolina. Some were even proposing that a bridge be built to Cape Lookout, and plans were made to subdivide property into lots near the lighthouse. The establishment of Cape Hatteras National Seashore in 1953 and Cape

Ocracoke beach road with Hatteras ferry to the north and Ocracoke Village to the south, 1955. Utility poles marked the path where the road would eventually be paved. (Photo by Martha McMillan Roberts, Standard Oil [New Jersey] Collection, SONJ 80698, Archives and Special Collections, University of Louisville, http://louisville.edu/library/archives)

Lookout National Seashore in 1966 ensured that the economic "golden egg" of pristine beaches remained part of the public trust for all citizens.

## THE PRICE

*What we have seen, we won't see no more. — Roy Parsons, Ocracoke*

Decades after bridges and ferries opened a new world to banks communities, many realize that opportunities can bring unwelcome consequences and reach a point of diminishing returns. The level of development in several of the Outer Banks villages — especially of "rental machine" houses that crowd the shoreline — is in stark contrast to the wild seashore all around. Even with the National Park Service's presence holding miles of these islands in the public trust, private enterprise has taken full advantage of the demand for coastal property.

A high-dollar condominium and marina project in Hatteras Village's

Hatteras Islander Roy McCarter and Leonard L. Browning Jr., husband of islander
Dixie Burrus Browning, on the Hatteras Village dock of Maurice L. Burrus (Dixie's
father) during the beginning years of deep-sea fishing on Hatteras Island, ca. 1950.
(Photo by Dixie Burrus Browning, part of Maurice L. Burrus Collection)

environmentally fragile Slash Creek area, complete with the planting of nonnative palm trees in place of the old twisted live oaks, is but one example of growth run amok. Slash Creek runs through the center of the village, and the project—begun at the start of the real estate boom in the early 2000s—struck at the very core of locals' identity. One of the Slash Creek developers, a multi-term state senator, told the *Independent* that those protesting his project had long objected to zoning and were, in essence, living with the consequences.

"I could build myself a nice Putt-Putt golf course in there if I wanted to," the senator emphasized. "Have a big orange tiger's ass revolving around for people to hit balls into. . . . [But I'm building] something nice so we can sell it and make some money." He added, "Those people are saying they are drawing the line in the sand, I say fine, just draw it on the other side of me."

Ernie Foster, who was moved to write an editorial called "Thoughts on Watching a Village Die," reflected on the arrogance of developments like Slash Creek and the difficulty of locals to fight big money. As he surveyed his vintage fleet of wooden charter boats, dwarfed by larger, newer vessels, he said, "Money never sleeps. The people of Hatteras can fight and fight, but we also have jobs and family to tend to. . . . Money, on the other hand, works 24/7."

Many families face the realities of living in a vacation destination while trying to maintain their traditional way of life. Rising land prices and real estate values have shifted the balance in many of these communities from mostly modest homes of fishing and boatbuilding families to high-dollar subdivisions catering to retirees or second homeowners. While this creates important tax revenues for coastal counties, it presents challenges for families who can no longer afford to buy land or pay property taxes in popular waterfront areas. As Carteret County commissioner Jonathan Robinson, a commercial fisherman from Atlantic, asked, "Is there going to be a place here for us?"

All twenty-one communities along the byway are unincorporated. Locals tend to bristle at the thought of zoning because they like the freedom of doing what they wish with their land. Especially in older parts of the villages, historical settlement patterns are evident. Someone may have a horse pen next to a church, which is beside a trailer with chickens in the yard and a boat repair shop out back. Next door could be a local art gallery with a shade-tree mechanic working in the side yard. That kind of free spirit has supported the economy here for generations. Bankers are the ulti-

Down East is that string of communities that follow along and near Highway 70 and then onto Highway 12 where you reach the "big water" of Pamlico Sound. It begins with Bettie, then Otway, and turning south takes you through Straits, Harkers Island, back through Gloucester and Marshallberg before heading northeast through Smyrna, Williston, Davis, Stacy, Sea Level, Atlantic, and Cedar Island.

Down East is thirteen communities of men born to be fishermen, boatbuilders, decoy carvers, hunting guides and of women born to be all those things if needed and everything else—mothers, community leaders, teachers, storekeepers, fish house worker, doctors, nurses, and preachers. Traditionally, women have been the backbone of these communities while the men fished, and that continues today. Here, there are no such things as rights without responsibilities and here everyone has a responsibility—to God, family, one another.

"But, change is a-coming." We hear that a lot Down East these days. We know it, we see it, we feel it. Every day a new name appears in our community, a new home, a new neighbor. Property values are rising much quicker than local folks' checkbooks can handle. People are worried about taxes, getting to the water, where to tie their boats, keeping community schools, where and how their children are going to survive in this new economy.

Down East Carteret County is a beautiful, natural, and until recent years, isolated and unspoiled landscape that had already survived all kinds of change including hurricanes, a world war, roads, and bridges. But those changes came at a pace and in a way that local people could still hold onto their homes, their communities, while maintaining a respect for the past and hope for their future and their heritage.

Regardless of what economic development reports may tell or not tell, commercial fishing remains the mainstay of Down East's heritage, the backdrop for its landscape, a shared bond among Down East people. When this industry is threatened, we all fear together for what this means for the fishermen, their families, and the communities they serve.

It is more than a livelihood that is at risk. It is what this way of life represents—the tradition, the character that has been instilled in each generation to work the water. It is the underlying and deep-rooted sense of independence and self-reliance that fishermen are made of that we hold dear, that reaffirms our heritage, holds us together as a community, and gives us hope for an uncertain future.

Now, as a people we face a future in a place we locals do not recognize, cannot afford, and feel helpless in warding off. First one bulldozer at the time and now in 10-, 20-, up to 90-acre tracts, marshland is turned into subdivisions that empty into productive rivers, creeks, and sounds. Fishermen and their families are wondering what this will do to the waters they depend on for their livelihood, their mortgages, their groceries, their children's education, their tomorrow.

Source: Karen Willis Amspacher, *Crossroads: A Publication of the North Carolina Humanities Council*, Fall 2008

mate entrepreneurs, and their backyards (and sometimes their front yards) show it.

Such freedom cuts both ways, however. Without restrictions, investors with deep pockets made their plans to build chain retail stores and high-dollar developments that would change the character of these small places. During the red-hot real estate market that sizzled until it fizzled in 2008, developers set their sights on the coast—not for the first time, of course—but property values were unprecedented. Subdivisions with three-story homes were proposed for areas Down East long considered too low and wet for construction. Family cemeteries and sacred places were crowded out as old home-places became "tear downs" in favor of rentable investments. Some locals cashed in on the opportunity, others lamented the change, and more than one did both.

Change has come more slowly Down East compared with Ocracoke and Hatteras, but local families up and down the byway face the economic realities of living in a vacation destination while maintaining "working family" incomes as fishermen, teachers, law enforcement or emergency personnel, service workers, or some combination of these. In the summer, the majority of local residents, especially the young families, hold several jobs to make up for the quiet but lean winter.

Questions relating to the quality of life, the sustainability of the landscape, and the future for the next generation began to circulate in small conversations amongst the locals and newcomers who came here for the same reasons the natives have stayed. Locals know there's been a great price paid

Saltwater intrusion tells the story of eroding shorelines and the ever-changing landscape of coastal communities. (Photo by Lillie Miller)

for the "progress" along these banks, and as the price becomes even greater, efforts to preserve and savor that closeness to the land, the water, and the people of this region are emerging.

## WHAT ABOUT TOMORROW?

*Sometimes we live on hope more than we do money. — Eddie Willis, Harkers Island*

What will tomorrow bring for communities along the Outer Banks National Scenic Byway? As residents look toward a new day, the signs are harder to decipher than those that their grandfathers read. Scientists studying sea level rise offer projections that put portions of the Outer Banks and Down East under water by the year 2100. Fishermen note shifts in the behavior of fish, with some cold-water species becoming scarce while warmer-water species are showing up in greater abundance. Storms are nothing new to coastal North Carolina, but warnings of more frequent and higher-energy storms in recent years are, in local words, "right discouraging."

Fishermen have an established track record of working with scientists,

Men "dobbing" chicken at the Gloucester Community Club, 2015.
(Photo by B. Garrity-Blake)

testing gear, studying spawning habits of crabs, and mapping historical oyster beds. Who better to help model the impacts of climate change than those who are on the water every day? North Carolina Sea Grant is helping link researchers with fishermen as well as farmers, who can show scientists where saltwater intrusion is already affecting food production and the health of natural resources. These collaborators are on the front lines of researching and planning for a more climate-resilient future.

As communities have changed, natives and residents who have moved in "from off" are building working relationships for the betterment of their now shared communities. Some retirees, young families, and other newcomers are willing to invest their time and talents in schools, churches, museums, and community efforts like festivals and fundraisers. Whether people are recent arrivals or have family roots "clear to the water table," residents are working together as a community to help support, protect, and celebrate the beauty of the landscape and the spirit of the people that make these communities worth the collective effort. This blending of old and new families with a common goal is key to the future sustainability of these fragile communities.

# KEEPING THE STORIES ALIVE

*They told the stories that gave meaning to the lessons I was learning.*
*— Joel Hancock, Harkers Island*

The days of mailboats and free-roaming livestock are gone forever. But the stories live on. Families with a long history in these communities have always made sure their children and their children's children keep the lasting connection to their ancestors and this place, inseparable, generation to generation. It remains true that "whose" you are defines "who" you are, and where you're from is much more important than where you're going.

"I grew up in a world of stories," reflected Joel Hancock of Harkers Island. "Old people told the stories, young people heard them, and I developed an appreciation that I've had ever since." He keeps a blog of stories told to him since the 1950s, called "The Education of an Island Boy" (http://jghislandstories.blogspot.com). The tradition of storytelling has risen to an art in recent years. Hatteras Island started an annual storytelling festival, the Ocrafolk Festival always includes storytellers, and Down East has its own characters who have lived the stories they tell every day.

*The Mailboat* journal was launched Down East in the early 1990s, recording stories and recollections about Diamond City, pony-penning, mailboat brides, Christmas traditions, and more, a direct outgrowth of the immensely popular Harkers Island cookbook, *Island Born and Bred: A Collection of Harkers Island Food, Fun, Fact, and Fiction.* Inspired by the *Sea Chest* publications of Hatteras a generation earlier, *The Mailboat* once again connected communities and people. Today the *Sea Chest* and *The Mailboat* writings are treasured firsthand accounts of life on Hatteras, Ocracoke, and Down East.

"We sort of laugh when people say, 'Oh, I don't have any stories to share,' because that's simply not true," Susan West said during an interview for the Coastal Voices oral history project (www.carolinacoastalvoices.com) that shares audio excerpts of people's stories from all over coastal North Carolina. This collection includes discussions on traditional dishes such as stewed shrimp and pie bread, recollections of memorable times in people's lives such as when the bridge over Oregon Inlet replaced the old ferries, and vivid accounts of surviving floods and storms.

Coastal Voices is part of a regional initiative made up of the twenty-one communities of Hatteras, Ocracoke, and Down East called Saltwater Connections (www.saltwaterconnections.org). Saltwater Connections, an outreach project of the Core Sound Waterfowl Museum and Heritage Center on Harkers Island, is a byway-wide community collaborative working on

## SPREADING *FOXFIRE*—HATTERAS ISLAND STYLE

A group of high school English students from North Carolina's Outer Banks in Buxton are carrying their studies beyond prepositions and participles into the unique seafaring culture in which they live. Their engaging experiment is patterned after *Foxfire*, a wildly successful concept that came down from the hills of Georgia to attract the attention of educators throughout the nation.

The tenth and eleventh grade English classes at Cape Hatteras School are gathering materials for a quarterly magazine call *Sea Chest* that they expect to be a treasure trove of Outer Banks lore, recording in words and pictures the fascinating and rapidly disappearing local culture. . . . Like the Georgia mountaineers, the Hatteras Islanders have a rich tradition of folklore developed during a long isolation from the mainstream of society.

*Sea Chest* staff members have begun to fill file cabinets with transcripts of interviews with lighthouse keepers, ship builders, ferryboat operators, and old-timers who recall the worst of the nor'easters that have swept across their narrow island. . . . There are folders full of notes on seafarers' superstitions, island crafts, recipes, sailors' weather signs, the lives of lighthouse keepers, and records from an old Coast Guard weather station. . . .

"These kids have always been proud of this land and its traditions," Mrs. Jenkins said. "The more they learn, the more proud they become."

There will be room in *Sea Chest* for discussion of the island's present and future as well as its past. The students want to devote one entire issue of the magazine to the tourists who flock to the Hatteras Island beaches every summer. The tourists play an important part in the economy of the island, but, as Mrs. Jeranko put it, "They do some really weird things sometimes."

Source: Kerry Sipe, *Coastland Times*, March 20, 1973

ways to enhance the quality of life and economy of the region without sacrificing the natural resources that sustain livelihoods. Local foods efforts, protecting working waterfronts, promoting fresh local seafood, and fostering school-based partnerships are just a few examples of work under way. Saltwater Connections also helped develop a new Outer Banks Heritage Trails system (www.outerbankstrails.org), helpful to both visitors looking to get "off the beaten path" and local businesses seeking to serve them.

On Ocracoke, the Ocracoke Foundation has led the effort to retain the

For generations, the "mailboat" was the primary means of communication, and oft' times, transportation as well, for the people of these isolated communities along the coast. It was their daily link to the rest of the world, before radio and TV, bridges and highways. By the mailboat, news came and went, as did visitors, doctors, missionaries, politicians, salesmen and the mail too! First by sail, then by motor, the mailboat was a vital connection to the mainland.

*The Mailboat* seeks to be a voice—a means of communication, like the mailboat of yesteryear. We want to help in the exchange of information and ideas; a sharing of all that is good about the Carolina coast—and how to hold onto it.

"The new mail route is on now and if the tides don't get better Capt. Cleveland will have to use an aeroplane or walk to the Light House wharf" (*Beaufort News*, January 7, 1926).

Captain Cleveland was Cleveland Davis of Harkers Island. The Light House wharf was at Cape Lookout. He "used" a boat to carry the mail.

The vessel was built by Carl Graham Gaskill of Straits and named for his son. The *Orville G* had carried freight and passengers from Down East Carteret County to Beaufort until sold to Mr. Davis and put into service as a mail carrier. Charles and Cleveland Davis and Kelly Willis were to "carry the mails" for years—by boat.

Carteret County has had fifty-eight separately named Post Offices, the preponderance of them served by boat. The County Seat, Beaufort, when laid out as "Porte of Beaufort," was situated on Taylor's Creek. With access to Bogue Sound and the Beaufort Inlet outlet to the Atlantic, here was a water-dominated settlement that was the location of Carteret's first Post Office (the first records of her Postmaster, John M. Verdin, is dated October 7, 1794).

From Beaufort the mail was distributed to outlying areas. Before the advent of motorboats, sailing skiffs were used to transport the mail. Thomas "Pat" Parkin's grandfather was such a carrier. If the wind did not blow he "poled," for if the "mail did not get through" he was penalized—his contract required that he pay a fine to the Post Office Department.

Only when the bridge was built to Harkers Island in 1941 did Kelly

Miss Pearl Whitley and friends aboard the mailboat *Pet*. Miss Pearl, a native of Harkers Island, was the last teacher at the school on Diamond City. (Photo from the Mailboat Collection, Core Sound Waterfowl Museum and Heritage Center)

Captain Kelly Willis standing on the cabin of the *Pet*, Harkers Island's last mailboat that made daily runs to Beaufort and Cape Lookout until the early 1940s. (Photo from the Patty Jean Lewis Taylor Collection, Core Sound Waterfowl Museum and Heritage Center)

character of the community with the purchase and restoration of the Community Square, at the heart of the village. Saving this property from getting into private hands for development keeps the architectural integrity of this working waterfront property for the community and public to enjoy.

## COMMUNITY FOUNDATIONS STILL STRONG

*It is hard to have a fishing village without the fishermen. —Morty Gaskill, Ocracoke*

Ocracoke faced the unthinkable in 2006: the prospect of losing its last remaining fish house. Always buzzing with activity, the fish house—located right in the center of the community on Silver Lake—closed and was put up for sale. For months fishermen had to truck their catch to the north end of the island, catch the ferry to Hatteras, and sell to a fish house there. Tired of their limited options, fishermen banded together and formed the Ocracoke Working Watermen's Association. They formed alliances with community members and nonprofits and secured the funds to buy the old fish house. Their enterprise, the Ocracoke Seafood Company, has restored the busy heartbeat of Ocracoke's working waterfront. The public can watch fishermen unload their catch and then walk into the retail market and buy the catch of the day. Ocracoke Seafood Company stands as a model for adapting new ways to carry on old traditions, thanks to the continued support of the community and seafood lovers who keep it in business.

Wind and tide are always at work molding Ocracoke's pliable shore. During the last 400 years, the island dwindled to a mere eight-mile stretch then grew to the fourteen miles of shoreline it has today, with most of it designated as a national seashore.

Ocracoke faces serious erosion on a different front: the loss of native culture. Although the island's living history is as colorful and captivating as its most famous visitor, the pirate Blackbeard, Ocracoke is not for every visitor. There are no chain stores or golf courses. But those who make the watery pilgrimage to this village of 800 year-round residents do so as much for what they leave behind on the mainland as for what they gain while here.

The inevitable give and take that accompanies growth and development has changed the face and even the voice of Ocracoke. The once robust dialect of native O'cockers, heavily influenced by Elizabethan English, has been watered down along with the familial bloodlines of the O'Neals, Styrons, and Gaskills. As real estate values continue to rise, many year-round residents work multiple jobs to pay the price of living here. The island's K-12 school recently expanded, but the local board of education has the difficult

Ocracoke Working Watermen's Association annual oyster roast, held between Christmas and New Year's, draws hundreds to the island to celebrate oyster season and show their support for Ocracoke's community-owned fish house. (Photo by Dylan Ray)

*Change*

task of recruiting teachers with no promise of affordable housing. Even the U.S. Coast Guard has reduced its island presence to limited seasonal operations, ending a year-round vigil that had endured since 1904. The doors of the Community Store, a favorite gathering spot for locals and tourists, were shuttered. Then in 2006, the island's last fish house was closed and put up for sale. Suddenly, in true O'cocker fashion, all hands were on deck in an effort to turn back the tide.

> A daily theater unfolds in small community fish houses: scenes of humor, advice, teasing, disappointments, obligations, expectations and familiarity. The players are fishermen, dealers, neighbors and kin, but roles blur and relationships intertwine in a small town. The wooden floors, one moment slick with scales and slime and the next hosed down clean, form the stage. Fish boxes stacked neatly, "polydac" rope snaking across the floor, and work gloves dripped here and there serve as props. The gurgle of diesel engines mixed with static from VHF radios plays a background symphony to the subtle dramas that unfold (from *Fish House Opera*).

A commercial fisherman without a fish house is like a farmer without a grain bin. And time is of the essence when you are battling the threat of fishing temperatures. One degree over posted regulations and every bit of the commercial fisherman's catch must be pitched. With the fish house closed, the Ocracoke fleet shrank to virtual non-existence. Those who did stay on motored northward to unload their cargo, the additional fuel charges sucking up their already dwindling profits. The closing also meant no dockside source of ice, and with each trip requiring 400 pounds of ice, both the commercials and recreational charter boats were left scrambling for cubes. To top it all off, with less real fishing activity on the docks, Ocracoke's tourism identity as a "quaint fishing village" was in jeopardy.

Community organizers met with the fish house owner who agreed to a one-year buy-out if the group could raise $325,000. In the meantime, the fish house was re-opened as the Ocracoke Seafood Company and managed by the fishermen themselves who had formed the Ocracoke Working Watermen's Association (OWWA), a part of the newly formed Ocracoke Foundation. Today more than 30 fishermen belong to the association.

Source: Heidi Jernigan Smith, *Carolina Country*, July 2007

Ocracoke's charter boat fleet hosts tournaments from spring through fall, offers daily trips, and provides fresh local offshore fish for area restaurants throughout the season. (Photo by Melinda Fodrie Sutton)

## FISH ENOUGH FOR ALL

*Sometimes they're scarce, and sometimes they're plentiful. That's the way fishing has always been.* — Roger Harris, Atlantic

"Fishing for fun" has been a part of the coastal economy since before Captain Ernal pulled in that blue marlin off Hatteras and Captain Stacy Davis of Harkers Island began putting weekend "would-be" fishermen "on the fish" during the months when he wasn't commercial fishing. Recreational fishing has grown very lucrative, enhancing the tourism economy throughout the region. Anglers on charter boats, head boats, private boats, ocean fishing piers, and the beach flock to the coast to catch anything from pinfish to "the big one." Whether for food, trophy, or simply bragging rights in the popular "catch and release" practice, recreational fishing and all the related marinas, tackle shops, tournaments, and clubs bring millions of dollars into coastal economies.

Conflicts between recreational and commercial fishing interests cast a shadow over the fun, however, as some angler clubs have petitioned for gamefish status of three species—red drum, striped bass, and speckled

*Change*

trout—which would take these commercially important fish off the market and off the plates of consumers. The call for gamefish status was defeated in 2013, as were earlier calls to ban gill nets and shrimp trawling. Fishermen fear, however, that it is just a matter of time before they are legislated out of business. In the meantime, fishermen work with state scientists to develop more environmentally friendly methods of harvest, and anglers and watermen alike participate in management efforts. Various commercial fisheries-related groups, often led by women from the community, wives and daughters of fishermen, are addressing the challenge of fostering collaboration among all who share an interest in healthy fish stocks and the long-term welfare of fishing economies. Cultivating collaboration among commercial and recreational fishermen, natural allies in advocating for healthy resources, will go a long way.

## SHARING THE OLD WAYS IN NEW WAYS

*Decoys are my way of holding on to the past.*
—*Joe Fulcher, Core Sound Decoy Carvers Guild*

As lifelong innovators, residents along the Down East and Outer Banks region are creating new traditions. Nicky Harvey of Davis Shore was a builder of nets and crab pots. As imported crabmeat flooded the market, prices plunged and fewer crabbers bought pots. So Harvey, inspired by his family's ideas, built a Christmas tree out of crab pot wire to place in his own front yard more than ten years ago. Then he made a few more for friends and neighbors. Before he knew it, requests came in from across the county and beyond. It turned out to be a wonderful mix of Core Sound history, Down East ingenuity, and the spirit of Christmas. The Core Sound Crab Pot Christmas Tree became a new creation from an old tradition, giving locals something to be proud of. As more and more yards, docks, and store windows filled with crab pot trees of all sizes and colors, writers from magazines and newspapers came to see what this story was about, and the rest, as they say, is history.

*Our State* magazine called Harvey's tree a "newfangled Down East tradition." Today 10,000 crab pot trees are built each year in the Down East community of Smyrna, and these trees are sold all over the world. The trees have become a proud symbol of Down East and the ingenuity of one man's willingness to adapt his traditional skills in new ways. It is a prime example of a local craft grounded in tradition, supporting local jobs.

New celebrations are also growing in number and popularity, integrat-

Nicky Harvey's original Core Sound Crab Pot Christmas Tree honors the season as well as a long commercial fishing heritage for Down East Carteret County. The community of Davis is the home-place of the crab pot trees and host to the Core Sound Christmas celebration held each holiday season. (Photo by Scott Taylor)

ing long-held traditions into emerging economies of heritage tourism. Hatteras's Day at the Docks festival, held each September in Hatteras Village to mark the anniversary of Hurricane Isabel, is a celebration of the perseverance of the working waterfront. The festival has brought in fishermen from Alaska to Maine, rekindling ties among watermen and providing a forum to discuss emerging opportunities in the seafood industry. A full day's activities focus on fishing, both recreational and commercial, and end with a Blessing of the Fleet. The tradition of honoring the seafood industry continues to expand. Gloucester is home to the "smallest seafood festival in the state," the Wild Caught Local Seafood and Music Festival held each summer, celebrating all things local. Ocracoke's annual Oyster Roast between Christmas and New Year's continues the message of how important the fishing industry is to this area.

Ocracoke Island's Ocrafolk Festival is the region's largest gathering of musicians and storytellers, bringing in artists from all over to draw on the island's homegrown creativity. Molasses Creek, an important force in keep-

The first weekend in June draws thousands to Ocrafolk Festival to enjoy the island's annual celebration of art, music, and good food. The Blue-Eyed Bettys are a favorite. (Photo by Melinda Fodrie Sutton)

ing the music traditions of Ocracoke and surrounding communities alive, envisioned this June event years ago, and it has now grown to include artists, musicians, and crafters from across the state as its summer season kickoff event. Throughout the year, this work continues with events and programs as part of the organization Ocracoke Alive!

Over the past thirty years, Down East has honored its waterfowl heritage with a weekend dedicated to the art of decoy making and the heritage of Core Sound. It all began with the Core Sound Decoy Carvers Guild organizing the Core Sound Decoy Festival in 1988, which drew thousands to Harkers Island the first weekend of December. The festival now includes the celebration of decoy carving and hunting at the Harkers Island School and a celebration of waterfowl arts and local traditions at the Core Sound Waterfowl Museum and Heritage Center just down the road. Thousands have come to buy, trade, and admire waterfowl carvings — both old and contemporary — from up and down the East Coast. The festival takes place on the first weekend in December, the beginning of waterfowl hunting season. Decoy carving has become a cottage industry for Down East and many outlying communities, securing the region's historic role along the Mid-Atlantic Flyway. Core Sound carvers now participate at events such as the

Carvers and artists share their "love of ducks" during the Core Sound Decoy Festival (at Harkers Island School) and Waterfowl Weekend (at the Core Sound Museum). Thousands come together during the first weekend of December to buy, sell, compete, and learn more about the waterfowling heritage of eastern North Carolina. (Photo by Dylan Ray)

Waterfowl Festival of Easton, Maryland, and the Ward World Championship Carving Competition in Ocean City, Maryland.

## IS IT LOCAL?

*You see a pretty picture of fishing boats at a restaurant and you assume you're getting local seafood. That's not necessarily the case. —Pam Morris, president of Carteret Catch*

Folks traveling to the coast assume that waterside restaurants serve local fish, shrimp, crabs, and clams right off the boats at the dock. The reality of our food system, however, paints a shockingly different picture. Over 90 percent of the seafood consumed in the United States is imported from distant countries, and access to fresh, local seafood on the coast is not a given. But in recent years the fishing industry has been working to counteract that trend, and consumers are increasingly asking where their seafood comes from.

New programs and initiatives have sprung up to further these efforts. NC Catch (www.nccatch.org), a collaboration of four local seafood-

Fishermen and -women keep the fish house at Ocracoke busy with fresh seafood throughout the season. (Photo by Dylan Ray)

branding programs along the Carolina coast (Brunswick Catch, Carteret Catch, Ocracoke Fresh, and Outer Banks Catch) is working with other agencies on educating consumers about the benefits of eating local seafood. NC Catch's outreach efforts across the state highlight the health value of local seafood, the importance of supporting small family fishing businesses, and the benefits of keeping local dollars in local economies. Much like the local foods campaign Know Your Farmer, NC Catch is making sure consumers have the opportunity to know their fisherman and know where their seafood was harvested.

New ways of selling seafood to inland customers are emerging. The Community Supported Fisheries model, borrowed from small farmers' Community Supported Agriculture programs, links seafood harvesters directly with consumers and offers "shares" of the catch in advance of the fishing season. Each week shareholders get a different selection of familiar and not-so-familiar products, from jumping mullet to shrimp. The watchword is "freshness," as proprietors guarantee right-off-the-boat quality seafood. Walking Fish (www.walking-fish.org) of Beaufort, for example, launched by Duke University students and now run by locals, delivers seafood to inland clients, often with cleaning and handling instructions and favorite recipes

Local catch groups located up and down North Carolina's coast work together to make sure that consumers know where and when to buy fresh local seafood.

included. They also deliver the "story" behind the seafood, as subscribers learn about the seasonality of products, the life history of the resources, and the world of commercial fishing families, right down to the names of children, boats, and dogs. Other Community Supported Fisheries are coming online throughout the state as North Carolina's desire for real local seafood increases.

"I was spawned and reared from the small fishing communities of Atlantic and Sea Level," said James Morris, a Ph.D. scientist with NOAA who specializes in coastal ecosystems, invasive species, and aquaculture. Dr. Morris is simply "James" Down East, where he spends his spare time growing oysters in floating cages for the lucrative half-shell market.

"Clam gardens," where clams are simply grown in estuary areas leased to private individuals by the state, are a time-honored tradition in North Carolina. In recent years, however, cultured oysters have become more popular and today represent a multimillion-dollar industry in the Chesapeake Bay. Pioneers such as James Morris are working on expanding the industry in North Carolina as well. James was recently awarded the Presidential Early Career Award for Scientists and Engineers by President Barack Obama. "I couldn't help but think what my grandfather would have thought," he reflected. "The same little boy who was out on a shrimp boat with him was shaking the president's hand." James fished out several oysters from a cage and began cracking the bivalves open with a knife for a small group of Duke Marine Lab students to taste.

"Why do you have this oyster farm if you work full time as a scientist for NOAA?" one of the students asked.

"I still like to grow things, you know?" he replied, downing a fat, juicy oyster.

*Change*

Duke Marine Lab student Ruici Ong checking oyster cages off Harkers Island, 2013.
(Photo by B. Garrity-Blake)

## THE WORK CONTINUES

On Ocracoke, the U.S. Coast Guard station, which sat abandoned for nearly a decade, is now the eastern campus of the North Carolina Center for the Advancement of Teaching. Known as NCCAT (pronounced "en-cat"), this program hosts weeklong seminars for teachers from across North Carolina to renew their love of learning. Another experience that draws more and more visitors is Ocracoke's Springer's Point, a beautiful thicket of maritime forest that was acquired by the North Carolina Coastal Land Trust for the public's enjoyment. Hikers walking through the 120 acres of maritime forest pass some of the island's largest and oldest oaks and reach the shoreline along Teach's Hole, where Blackbeard met his demise.

Explorations in culinary fields, maritime trades, and marine science once discontinued from local curriculums are now being offered, as educators prepare the next generation for careers that are applicable in their home communities as well as the wider world. At East Carteret High School at the entrance to Down East near Beaufort, Harkers Island native Heber Guthrie is teaching traditional wooden boatbuilding skills. At Cape Hatteras High School in Buxton, Evan Ferguson is building a local foods movement within the

Jay Styron has an audacious mission: to provide high-quality half-shell oysters to the world.

That's a pretty bold notion for someone who raises oysters in a mere 500 cages floating in estuarine waters off Cedar Island in Carteret County. "I like to think big," he tells you with a sly grin.

Don't be too quick to call him a dreamer. There are those who would call him a visionary—one who sees the role marine and freshwater aquaculture collectively must play to provide healthy and sustainable seafood for a global market.

Today, over half of the seafood consumed around the world is produced by aquaculture, a statistic cited often by Styron and Chuck Weirich, North Carolina Sea Grant marine aquaculture specialist.

The National Oceanic and Atmospheric Administration also notes that over 90 percent of all seafood is imported in the United States. Currently, domestic aquaculture supplies only about 5 percent of the seafood Americans consume, and the remaining 5 percent is wild caught.

In North Carolina, aquaculture accounts for only a small fraction of the annual total agriculture industry revenue, according to the N.C. Department of Agriculture and Consumer Services, or NCDA&CS.

Still, the potential for North Carolina's aquaculture is strong because current and prospective producers don't have to go it alone. In fact, anyone looking for a working definition of science and technology transfer need look no further than the state's aquaculture industry and its network of partnerships.

The 1989 N.C. Aquaculture Development Act provides a framework for partnerships that connect growers with university researchers, field faculty, and N.C. Cooperative Extension and Sea Grant specialists, as well as experts from the U.S. Department of Agriculture and NCDA&CS.

Styron, who leads the N.C. Shellfish Growers Association, knows firsthand how research partnerships help fine-tune the efficiency of growing oysters for the half-shell trade. His business, Carolina Mariculture Co., occupies two acres of a family-held, 10-acre traditional oyster-bottom lease.

It is one of several commercial demonstration sites within a project led by Weirich and funded through the NOAA Extension and Technology Transfer Program. Other partners include researchers from the University of North Carolina Wilmington and Carteret Community College in More-head City.

The team is comparing growth of oysters native to distinct N.C. waters. Ami Wilbur, director of the UNCW Shellfish Research Hatchery, had identi-fied the strains in an earlier Sea Grant–funded collaborative study.

In the current project, the participants also are comparing four types of off-bottom gear used to grow half-shell oysters. In addition, they are evalu-ating the culture of sunray venus clams at the sites as a potential means to diversify the industry.

Through an earlier collaborative study, Styron learned to stagger the planting of his hatchery-raised spat. That has enabled him to manage each class closely from start to harvest, every 14 to 16 months. "Rotating our crop means our oysters are available nearly all year round, not just in months with an R," he explains.

Each harvest yields about 30,000 individual oysters — delicacies that have earned national attention and year-round demand.

Styron and his wife, Jennifer Dorton, have been featured on *A Chef's Life*. In an episode of the award-winning PBS show, they described their operations, and showed off oyster-opening techniques, to celebrity chef Vivian Howard. Her Kinston restaurants — The Chef and the Farmer, as well as The Boiler Room — are among those eager to serve Carolina Mari-culture oysters.

Source: Pam Smith, "Aquaculture: Science Working for the Economy,"
*Coastwatch*, North Carolina Sea Grant College Program, Holiday issue 2012
(updated April 29, 2016, online blog, www.ncseagrant.ncsu.edu)

school, growing vegetables and partnering with local agencies to encourage healthy eating community-wide. Cape Hatteras and East Carteret schools are sharing recipes and traditions from one island to another, while the shop class at East Carteret, led by commercial fisherman and teacher Zack Davis, built a fish-cleaning table for students at Hatteras. Ocracoke School worked with linguist Walt Wolfram to develop a curriculum on the coastal dialect. Plans for a regional STEM (science, technology, engineering, mathematics) education initiative are under way, looking for ways to encourage local stu-dents to consider marine education and place-based science occupations that will allow them to return home to well-paying careers after their college years.

Fisherman Aron Styron with Duke Marine Lab students off Cedar Island, 2013.
(Photo by B. Garrity-Blake)

These educational efforts try to keep students engaged with the local heritage while preparing them to frame a better future. The "brain drain" of young people leaving the coast for careers in urban areas is a concern, as fewer youth are available to fill the shoes of firefighters, teachers, fishermen, and other roles that keep a community viable. Local leaders look for ways to grow well-paying, year-round jobs for those who would like to stay in their home communities. Initiatives that connect coastal marine science institutions with local schools show promise, incorporating students' love and knowledge of the natural world.

Today coastal communities boast excellent twenty-first-century schools, university-based health care services, improved roads, more frequent ferries, and new bridges. Communications, especially the Internet, have brought villages into a new world that only a few would trade for those mailboat days. It's no exaggeration to say that the people of the Outer Banks live in two worlds, one of heritage in a "close to the bone" environment and one of modern conveniences and new horizons.

Those who have lived through this evolution from isolation to connectedness will tell you that balance is the key. How to welcome new oppor-

Summer science camp at the Core Sound Waterfowl Museum and Heritage Center brings kids of all ages to the "end of the road" to learn more about marine science and the importance of good stewardship. John Waszak, one of the area's favorite science teachers, makes learning an exciting, fun experience. (Photo from the Core Sound Waterfowl Museum and Heritage Center Collection)

tunities without sacrificing cultural integrity while retaining the values of the past and still exploring new ideas is no easy task. Nonetheless, these old communities are determined, more conscious of their fragility than any generation before them, to make sure their legacy will be worthy of the next generation's inheritance, kept safe, and honored for their children and their children's children.

## LOOKING FORWARD: CHANGE KEEPS COMIN'

Life is change, and here on the Outer Banks, change comes daily, with the tide, the ferry, the weather, the season. "A Change Is Gonna Come," Sam Cooke sang, but for this place and these people, change has always, *always*, been the constant.

Each generation has adapted in its own way, and this generation will be no different. In today's world though, the change happens at such a pace and with such completeness that it is difficult to comprehend the consequences. As a global economy floods markets with imported seafood, a housing boom crowds traditional neighborhoods, and corporate chains threaten locally owned stores, many feel at risk of losing all that truly matters. The next generation of fishermen, entrepreneurs, and community leaders fight to adapt while keeping their long-held traditions, preserving the natural beauty of the landscape, and protecting the water quality on which they depend. Locals and visitors alike cherish the sense of place that still holds families and communities tied to this place, and they're willing to work to keep it that way.

Local leaders agree that "what we have is hard to find. We have watched other resource-rich coastal communities, like mountain communities, disappear in the name of 'progress,' lost to the highest bidder for the so-called highest and best use, and we wonder, whose best use?" wrote an islander in an emotional letter to the editor several years ago.

The people of the Outer Banks are seeking ways to balance progress with preservation, and community-minded residents are learning of other places where heritage has held communities together for hundreds of years, and still does: Places where residents treasure, support, and share their heritage with one another and with travelers from around the world who are willing to go the extra mile, to spend that extra dollar to "keep it local" and experience and protect this country's rich cultural and natural legacies. The Outer Banks National Scenic Byway is such an effort, showing that these twenty-one communities connected by seemingly endless miles of open beach and saltwater still have enough character, spirit, and beauty to be such a place.

This is a sacred place, worthy of care and protection from all of us. Whether you are visiting for a day or spending a lifetime, we ask you to help us weather this change, help us hold on to the reasons why we linger, here at the edge. We share it with the hope that together we can find a way so that our future resembles our past and our people can continue working to raise their families here. Our landscape may have changed, but our values haven't. This is still home for thousands of families all year-round and a favorite place for tens of thousands to visit again and again, coming to the edge to soak up sun and salt and to be part (if only for a moment) of a place and a people "set apart." Why would we want to change it?

Change is nothing new. These banks have been changing for centuries as high land and deep water ebbed and flowed. Channels come and go daily, dunes can disappear overnight, and a slick ca'm day can turn into a howling northeaster in a matter of hours; change is part of all this place is, and we are shaped and strengthened by it.

Change in the social fabric of a place is sometimes not that easy to accept. This change comes slower and is harder to see—until it's too late. In the past 100 years, bankers have been welcoming new people from all over the world to our communities. We have benefited greatly from the contributions of many who have moved here and become part of us. We have learned from everyone, and hopefully, they have learned from us. New people have come and become "investors" in our churches, schools, and organizations, giving of their time, talents, and resources; now they are leaders and givers, and we are stronger for their efforts. We are thankful for their commitment to our shared vision for a future that retains the very reasons they came and we have stayed. Thank you for holding on *with* us.

We welcome all who will come to be part of us and choose to take the time to listen, to hear and see, to taste and feel. There is much to experience here: the power of the water, the evolving landscape, the substance of the people and their heritage, and the combination of all these elements that makes living here on the edge a constant, changing process. So slow down, wait, listen, and take it all in; the road at the edge takes time.

# Crossings

# 5

# Crossing Oregon Inlet

*Hatteras Island's most popular icon, the black-and-white, spiral-striped Cape Hatteras Lighthouse, keeps watch over the stretch of the Atlantic where the Gulf Stream and the Labrador Current collide to create a culture indelibly shaped by a dynamic maritime environment.*

*The weather, water, and waves hold sway over life on the island in large and small ways that were wholly unfamiliar to me when I moved here in the 1970s, seeking refuge from the suburban sprawl that was swallowing my hometown. Within weeks I traded my umbrella, useless in Hatteras winds, for a bright yellow foul-weather jacket and bought my very first weather-band radio so I could monitor hurricanes and northeasters.*

*Hatteras Island is a place far removed from the rest of the world. Sitting as far as thirty miles out to sea from the mainland, the villages are bonded to the ocean and the sound in a practical intimacy that outstrips the influence of any ideology.*

*Somewhat paradoxically, the island's geography has also thrust it onto center stage as the setting for events of international significance. The first Union victory in the Civil War, Reginald Fessenden's early radio communication, Billy Mitchell's test of air-powered bombing, and German U-boats torpedoing Allied vessels during World War II took place here.*

*The island doesn't flaunt its heritage and culture, but the stories are there for travelers to discover.*

SUSAN WEST, BUXTON

Crossing Oregon Inlet. (Photo by Baxter Miller)

## THE NORTHERN ROUTE OF THE
## OUTER BANKS NATIONAL SCENIC BYWAY

*Driving in the sand, you were probably pushing as much as you were riding.*
*— Dale Burrus, Hatteras Village*

Once the resort town of Nags Head is in the rearview mirror, travelers heading south on Highway 12 enter a mesmerizing, otherworldly stretch of the Cape Hatteras National Seashore. A certain state of mind sets in while rolling past mounds of sand, grains streaming onto the road and sweeping to and fro with each passing car. Vivid blues of ocean and sound appear between the earthy hues of dunes. Few things are as humbling and magnificent as having two vast bodies of water within a stone's throw as you drive along a narrow bank of sand.

The road to Cape Hatteras National Seashore begins at Whalebone Junction, located at the intersection of US 64, US 158, and Highway 12.

*Crossing Oregon Inlet*

Whalebone Junction is so named because Alexander Midgett found a whale skeleton on Pea Island in the 1930s. He managed to load part of it into the back of his Model-T truck and hauled it north across Oregon Inlet on Toby Tillett's ferry. Midgett, one of the first with an eye for attracting tourists, dumped the skeleton across from his gas station and called it Whale Bone Service Station. The bone and the station are long gone, but the name lives on as a gateway to the wilds of barrier island life.

Whalebone Junction is on Bodie Island, the southern end of Currituck Banks. Bodie (pronounced "Body"), like Pea Island, was once a separate bank until an inlet filled with sand. The origin of the name Bodie is unclear. Local lore attributes it to shipwrecked bodies washing ashore, but Roger Payne, author of *Place Names of the Outer Banks*, suggests a family surname, a shipwreck, or a reference to a "body" of land.

Bodie Island Lighthouse, ten miles south of Whalebone Junction, comes into view on the west side of Highway 12. The stately tower with its horizontal black-and-white stripes was built in 1872 to replace a lighthouse destroyed by Confederate troops who feared the Union would make use of it. The Bodie Light stands 165 feet tall and casts a beam that is visible for nineteen miles. You can find the National Park Service–maintained lighthouse and keeper's quarters at 820 Bodie Island Lighthouse Road. The tower is open from mid-April to mid-October for climbing. Check the website for details (https://www.nps.gov/caha/planyourvisit/bils.htm).

Across from Bodie Light on Highway 12 is Coquina Beach, a swimming area with a bathhouse. Near the access point on the beach are the remains of the *Laura Barnes*, a four-masted schooner built in Camden, Maine, that wrecked in 1921. The eight members of the *Laura Barnes* crew were rescued by surfmen of the Bodie Island Coast Guard Station. Only six years before, in 1915, all Coast Guard stations that dotted the coast had been Lifesaving Service stations established after the Civil War. The timbers of the *Laura Barnes* appear and disappear at the will of the wind and sand.

Five miles south of Bodie Island Light is the fearsome Oregon Inlet, spanned by the Herbert C. Bonner Bridge. When the ill-fated Lost Colonists tried to establish a foothold on Roanoke Island in 1587, Oregon Inlet did not exist. Instead, the explorers sailed through Gun or Gunt Inlet, opened from 1585 to 1798. Oregon Inlet, just south of the former Gun Inlet, was cut in 1846 by a hurricane and was named for the first vessel that navigated through it, the side-wheeler *Oregon*. At first the inlet was deemed a nuisance, as it separated Hatteras Island from the rest of the northern banks. But it proved to be a good thing for fishermen, who gained a new access point to the ocean.

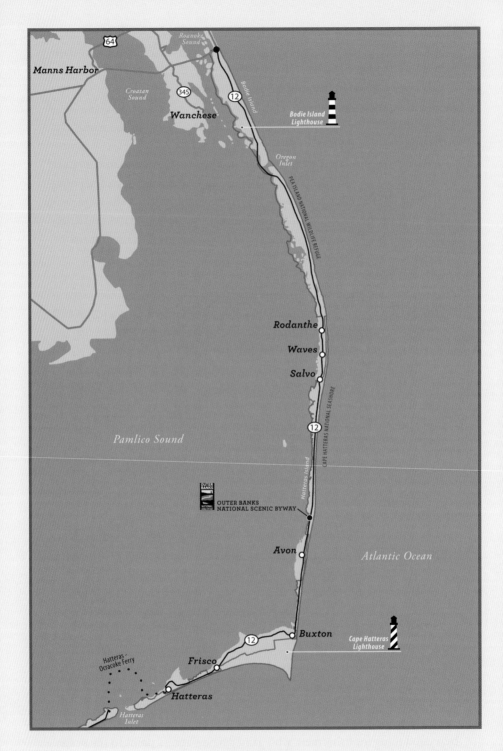

HATTERAS ISLAND

The inlet is ranked as one of the five most treacherous inlets along the Atlantic Coast. Fierce currents, winds, and ever-migrating shoals have spelled trouble for mariners. In recent years, shoaling has become so common that large trawlers can no longer pass through the inlet to the fishing community of Wanchese. Even captains of smaller charter fishing boats must pay close attention to the day-to-day status of the inlet when working out of the Oregon Inlet Fishing Center, located at the northern foot of the bridge. The fishing industry has lobbied unsuccessfully for Congress to approve a jetty to stabilize the south-drifting inlet. Dredging continues in an effort to keep the inlet passable.

The Herbert C. Bonner Bridge is a graceful, two-and-a-half-mile-long arc that lifts travelers high over the turbulent waters of Oregon Inlet. The southern foot of the bridge is on the northern end of Pea Island, a single land mass with Hatteras Island since 1945. The Bonner Bridge, built in 1963, has far exceeded its thirty-year lifespan. Plans for a new bridge were delayed due to legal disputes over length, placement, and costs. A settlement was reached in 2015, clearing the way for a slightly longer bridge to be constructed just west of the original bridge. The new bridge, with a 100-year lifespan, is slated to open in November 2018.

The Bonner Bridge and paved highway on Hatteras Island and Ocracoke brought tremendous change to the Outer Banks in the 1960s. Not only did islanders gain quick and convenient access to the mainland; a pipeline for tourism on the banks was opened. Photographer Aycock Brown worked as director of the Dare County Tourist Bureau at the time. He tirelessly promoted the Outer Banks, sending stories to as many as 170 newspapers a week. Brown's efforts fueled a tourism boom that exploded in the 1970s and continues today.

"We knew that life was going to change," reflected Gail Quidley Scarborough of Frisco. Although terribly excited to take her first trip over the bridge in 1963, she recalled experiencing mixed emotions. "When I looked over and saw the ferries sitting there, I got sad." Scarborough was referring to the humble wooden ferries, such as the *Oregon Inlet* and *Barcelona*, put in service to shuttle cars back and forth since the early 1920s. "It felt like I was abandoning something," she added.

The now-decommissioned Oregon Inlet Lifesaving Station, appearing rather forlorn on the windswept north shore of Pea Island, keeps a ghostly watch over the turbulent inlet. Listed on the National Register of Historic Places, the station is located on the east side of Highway 12 and is visible from the bridge. Built in 1883 and rebuilt in 1887, the structure was vacated by the U.S. Coast Guard in 1988. Now state property, the station was almost swallowed by sand until renovations began in 2008. The Oregon Inlet Lifesaving Station is not open to the public and awaits further renovations, pending funding. Lifeboat Station Road on the east side of Highway 12 allows visitors to pull over and take in the dramatic scenery.

Just south of Oregon Inlet is the Pea Island National Wildlife Refuge, a birder's paradise managed by the National Wildlife Service. Made up of more than 5,800 acres, the refuge is an excellent area to view migratory waterfowl such as snow geese and tundra swan in the winter months and oystercatchers, plovers, skimmers, and other feathered delights year-round. The Pea Island Visitor Center, with its staff of dedicated volunteers, is located six miles south of the inlet on the west side of Highway 12. It offers interpretive exhibits, nature trails, wildlife observation stands, and public restrooms.

Although no trace of it remains on the island today, the Pea Island Lifesaving Station was located near the present site of the Pea Island Visitor Center. The Pea Island Lifesaving Station was the only station in the United States served by an all–African American crew. Captain Richard Etheridge, born into slavery, served as an officer in the Union Army before becoming the first black lifesaving station keeper in 1880. In 1996, 100 years after the fact, the Gold Lifesaving Medal was awarded posthumously to the Pea Island crew for their heroic rescue of the crew of the *E. S. Newman*, a three-masted schooner. The original Pea Island Lifesaving Station, built in 1871, was destroyed in a suspected act of arson in 1880 but was rebuilt the same year. The station continued to be manned by an all-black crew until it was decommissioned in 1947. The cookhouse was eventually salvaged and moved, along with other artifacts, to Collins Park, 622 Sir Walter Raleigh Street in Manteo. Tours are available Mondays, Wednesdays, and Fridays until 3:00 P.M.

The Pea Island lifesaving crew were stationed in a beautifully stark place. Until closed by storm in 1945, New Inlet separated the Pea Island surfmen from Hatteras Island villages to the south. Oregon Inlet separated them from Currituck Banks to the north. Mary Meekins of Avon remembered the Pea Island crew when she attended school in Manteo in the 1920s. Her father would take her to Oregon Inlet, where she'd sometimes board the boat with the surfmen. "They'd take me over to Manteo," she said. "They'd be going on liberty and I'd go across with them."

The name Hatteras is derived from an Algonquin word meaning "area of sparse vegetation." High winds and salt spray on the northern part of the island keep vegetation in check. Just before reaching the village of Rodanthe, travelers encounter the notorious "S" curve of Highway 12, a "hot-spot" of frequent ocean overwash that seems determined to become an inlet. The curve was once New Inlet, and remnants of an old bridge can still be seen just to the west. New Inlet was filled with sand during the hurricane of 1944, turning Hatteras and Pea Islands into one sandbank. More recently, *New* New Inlet was punched open by Hurricane Irene in 2011 and spanned by a temporary fix locals dubbed The Lego Bridge. The area is steadily filling in, compliments of Mother Nature.

The contrast between wild parkland and beach development within village borders is quite obvious on the approach to Rodanthe. Large rental "cottages" loom up on both sides of Highway 12 in the northernmost village. This inhabited section of Hatteras Island is called the "tri-villages" by locals, as the communities of Rodanthe, Waves, and Salvo are side by side and nowadays are hard to distinguish. The region has long been known as Chicamacomico (Chic-a-ma-COM-ico), derived from an Algonquin term meaning "sinking down sand."

Civil War buffs might be familiar with the term Chicamacomico Races, the two-day ordeal that occurred in August 1861 when Yankee forces occupied Hatteras Island. Confederate troops, wading ashore from "Mosquito Fleet" vessels in Pamlico Sound, chased a Union regiment from Live Oak Camp at Chicamacomico clear to Cape Hatteras — on foot, in the sand, for some twenty-five searing-hot miles. The next day, after Union troops took refuge at the lighthouse, federal reinforcements arrived and drove the Confederates back up the banks. The event, which compelled many villagers to abandon their homes and also seek refuge at Cape Hatteras, thus became known as the Chicamacomico Races.

## RODANTHE

*My brother caught bluefish to pay his taxes.* — Carroll Midgett, Rodanthe

Rodanthe (Ro-DAN-thee) is the first settlement travelers reach when entering Hatteras Island from the north. It's also the easternmost point of North Carolina. The village post office opened in 1874, and because the government rejected the name Chicamacomico, the name Rodanthe was chosen, since it was considered easier to pronounce and spell. Rodanthe became a household name with the release of the Warner Brothers film *Nights in Rodanthe*, starring Diane Lane and Richard Gere. An adaptation of Nicholas Sparks's best-selling novel, *Nights in Rodanthe* was partially filmed in the village, and the Rodanthe-Waves-Salvo Community Center served as a staging area. Locals were hired as extras, and Serendipity, the beach house depicted in the movie, was purchased and moved after filming was complete; thus it was saved from falling into the ocean. It's now a vacation rental called the Inn at Rodanthe.

The northern tip of Rodanthe is called Mirlo Beach, named for the British tanker SS *Mirlo* that exploded offshore in August 1918, a real-life drama that stands out in Outer Banks maritime history. Central to the story is Chief Warrant Officer John Allen Midgett, descended from Matthew Midgett, who washed ashore in a shipwreck at Chicamacomico in the early eighteenth century. As described by Nell Wise Wechter in *The Mighty Midgetts of Chicamacomico*, John Allen Midgett led his six-member crew of the Chicamacomico Lifesaving Station into a fiery sea after a World War I German submarine blew up the *Mirlo*, which was carrying more than 6,500 tons of fuel. They rowed five miles through the smoke and flames, singeing their hair and blistering the paint on their surfboat, to the hell-like scene. It took them four trips, shuttling victims to shore, to save all but nine of the fifty-one-man crew. Each of the six rescuers earned a Gold Lifesaving Medal from the British government and the Grand Cross of the American Cross of Honor from the Coast Guard. "In the seventy-year history of the Coast Guard," Wechter noted, "officials have awarded only eleven Grand Crosses."

The Chicamacomico Lifesaving Station is located at its original site in the heart of Rodanthe. Open to the public, it is the most complete station complex in the nation, with eight original buildings. This was the first operational station in North Carolina, active from 1874 until 1954. Once the station was decommissioned, the National Park Service assumed responsibility of the site. By 2002, it was deeded to the Chicamacomico Historical Association, a nonprofit organization dedicated to the preservation of the buildings, equipment, and history associated with the station. The Chicamacomico Lifesaving Station is the only place in the country where visitors can witness the breeches buoy rescue, reenacted each summer by active-duty U.S. Coast Guard members. Check their website for details (www.chicama comico.org).

Memories of simpler times, when social life revolved around the harbor, church, and school, still linger in the minds of the older residents of Rodanthe. The Rodanthe School was the first to consolidate on Hatteras Island, bringing in students from neighboring Waves and Salvo in the 1930s. The three-room school ran through tenth grade until it was accredited as a high school in the late 1940s. Previously, students planning to graduate had to leave the village and board elsewhere to finish high school. Some went to Hatteras Village while others went to Manteo or Elizabeth City. By 1955 all the Hatteras Island schools had consolidated to Cape Hatteras School in Buxton.

"Dad or Mother never really made us go to church," Anderson Midgett recalled. "But if you didn't go to church you didn't go nowhere else." Before the Methodist churches unified, the Northern Methodist congregation met on the border of Rodanthe and Waves, while the Southern Methodists met in Salvo. In 1927, when the Assembly of God was established in Salvo, congregations from both Methodist churches in Chicamacomico lost members to the fiery sect. Carroll Midgett recalled that the line between Rodanthe and Waves was very much expressed at the Northern Methodist Church. "Years ago the boundary was the Methodist Church—one side was Rodanthe, one side was Waves." He added, "People from Rodanthe sit on the north side, people in Waves sit on the south side of church."

The U.S. Coast Guard dug a channel and harbor on the sound side of Rodanthe in 1936, presenting a great convenience for local fishermen. There were as many as three fish houses and buyers in Rodanthe, who would compete for the long-haulers' catch in a bidding war. Boats would sit in the middle of the harbor, Rudy Gray explained, and buyers would shout out their bid. "Whoever was the highest bidder, that's where that boat would go and unload."

Ignatius "I. D." Midgett recalled that before the harbor was dug, the mailboat offloaded letters, packages, and passengers offshore. "Somebody would shove or row out and pick up the mail." The *Hattie Creef* was a fifty-five-foot oyster boat built by George Washington Creef of Manteo in 1888, named after his daughter and used as a fish buy boat for Globe Fish Company by 1915. "A fish boat called the *Hattie Creef* come in and picked up fish, brought passengers, and made regular runs," I. D. Midgett reflected. "She would leave Elizabeth City and come to Wanchese, then from Wanchese to Rodanthe." In its waning years, the *Hattie Creef* was pulled ashore and turned into the Hattie Creef Drive-Inn restaurant in Salvo in the 1970s.

Joseph "Mac" Midgett owned the Island Convenience store in Rodanthe until he passed away in 2006. Mac Midgett had a larger-than-life persona with his stout build, bushy beard, and pirate-like swagger. Although he cut a gruff figure, he was known to extend credit to residents who needed it and to forgive debts of those who had fallen on hard times. Midgett also ran a garage and towing company behind Island Convenience, and the sandy ridges behind the store were strewn with junk cars. He had a few torn-up, greasy chairs in the garage, and the most important community business

Rodanthe is one of the few places left that celebrates Old Christmas, also known as Twelfth Night, in the United States. This long-held tradition can be traced to England's adoption of the Gregorian calendar in 1752, which shortened the year by eleven days. The change was resisted by isolated groups of Protestants, including the people of Rodanthe, who marked Jesus's birthday as January 5 (Twelfth Night). To this day, people who participate in Old Christmas in Rodanthe talk about celebrating "two Christmases."

In the old days, Old Christmas began with a pre-dawn racket, as a rowdy band of villagers marched along playing fifes, drums, and assorted noisemakers. People in costume joined the procession through the village of Chicamacomico. They'd eventually end up at a table loaded with chicken, oysters, pies, and other Christmas fixings. At the lifesaving station, a test of marksmanship would commence, including a surfman with a .22 rifle shooting an apple off the head of a man.

Over the years, Old Christmas migrated to the Rodanthe School, which has since been renovated and enlarged to serve as the Rodanthe-Waves-

Elvira Payne drums up Old Christmas in Rodanthe, 1957. (Photo by Aycock Brown, David Stick Collection; courtesy of the Outer Banks History Center, State Archives of North Carolina)

Climbing aboard Old Buck for a good-luck ride.
(Photo by Aycock Brown, David Stick Collection; courtesy of the
Outer Banks History Center, State Archives of North Carolina)

Salvo Community Center. Brawling was common at Old Christmas celebrations, as folks would settle old scores and start the new year with a clean
slate. The highlight of Rodanthe's Old Christmas was the appearance of
Old Buck, a mythological bull that was said to be shipwrecked on Hatteras
Island. No one is sure when Old Buck became a part of the celebration, but
by the turn of the twentieth century, the procession was led by a blanketed
creature with a steer's head, horns, and four legs that looked suspiciously
human.

Old Christmas today is held at the Rodanthe-Waves-Salvo Community
Center at the harbor (23186 Myrna Peters Road) on the Saturday closest to
January 6. By all accounts, today's Old Christmas is a tamer affair than those
of times past. A shooting contest takes place outside on the basketball court
in the afternoon with the winners receiving buckets of oysters. There is an
admission fee for the evening event, which includes a homemade chicken
and pastry dinner, roasted oysters, and dancing to a live band. The highlight
continues to be the appearance of Old Buck, who is led once around the
dance floor as adults dare their children to touch him for good luck.

and gossip took place there among the men who sat with sodas or lunch in hand. His influence was evident in the 2004 election, as Mac Midgett won a seat on the Dare County Commission for the second time, beating a popular incumbent. At the end of his first eight-year stint in politics, he said, "I appreciate the people who supported me. I don't very much appreciate the people who didn't."

Mac participated in all sorts of commercial fisheries, including launching a small dory through the surf to seine striped bass. He told a story about one of his distant fishing jaunts to Core Banks, south of Hatteras and Ocracoke in Carteret County. "Once, we run a twenty-foot boat across Drum Inlet from Atlantic to Portsmouth Island—it was rough, but we had to cross it. We eventually get home to Rodanthe. After a while the phone rings. My wife answers it and it's the Coast Guard. They say, 'We're sorry to tell you that your crowd is missing and possibly drowned.' She turns to me and says, 'You ain't missing, are you?'"

The Island Convenience store is still run by the Midgett family and is a great place to gas up, get refreshments, and ask about Chicamacomico history and events, including the annual Old Christmas celebration. The store is located at 23532 NC 12 on the west side of the road.

### WAVES

*If you was out in the sound and looked back at the shoreline you would see three clumps. Waves was the middle one. —Lance Midgett, Hatteras Island*

Waves is directly south of Rodanthe, the middle community of the tri-village area, although it is very difficult to tell where one village ends and the next begins. Waves was called South Chicamacomico and South Rodanthe before Waves P.O. was selected in 1939. Anna Midgett was the first postmistress. Her nephew explained that she chose the name because the community does "have a lot of waves."

Waves was once a sleepy fishing village. A local fisherman remembered watching his great-grandmother tying nets from a skein of cotton twine, a common industry among islanders until nylon was introduced in the 1950s. His great-grandmother "could get her hand going so fast tying that net that you could hardly see her hand or the needle," he recalled. "My grandfather would make the gauges for her, and that would determine the size of the mesh that the net would be." Nets were hung in the yard, on the porch, or—during the winter—right down the center hall of the house, from a nail driven in a window sill.

Small dories can still be observed crashing through the ocean surf in the cold winter months in search of migrating schools of fish. Waves fisherman I. D. Midgett has long participated in "beach fishing" or the haul seine fishery, where crews patrol the shore in trucks, searching for signs of bluefish, red drum, or striped bass. Once fish are spotted, the dory is pulled off the trailer and launched like a waterborne rocket through the crashing waves. The crew pays out one end of a long seine net, while the other end is secured onshore, tied to a truck. The net is hauled straight offshore to intercept a school of fish. The dory then circles back to shore in a U-pattern. The truck is used to help pull in the seine that fishermen hope is loaded with fish.

The catch is trucked to market, and the fishermen might take a fish or two home for supper. Red drum is a local favorite, although today the large "old drum" favored by locals for a baked dish called a "muddle" is off limits. "You got to have those big fish to make that drum muddle," said a fisherman. "We'd take and thicken ours and make a gravy to put it over the top of the cornbread."

"The inspiration here was eating me up," said Waves photographer Michael Halminski. His work has captured the excitement of dory fishing and countless other aspects of life on the Outer Banks. "My photography just sort of snowballed." Like many others, he visited Hatteras in the 1970s to surf but couldn't tear himself away. He has documented decades of storms, including the stages of Hurricane Irene, with photographs on his blog of a creek sucked dry as the water blew westward across Pamlico Sound, a returning wall of water, and sixty-six inches of tide in his yard. "Irene is the new benchmark for soundside flooding in our villages," he noted on his website (www.michaelhalminski.com). His studio on Pamlico Sound is open Monday through Saturday from 10:00 A.M. to 6:00 P.M. during the warm-weather months. Michael Halminski has witnessed much change on the island, and his love for his island neighbors shines through his photography.

Charter boat captain Rudy Gray has fond memories of growing up in Waves as the son of the "Pepsi Cola man." His father trucked soda pop from Elizabeth City across the ferry to the villages of Hatteras Island. He kept a couple of boards underneath his truck for use in soft sand. If stuck, he'd lay out a board in front of the truck, drive its length, stop, get the second board, and drive that length, until he was free of the mire. Rudy Gray often accompanied his father on deliveries to the little family-run stores so common in the 1940s and 1950s. "The grocery stores is where all the older men would hang out in the afternoon," Rudy Gray recalled. "Ten, twelve, fourteen men

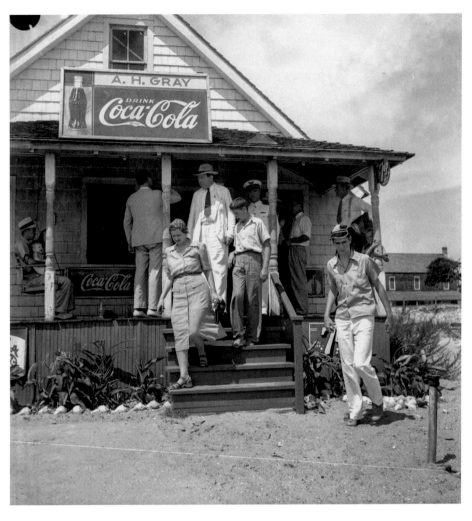

Governor J. Melville Broughton visits Hatteras Island for a speech at the Cape Hatteras Lighthouse in 1941. There were no paved roads at the time. (Photo by unnamed photographer, Victor Meekins Collection; courtesy of the Outer Banks History Center, State Archives of North Carolina)

in the afternoon sitting around talking, some of them playing dominos or checkers."

On Midgetts Mobile Court Road in Waves, amid a small collection of sandy graves, is a humble headstone for another "Mighty Midgett" of Hatteras: Erasmus "Rasmus" Midgett, whose heroic rescue earned him the Gold Lifesaving Medal of Honor. The San Ciriaco storm of 1899 had just hit, driving people off the southern banks and dooming several ships off the

*Crossing Oregon Inlet*

coast of North Carolina. Out of the pre-dawn darkness, Rasmus Midgett noticed debris washing up along the beach and then heard voices crying out in the distance. The 643-ton barkentine *Priscilla* had wrecked just offshore. Surfman Midgett decided to attempt the rescue himself rather than lose hours fetching his crew at the Gull Shoal station. He famously waded into the surf and ferried ten survivors to safety, one by one, including the ship's captain, who had already lost his wife and small son overboard.

## SALVO

*I'm the last generation that's going to know the names of creeks. —Burt Hooper, Salvo*

Salvo, just south of Waves, is the last populated village in the Chicama-comico region. South of Salvo is twenty miles of wild beach until travelers reach Avon. Salvo was once known as Clarks or Clarksville. During the Civil War, a Union ship commander is said to have spotted the settlement from sea and asked his crew for the name of the village. Finding no name on the chart, the captain ordered his men to "give it a salvo anyway" and fired the cannons. A crewman wrote "salvo" on the map, and the rest is history. In the mid-1950s, a geographer dubbed Salvo "a fishing village, [with] little cause for tourists to stop." Today this is no longer the case, as motels, campgrounds, and rental homes attest to its popularity.

"They pulled their sail skiffs up every Saturday morning," Burt Hooper said, recalling his boyhood days when fishermen built and sailed wooden skiffs. "Scrubbed 'em inside and out. Sunday you went to church, and Monday morning they're setting their nets again." He said that fishermen from Salvo and Waves carried their catch to Rodanthe and sold to Globe Fish Company.

"I worked for forty-nine years but only got credit for seventeen," said Edward Hooper, explaining that he worked part time for the U.S. Postal Service before becoming postmaster at Salvo. The Salvo Post Office was so tiny, Hooper exclaimed, that "it tied for first place in the national Smallest Post Office Challenge!" The eight-by-twelve-foot structure was larger than an outhouse, but Hooper shared a story of a visitor who kept asking him if it was a bathroom. "The third time she asked she rub me the wrong way," he laughed. "I said, lady, you see all these bushes out round back? If you need to go, you help yourself—that's where I go!"

The tiny Salvo Post Office building was decommissioned and moved to Hooper's front yard. "[People] still come by wanting to mail a letter," he said in 2002. "Some of them sticks letters under the door." After Hooper's house

Retired postmaster Edward Hooper (*right*) and his brother William Hooper in front of the Salvo Post Office, 2002. (Photo by B. Garrity-Blake)

was flooded in Hurricane Irene, the old post office was moved to the Salvo Volunteer Fire Department at 27209 Roth Road, where it can be seen today.

Edward Hooper's aunt Lucy Hooper was preacher at the Salvo Assembly of God Church, which once had a sign that read, "Welcome to the Little Church with the Big God." Lucy Hooper, originally a Methodist, was saved during a revival led by missionary Myrtle Chambers, who imported the charismatic faith to Salvo and Avon in the mid-1920s. Lucy Hooper and her husband, Leonard, organized an effort to salvage timbers from the grand *G. A. Kohler* to build the Assembly of God church. The 212-foot-long, four-masted schooner had been en route from Baltimore to Haiti when it beached near Salvo in the '33 Storm. A carpenter herself, Lucy Hooper helped with construction, and a church history noted that the "building [rose] from the wreckage of a schooner." Edward Hooper recalled that his aunt also built boats and "fished and everything just like a man."

The *Kohler* timbers were also used to build a barbershop and numerous

*Crossing Oregon Inlet*

banks houses and additions. The ship lay on the beach for ten years until it was burned during World War II for its iron fittings. To this day storms periodically uncover what remains of the wreck along the beach south of Ramp 27 between Salvo and Avon. Another shipwreck visible from Salvo is a metal paddle wheel shaft that sticks prominently out of the surf just off the beach from Sand Street. Some suspect it is the remains of the *Pocahontas*, an 1829 sidewheeler, while locals call it the *Old Richmond*. According to NOAA, the engine does not match that of the *Pocahontas*. If it is indeed the USS *Richmond*, the ship was an American blockade-runner from New York built in 1848. An illustration of the iconic wreck graces the cover of the Salvo Volunteer Fire Department cookbook.

Surfing is one of the Outer Banks's longest-running sports. Just as the region is a premier fishing area, it's also renowned for its world-class waves. Surfers from all over seek the perfect break off the jetty at Cape Hatteras; near the S-curve at Rodanthe; along the Frisco, Avon, and Rodanthe pier sites; and at numerous other spots. Mr. Leslie Hooper of Salvo, now deceased, and his friend Gaskill Austin claim to be among the first surfers to ride the waves off Hatteras Island, before surfing became a recognized sport in the 1950s. The Salvo boys collected old planks — "dunnage" — that washed ashore and converted them to makeshift surfboards.

"One day, I got too far out on a wave and curled, and the board dipped in the sand, rode me over and I slid off," Austin recollected. "A piece of the board . . . went up my armpit and came out through the back of my shoulder. I got stabbed good." His "treatment" was typical of the no-nonsense self-sufficiency of the Outer Banks. "My uncle held me down, put his foot on my shoulder, and yanked the thing out. I went back in the ocean and soaked it in saltwater."

The Salvo Day Use Area, located at the southern border of the community on the west-side shore, provides excellent access for those who wish to experience calmer, sound-side waters and activities. A former campground, the Salvo Day Use Area is maintained by the National Park Service as a park, complete with picnic tables and short trails to the shore. The area is popular for wading, windsurfing, fishing, and kiteboarding. The Day Use Area has an interpretive sign about the capture of the *Fanny*, a Civil War–era Union tug that was overtaken by North Carolina's Mosquito Fleet of Chicamacomico Races fame. The *Fanny* represented the first Confederate capture of a Union warship during the war.

At the Salvo Day Use Area is a cemetery, the resting place of long-departed villagers, including postmaster Kenneth Pugh (b. 1861), Dorothy

"Dortha" Midgett (b. 1828), and Sparrow Midgett (b. 1897), son of Pharoah Farrow Midgett (b. 1848). The oldest surviving grave is of Watson Midgett, born in 1822, son of Banister Midyette. Military veterans, lifesaving station surfmen, and Coast Guardsmen are interred here on the banks of the Pamlico. Sadly, severe erosion is taking its toll. Some graves have been unearthed, and headstones can be found in the water. An online "gofundme" site, established to raise funds to shore up the graveyard, states, "We are literally watching these people wash out to sea." This has been a common fate for many graves along the storm-prone Outer Banks.

### AVON

*The big livers around Avon at that time were the Coast Guard. —Willard Gray, Avon*

The community of Avon sits alone on an open stretch of barrier island wilderness. Located twenty miles south of Salvo and eight miles north of Buxton and Cape Hatteras, Avon represents the geographical center of Hatteras Island. Avon was originally called Kinnakeet, from an Indian term meaning "that which is mixed." This is appropriate today, given the "two Avons" that coexist within village boundaries: One is made up of modern businesses, homes, and rental cottages on the highway and ocean. The other, marked by "Kinnakeet" painted across a water tower, follows the old roads and twisting paths of the sound-side village.

There was once a settlement known as Little Kinnakeet a little more than two miles north of Avon. It was home to the Little Kinnakeet Lifesaving Station, active from 1874 to 1954, north of the Big Kinnakeet station at Avon. Emma Gray, born in Little Kinnakeet in 1898, said that the settlement had its own school, which she attended until age fifteen, but no store. "We used to have to walk down here [to Avon] from Kinnakeet Station . . . and take our groceries back up," she explained. Her family bought flour, cornmeal, sugar, coffee, lard, beans, peas, canned tomatoes, and canned beef but procured their own eggs and fresh meat, as well as milk from their cows Levy and Brighty. Willard Gray recalled that dead and dying victims of a shipwreck following the '44 Storm were laid out at the Little Kinnakeet Lifesaving Station. "They had four, five of them stretched out in a Little Kinnakeet boathouse [because] they all drowned. There was one of them they didn't find. They said he wandered off into the woods to die."

The Little Kinnakeet Lifesaving Station is in the process of getting restored by the National Park Service. Although the proud little station and outbuildings are surrounded by a chain-link fence, it is possible to see them.

They are located on the west side of Highway 12 off a side lane, nine miles south of the Salvo Day Use Area and 2.3 miles north of Avon.

In Avon, the old village of Kinnakeet can be found on the west side of Highway 12 down Harbor Road at the northernmost traffic light in Avon (there are only two traffic lights on Hatteras Island, both in Avon). The heart of the old village is organized around the harbor, dug by the U.S. Army Corps of Engineers in 1947. Before the harbor was complete, fish houses and an icehouse stood on stilts offshore near deepwater channels in Pamlico Sound. Fish houses then relocated to the harbor and served as a beehive of activity for Avon until very recently, when the last fish house shut its doors. Locals still call the village Kinnakeet and proudly call themselves Kinnakeeters.

Manson Meekins, born in 1916, described the home in which he was raised. The two-story, five-bedroom bungalow was T-shaped with a kitchen annex. The house was furnished, in part, with mahogany furniture from the *G. A. Kohler*, wrecked in the '33 Storm. The Meekins family had both a front and a back porch, important for the neighborhood tradition of "visiting." Like most of the Outer Banks homes, it was a continuous work in progress, with modifications and additions, a testament to the adaptability and thriftiness of the islanders. As one Avon resident put it, "I've been quilting on [my house] all my life." The family cooked with a woodstove. There was no heat upstairs.

"We had feather beds made from goose, brant, and duck feathers," Manson Meekins recalled. "And after you shivered about three or four minutes, you'd settle down to a good night's sleep."

Kinnakeet native L. P. O'Neal recalled when his mother got her first oil stove. "My mother told Daddy, 'If you want me to cook again next year you better buy me an oil stove, because I'm not going to have this woodstove.'" His father bought her an Aladdin oil stove. "It was beautiful—it was off-white and green." A Hatteras storekeeper named Shank Austin acquired several oil burners that could be attached to the Aladdin stove. The burners "had a little glass jar" for oil. "Everybody come in here looking at that stove."

Few people would know what a "sea oar" is, let alone a sea oar *house*. Eelgrass, once abundant in Pamlico Sound until a disease decimated it in the 1930s, was called sea oar by locals for reasons long forgotten. The community of Avon was unique in developing an eelgrass or sea oar industry, as dried grass was used to stuff mattresses and furniture. Villagers collected great mounds of eelgrass and spread it out on drying racks. Local boys were paid 50 cents a day to turn the grass with pitchforks and then press it into

## CARRIE GRAY, NEW BRIDE TO AVON

Carrie Gray was a seventeen-year-old bride from New York when she moved with her husband to Avon in 1932. She paints a vivid picture of what the village was like when she arrived and of the shock of trading big-city life for her husband's windswept barrier island home. "No roads nowhere—sandy car ruts, and the cattle and horses were roving free," she exclaimed in a 2003 interview. She was interviewed on the front porch of her modest home, the former Northern Methodist Church building. "After we bought the old church and moved up here, the outhouse was back there in the marsh." She shook her head. "I went to the outhouse, and when I turned to come back there was this old brindle bull between me and the house, and I was stuck out there for about two hours! He was a gentle old thing, but I was from New York and I didn't know nothing about gentle bulls."

Her husband's family treated her like their own, however, and "everyone was nice and wonderful." She noted that all the women wore sunbonnets. It was disconcerting, however, when "the cattle would come and scrape their horns at night on the side of the house," as her house was near a watering hole. The area was called Frog Marsh, and "good, fat, hoppy toads, hundreds of them in the evening, come up here in the yard."

Carrie Gray's first experience fishing with her husband was memorable. "He was going to take us out in the boat in the middle of the day, on a little picnic. I was from New York, and I never drove a boat!" He handed her the wheel and told her to go starboard. "I didn't even know what 'starboard' meant!" she exclaimed. She ran the boat aground on a shallow shoal, whereupon they were stuck until the tide rose. "We stayed aground for I don't know how long, and his mouth was a-going continually."

100-pound bales. "They would take the bales on freight boats to places like Elizabeth City," Manson Meekins explained. The freight boat *Julia Bell* was often used to transport the bales to buyers for furniture companies.

Ruby Williams recalled sneaking into the sea grass warehouse, known as the sea oar house, to have impromptu square dances. The teens played harmonica, banjo, and drum while another called the dance. Sometimes a worried parent would come looking for them. "We'd blow the lights out, and every one of us would go get behind the bunches of sea oars. . . . We was hiding all around."

Avon is a gathering place for surfers, anglers, and creative types of all kinds, including potter Antoinette Gaskins Mattingly, great-granddaughter of Carrie Gray. Antoinette, a fourth-generation Kinnakeeter, is owner of Kinnakeet Clay, an art studio located at 40462 North End Road in the heart of the old village. The gallery showcases a colorful collection of local and regional art. Antoinette is as passionate about her heritage as she is her creations. "It takes a certain kind of salt to live here," she reflected, happy to have returned to her island home to raise a family and open an art studio.

Antoinette has launched a Coastal Voices oral history project about the nonfiction book *Kinnakeet Adventure*, by Stanley Green. Green was a mainlander who, upon graduating from the University of North Carolina, found himself employed as school principal in Kinnakeet from the Depression era to World War II. Antoinette and others are documenting stories of villagers who remember that era and the old place names unfamiliar to young people today. "We hope to write a reader's guide," said Antoinette. "I think every high school student at Cape Hatteras School should read *Kinnakeet Adventure* to understand where they are and where they come from."

"To them," Stanley Green wrote about the Kinnakeeters, "the world was made of sand and water, while the salt was in their blood."

Water sports enthusiasts may be less familiar with the term "Kinnakeet" than they are with "Canadian Hole," a site four miles south of Avon known officially as the Haulover Day Use Area. The National Park Service maintains the sound-side parking area and bathhouse, which has become wildly popular among wind surfers and kite surfers. Visitors from Canada seem to especially love the site, which is how it got its nickname. The name "haulover" is historical, as the site represents the slimmest point between sound and ocean and was the place where boats were literally "hauled over" from sound to ocean and back with log rollers, ropes, and capstan.

## BUXTON

*The lighthouse is cracked all the way down but it's still standing.* — Joe Farrow, Buxton

Buxton, six miles south of Avon and just north of Frisco, was listed as Cape Hatteras Indian Town on early maps, as indigenous people of the Croatan chiefdom dwelled, hunted, and fished at the cape until the late 1700s. An 1882 post office inspired the change in name to Buxton, in honor of Judge Ralph P. Buxton. Inhabitants continued to refer to the region as "the Cape," however, and according to Stanley Green's *Kinnakeet Adventure*, residents of Buxton were called Capers at least through World War II.

Buxton, just west of the elbow of Cape Hatteras, is in the thickest, lushest part of Hatteras Island. Buxton Woods, a 1,000-acre reserve, shades a large swath of the region, covering a system of ridges of ancient sand dunes. As the cape juts out toward the warm Gulf Stream, Buxton Woods supports the northernmost frontier for subtropical plants and the southernmost edge of temperate plants. The forest provides habitat for deer, foxes, raccoons, rabbits, and other animals. One can stand in the deep woods at night, see the sweep of the Cape Hatteras light through the trees, and hear the peeping of frogs harmonize with the rumble of ocean waves.

Because Cape Hatteras is so close to the Gulf Stream, the warm climate supports the last thing newcomers would expect to grow on a sandbank in the blustery mid-Atlantic: citrus trees. The Orange Blossom Bakery, a Buxton mainstay famous for its "apple ugly" pastry, got its name in the 1950s from an orange grove that surrounded what was then the Orange Blossom Motel. Although the grove is long gone, the owners of the bakery can fill you in on the history of the Orange Blossom over coffee and an "apple ugly."

The village of Buxton, at ten feet above sea level, has long been a desirable place to live for Hatteras Islanders. Some Avon families moved to Buxton after the devastating floods wrought by the '44 Storm. Buxton is the most populous village of Hatteras and is the island's informal capital of sorts. Cape Hatteras Elementary School and Cape Hatteras Secondary School of Coastal Studies, both in Buxton, serve the student population of all seven Hatteras Island communities. The students at Cape Hatteras Secondary School have a maritime focus; not only was the school home of the famous *Sea Chest* journal of coastal traditions, but today students can learn about marine ecology, aquaculture, and local seafood preparation and marketing.

With the launch of the *Sea Chest* in 1973, students began to record and better appreciate island traditions like fishing, old remedies, boatbuilding, and hunting. Generations later, former students would recall the experiences of their *Sea Chest* project. "Armed with tape recorders and cameras, we students opened many doors otherwise destined to stay closed forever as the older generation graciously reflected on the past to us," remembered Danny Couch, former *Sea Chest* editor, who now serves as one of Hatteras Island's most respected historians. Couch offers highly informative and entertaining tours of his beloved island. Information about his Hatteras Tours can be found on his website: www.hatterastours.com.

The seclusion and protection provided by Buxton's snug location is in vivid contrast to the powerful elements forever conspiring to brew up

*Crossing Oregon Inlet*

## EDNA GRAY, LIGHTHOUSE KEEPER'S DAUGHTER

Edna Gray of Buxton, born in 1908, was interviewed in 1988 about grow-ing up as a lighthouse keeper's daughter. Her father, James Casey, worked on offshore screw-pile lighthouses and, later, at the Cape Hatteras Light. Screw-pile lighthouses, run by the Coast Guard, were typically octagon-shaped houses on stilts in the shoal waters of Pamlico Sound. Edna Gray often accompanied her father to these water-bound stations and lived for several years at the Cape Hatteras Light. She and her sister slept upstairs in the keeper's quarters, where they'd "take the screen out the window nights and lay there and watch the rays . . . the old, lovely [light] rays that go from the tower and light everything up."

On an especially stormy night when her father was having trouble keep-ing the light on, her mother realized he had forgotten his lantern and sent the daughter to deliver it. "She bundled me up and gave me the lantern and extra matches, and I had to almost bend double to walk against the wind. But I got up there and he was so glad. On the way, we both heard a cat meow, and we searched that tower over and never did find that cat. My daddy was not a superstitious person and he said he couldn't account for it unless it was just on the ledge and blew off after it meowed. We never did find him."

On stormy nights, shorebirds would hit the light and fall on the tower's balcony. The next morning Edna Gray's father would tell her, "Bring me a bucket." They'd collect the birds and her mother would prepare them for dinner. "They make the nicest pot pies, you know."

trouble just offshore. Cape Hatteras, of course, points to the number one reason North Carolina's coast is called the Graveyard of the Atlantic: Dia-mond Shoals. The mightiest of ships have broken apart on Diamond Shoals, jutting twenty-five miles off Cape Hatteras in a three-tiered diamond shape. The distant Outer Diamond, the Inner Diamond, and Hatteras Shoals are separated by sloughs, underwater conveyors of currents, migrating schools of fish, and all-around aquatic muscle that creates a chopping and roiling sea. What is more, Cape Hatteras is the point of confluence where the warm Gulf Stream meets the cold Labrador Current, the "weather-breeder hatch-ery" for the East Coast. Mysterious and unpredictable, out of thin air and thick sea emerges big weather, rolling up the Atlantic Coast.

The Cape Hatteras Lighthouse keeps watch over it all. Hatteras Island's

1940s U.S. Coast Guardsmen at the Cape Hatteras lifeboat station. On left is
Sam Maurice, who, like many young Coast Guardsmen stationed on Hatteras Island,
married a local girl. Sam married Lucy Allen Burrus of Hatteras Village.
(Photo from the Sandra Maurice Oullette Collection)

most prominent and popular landmark, the black-and-white spiral-painted
brick tower is the tallest in the country. From ground to peak, the lighthouse
measures 193 feet and today sits 210 feet above sea level. The National Park
Service manages the lighthouse and keeper's quarters, the latter containing
a visitor center and museum. Access to the top of Cape Hatteras Light is
open seasonally, so check ahead (www.nps.gov/caha/). Climbers navigate
257 steps to reach the spectacular view of the banks from the pinnacle.

The lighthouse is quite visible as one approaches Buxton. Yet, to the
amazement of islanders, first-time visitors sometimes have a hard time finding the lighthouse once they are inside the village. "You didn't see the Cape
Hatteras lighthouse?" Dwight Burrus's grandfather would ask incredulously
when travelers inquired as to its whereabouts. "That lighthouse marks some
of the most dangerous shoals in the world!"

"Papa, that's a car," Dwight Burrus would respond. He laughed at the
memory of having to remind his grandfather that tourists in automobiles
were not in danger of running aground on the Diamond Shoals.

Thousands of people made their way to the lighthouse in 1999 when
the unthinkable unfolded: the lighthouse was moved. An eroding shoreline put the Cape Hatteras Light dangerously close to the pounding surf.

*Crossing Oregon Inlet*

When the park service proposed moving it to safer ground, many locals were adamantly opposed. Some thought the move would be too risky for the aged structure and felt it best to leave well enough alone. Mariners had long oriented themselves according to the lighthouse and did not want an important landmark moved. For others the relocation was symbolic of the villagers' own tenuous hold on their island and culture. "If they can move the lighthouse they can move us," said a Buxton fisherman.

Nonetheless, the 5,000-ton lighthouse, in an unparalleled feat of engineering, was moved 2,900 feet from the site it had inhabited since 1870. Professional house movers used hydraulic jacks to lift the tower off the original foundation onto steel beams. A high-tech version of the old "bedways and rollers" system of moving banks houses was employed, as the tower was slowly coaxed along steel mats using rollers and horizontally mounted push jacks. Sixty sensors installed in the lighthouse measured tilt, vibration, and other conditions. Locals and visitors from around the world watched as the tower was moved five feet at a time. The move was completed in just twenty-three days. Cape Hatteras Light, which had been in danger of falling into the sea, is now 1,600 feet from the ocean. The keeper's quarters, oil house, and cisterns were also moved. Books about the lighthouse and Cape Hatteras maritime history can be found at the visitor center in the keeper's quarters. Another great selection of books on Outer Banks history, coupled with years of local knowledge and great conversation, can be found at Buxton Village Books, 47918 Highway 12, a gathering place of locals and frequent visitors.

A British cemetery is located close to the lighthouse on Lighthouse Road. This is one of two British cemeteries on the Outer Banks; the other is located on Ocracoke. The land on which the graves are interred is leased to the British government. The Buxton cemetery is the resting place of two British casualties of World War II: one washed ashore after Germans destroyed the *San Delfino*, and the other was found a year later shortly after the HMS *Bedfordshire* went down off Ocracoke. A ceremony complete with a twenty-one-gun salute honors the dead each May 12 at both sites, with the British Royal Navy, U.S. Coast Guard, and National Park Service officiating.

One of the most coveted areas of Cape Hatteras is the remote Cape Point, which serves as a surf-fishing mecca of the entire East Coast. Cape Point is sacred ground for locals and visitors alike and, as such, evokes strong feelings when access is restricted. When the National Park Service began developing a beach-driving management plan, many anglers and business owners were upset, fearing loss of access to a wildly popular fishing ground.

"No Easy Job," by Jimmy Pitetti and Johnny Williams, Jr.

Johnny Williams, Sr. and Calvin Burrus, Jr. of Buxton have been earning their living fishing just about all of their lives. These fishermen have to battle with rough seas, torn and damaged nets, and the constant rise and fall of fish prices. Their day starts at daybreak and ends whenever the job is done.

In this interview we learn how these two men get started each season, how they fish their nets, and how they carry fish to market.

"Usually we try to set side to the current. For instance, if the current is running to the west we run our nets north and south. . . . Mostly trout and croaker are caught in the summer. One fish that has hardly been caught in pound nets are speckled trout because if a fish has a brain they are a little smarter."

"A Nice Little Bunch of Children," by Caroline Smith

Mrs. Eliza Midgett Edwards was a teacher at the old school house in Rodanthe from 1928–1936. She was born and raised across the street from where she and her husband, Murray, now live in Wanchese.

Mrs. Edwards said that the old school house is the present day Community Building, but it was a lot smaller then than now.

"There was three rooms and three teachers when I was there. First I taught the fourth, fifth, sixth, and seventh grades, and later on I had the primary grades: the first, second, and third grades.

"You know, they were a nice little bunch of children, they really were," recalls Mrs. Edwards. "It's not just something I'm saying now that I've got old and mellow, but at the time, they were good."

Source: *Sea Chest*, Cape Hatteras School, Spring 1979

---

Others were relieved, glad to see the nesting grounds of endangered shorebirds and sea turtles protected. Today driving on any of the beaches of Cape Hatteras National Seashore is restricted and requires a permit, so check in advance (www.nps.gov/caha/). Whether to fish or not, access to Cape Point is a great privilege; the opportunity to stand at the tip and take in the sheer power and beauty of clashing currents and crashing waves is unforgettable.

The windswept plains of Hatteras have provided opportunities for research and innovation. At the turn of the century, Reginald Fessenden, former chief chemist on Thomas Edison's staff, worked for the U.S. Weather Bureau and undertook wireless telegraphy experiments from a fifty-foot tower constructed in Buxton. In 1902, he successfully transmitted a wireless message from Buxton to Roanoke Island. His work led to the first public broadcast of a radio voice transmission in 1906. Guide-wire anchors are still visible at Fessenden's tower site, and the community has since built a community center in his honor near the original location (46830 NC 12).

Perhaps taking their cue from Fessenden's success, Hatteras Island fishermen rigged a makeshift phone line to communicate with fish houses from camps along the banks. "They strung wire through the woods, on the ground, on the trees, across the beach hills, and they had a telephone," Rocky Rollinson told Cape Hatteras High School students in a *Sea Chest* interview. "They'd ring over and tell Burton Smith, who had a little store in Buxton, that they had a load of fish, and he would send horse and carts out to bring the fish." Fish house owners, he added, communicated to fishermen by flying flags above their fish houses, spreading the bad news that they were not accepting more fish that day.

Medical care on Hatteras was long dependent on a combination of local medicine and healing methods and imported physicians. In the early 1920s, Maurice Bernard "Doc" Folb served as chief pharmacist's mate for the U.S. Navy after his predecessor died in the flu epidemic of 1919. Folb also served lighthouse and Coast Guard personnel as well as Hatteras villagers, making house calls from one end of the island to the other.

"I couldn't have done it if the Coast Guard hadn't helped to pull me out of swamps [and] get me out of bad places," Folb recalled. Building on the independence and self-reliance of the banks people, Folb and a nurse taught locals in each village how to do emergency work. By the same token, Folb learned from islanders how to make do with materials at hand. "Had one boy in Kinnakeet who broke his leg playing baseball," Fold said. "I was there without any tools, but they were building a house next door and I took a shingle and wrapped it in cotton and made a splint for him."

Historian David Cecelski came across evidence of an extraordinary relationship between a self-taught Hatteras Island midwife named Bathsheba "Mis' Bashi" Foster and "lady doctor" Blanche Nettleton Epler, who graduated from Johns Hopkins. Dr. Epler was the first woman appointed to the U.S. Coast Guard. In his book *A Historian's Coast*, Cecelski explained that

Calvin Burrus Sr. was the Coast Guard linesman from Hatteras Village who installed and maintained the phone lines to the Coast Guard stations on the island. He was driving a USCG 1928–29 Ford Model-T with daughter Marcella, speaking to his nephew Octavius Coke Fulcher Jr. of Buxton, early 1930s. (Photo from the Octavius Coke Fulcher Sr. and Lula Dean Burrus Fulcher Family Collection)

Epler had accepted a post at Cape Hatteras from 1923 to 1925 to serve as the only doctor on the island. The doctor and midwife worked together, blending traditional healing methods with the latest in medical training. Cecelski shared an excerpt from a 1933 article by Dr. Epler in *National Geographic* describing Mis' Bashi as a capable or "couthy" woman who rode her sand pony Napoleon up and down the banks, attending to the births and medical needs of villagers.

"One midnight I had returned from a trip across the sedge," Epler wrote. "I had just extinguished my lantern when four men brought in on a sail Mr. Nevada." Nevada was a fisherman with a sting ray spine embedded in his leg. The doctor's medical equipment had not yet arrived, but drawing on the know-how of Mis' Bashi, the two women improvised "utensils out of cutdown lard and coffee cans," sterilizing everything with water, soap, turpentine, and coal oil. "We placed Mr. Nevada on Mis' Bashi's kitchen table. . . . [Her] nimble, clean hands aided as the villainous prong was cut away."

*Crossing Oregon Inlet*

# HISTORY OF CAPE HATTERAS NATIONAL SEASHORE

CAPE HATTERAS NATIONAL SEASHORE PARK: THE VISION
*Call this ocean front a national park, or a national seashore, or a state
park or anything you please—I say that the people have a right to a
fair share of it.* —Secretary of Interior Harold Ickes, 1938

Nineteen thirty-three was a tough year for Outer Banks communities. Like the rest of the nation, the region had been mired in the Great Depression, and newly elected president Franklin D. Roosevelt had only just unveiled his New Deal programs. Modern conveniences like electricity, telephone service, and paved roads had not yet entered the lives of barrier island families. Not one but two fierce storms tore the coast apart in 1933. A category 2 hurricane hit the northern banks on August 22. A category 3 storm hit the southern banks on September 15 and traveled up Pamlico Sound, flooding cities, towns, and villages; that one, known as the '33 Storm, claimed twenty-one lives. The fishing economy was in shambles. Hunting lodges and camps were damaged or destroyed in the back-to-back storms. What would the future hold for the ever-so-vulnerable sandbanks communities?

"A Coastal Park for North Carolina and the Nation" read a July 21, 1933, headline in the *Elizabeth City Independent*. The article served as a public unveiling of Frank Stick's vision for the Outer Banks. Stick, father of Outer Banks historian David Stick, moved to the northern coast of North Carolina in 1929. Frank Stick was a commercial wildlife artist, outdoorsman, and conservationist. Ironically, given that he did indeed envision the country's first national seashore park, he was also a real estate investor, buying property up and down the northern banks.

According to park historian Cameron Brinkley, Frank Stick realized that "unrestricted development would eventually destroy the Bank's basic appeal, which was as a recreational paradise." Stick cited the need for recreational opportunities, a refuge for migratory wildlife, and a more secure coastline should war break out. Rather than displacing existing communities on the banks, Stick firmly believed a national park would bolster the economy for villagers, and he advocated for their employment in New Deal work-relief programs. At the top of his list was dune construction and grass planting to combat erosion from storms and livestock grazing; he saw such efforts as benefiting communities as well as seashore parkland.

Events seemed to line up perfectly for the realization of Frank Stick's dream—at least at first. The National Park Service began supervising New

Deal Civilian Conservation Corps work-relief projects. By 1934, labor camps were setting up shop on the banks so that erosion control efforts—mainly sand fence building and grass planting—could begin. In 1935 North Carolina designated the region as a state park, anticipating a large land donation from the wealthy Phipps family who owned more than a thousand acres of hunting grounds at Cape Hatteras. The state also put a ban on free-range grazing in Dare County in an effort to help control erosion.

On August 17, 1937, President Roosevelt signed a bill authorizing the Cape Hatteras National Seashore. Restoration work continued, including renovation of the Cape Hatteras Lighthouse. More land was acquired as well. But park development came to a screeching halt with the onset of World War II. Restoration efforts ceased, Civilian Conservation Corps camps were shut down, and attention turned to protecting the coastline from enemy attack. The wartime economy gave rise to new oil exploration efforts, including on the Outer Banks. Oil companies secured land-based and offshore oil leases. Although no oil was found, some people turned against the idea of a park, fearing it would stymie future economic possibilities. Opponents circulated petitions calling for the land acquisition process to be halted.

By 1950, momentum for the park began to revive. Although some villagers feared that they'd lose the ability to hunt and fish, and others—including some hunt club owners—fought the government's land acquisition efforts, many landowners were willing to sell, as open stretches of barrier island had become all but useless once free-range livestock was outlawed. A fortuitous donation by the Mellon family put the goal within reach, as did the hard work of Congressman Herbert Bonner, namesake of the Bonner Bridge. In the end, the prospect of a paved road, a bridge, and economic links with the outside world held sway with villagers.

Cape Hatteras National Seashore was officially signed into existence in 1953 under the new Eisenhower administration. With some 13,000 acres secured for park use, excluding village boundaries, which were drawn liberally to allow communities to expand, Frank Stick's dream was at last a reality.

"Hold your lands within your communities," Conrad Wirth, director of the National Park Service, wrote in an open letter to the people of the banks villages. "Don't let outside speculators come in and take over. . . . Enjoy the prosperity that you so rightfully deserve because of your long occupancy of these lands." He also assured them that their fishing and hunting rights would remain "reserved to the people." That assurance has been cited repeatedly in recent years by banks residents and visitors, as many believe it to be a "broken promise" in light of increasing management restrictions.

Fifty years later, relations between the National Park Service and neighboring villages can hardly be characterized as harmonious, and some have likened it to a "shotgun marriage," with all the tensions inherent in such a union. The park's very mission of preserving the natural environment while providing recreational opportunities contains the seeds of conflict. Trying to balance the needs of barrier island ecology with a booming visitor population on sandbanks inhabited by working families and retirees makes for an interesting job.

"Sailboarders were cutting our nets," complained a commercial fisherman from Waves. "They didn't mean to do it, but they'd approach our net and tilt their board so the fins would hit the top of the net and cut it." As an example of locals' frustration with the federal government, he described approaching the park service about starting a program to educate visitors and recreationists about commercial fishing. He found park employees reluctant to get involved. "They said, 'We can't make public speeches like that.' I said, 'Why can't you? You tell them about shorebirds, the lighthouse, turtles. . . . You can't educate them about us?'"

The park service does, in fact, work to preserve and interpret the cultural history of the Outer Banks, from maintaining historical structures and artifacts to collecting oral histories. At times, however, politics overshadows their contribution, and park personnel get caught in the crossfire of problems too big to contain. Such was the case of the widely publicized effort to get a handle on where and when people can drive on the beach.

"Piping plover tastes like chicken!" read the bumper sticker on a large "beach buggy" SUV parked on the shoreline of Cape Point. Such slogans became common in 2010 when the park service announced plans to develop an ORV (off-road vehicle) management plan to address concerns that beach drivers posed a threat to nests of piping plovers and other endangered shorebirds and sea turtles. Environmental groups had threatened legal action if the ORV plan, which was a federal requirement, wasn't put in place.

Not only were recreational anglers upset at the prospect of losing access to their favorite fishing spots, but local tackle shop, motel, and other business owners feared loss of tourism revenue if people couldn't drive to Cape Point. In the five years it took to finalize the beach driving plan, which curtailed but did not stop access to choice fishing areas, tensions between the park and the public were never higher.

Although sore feelings linger, and signs and bumper stickers continue to remind us of the "war" over beach driving, park service staff—and many locals—are keen to put the issue behind them and work toward healing old rifts.

## FRISCO

*If it wasn't for the park service, you wouldn't be able to go on that beach, because it would be owned by private individuals who would not allow it. —Douglas "Chubby" Dorris, Frisco*

On the western side of the cape elbow of Hatteras Island is Frisco, originally called Trent or Trent Woods. Local historian Danny Couch names Trent as the oldest settlement on Hatteras, dating back to the 1690s. The community expanded with the establishment of Creeds Hill Lifesaving Station in the 1870s. The surfmen "built little houses up there for their families and they just started growing," explained an islander. A prominent feature of Frisco was the thick, forested area from the southern border of the community into Buxton Woods. Hurricane Emily in 1993 destroyed much of the forest. "We had forty-two trees down," said Margaret Willis. "We sit here in the swing and watched the trees pop off."

Frisco has more than one legend associated with the woods. The village itself maintained a mysterious, almost fairy tale quality, thanks to the dense forest. Trent Woods was the home of Rodanthe's mythological Old Buck, the giant bull that appears at Old Christmas. Local legend describes a witch named Polly Poiner who lived in Frisco Woods and cast spells on cattle and horses. A local stockman, blaming her for his sick livestock, stormed into her hut and "broke her neck," author Nell Wise Wechter recounted. The stockman was tried and hanged on mainland Hyde, inspiring a ballad: "Oh, the yaupon scrub and scraggly oak, quivered on the dunes when Polly spoke. A madman turned a trick quite neat, but the noose hung high in Mattamuskeet." Wechter also wrote about the fisherman who started each day with a holler in the 1930s. "Dave 'Eddered' would burst forth with his eerie slave call," she recounted. "Its notes echoed and re-echoed throughout Trent Woods, bringing a startled awakening to light and heavy sleepers."

Some, including the founders of the Frisco Native American Museum and Natural History Center, feel a deep connection to the woods that once sheltered early indigenous populations. Celebrating American Indian culture and local ecology, the museum is a fascinating and funky mix of artifacts, specimens, and historical photographs. Carl Bornfriend and his wife,

My brother Larry was born just after the '44 storm. He had spina bifida. The night he was born, he was kicking just like any other little baby. He had a little place on his back about the size of a marble. But within a month's time, he didn't kick no more, and he was paralyzed from the waist down.

We carried him to Duke's hospital. We had to go across Pamlico Sound to Engelhard on the *Hadeco*. It was a freight boat. From Engelhard, we took some kind of a bus to Raleigh. Then we walked from there to the medical center. They told Mama that they couldn't do anything for him. They said he wouldn't live more than two or three years, and that she should put him in a home. He lived 10 years and wouldn't have lived that long if my mom hadn't taken such good care of him.

He was just our life then. We spent all our time playing with him. I would sit and rock him until my arms ached, just so he could sit up. He learned everything we learned in school. He was real happy, and he was smart. The Methodist church here in Hatteras used to buy his alcohol and gauze pads to go on his back. They made all of his gowns and things that he wore when he was little.

Source: Barbara Garrity-Blake, "Sound Stories," *Our State*,
September 2011; reprinted by permission of the publisher;
"copied with permission of *Our State* magazine"

Joyce, retired educators, have owned and operated the museum since 1987. Chatting with them about island life and challenges is worth the price of admission. The building is a low, sprawling compound of many additions and renovations, bouncing back after calamities such as Hurricane Emily, which put more than two feet of water in the museum. A natural trail and dance circle area is behind the building. The Bornfriends host occasional intertribal powwows on the island.

The wooded region of Frisco was once so thick with yaupon that it was harvested and sold. John Whedbee of Frisco processed yaupon tea until the 1930s. His daughter explained that Whedbee would place the yaupon branches in a trough and "twig" them with a knife. Careful to remove the poisonous berries, he would then chop the twigs into small pieces with an axe. He'd heat ballast stones in a fire and place yaupon and hot stones in a barrel, or "hogshead," in alternating layers. The barrel was buried in the sand and left for three days. Once the yaupon was cured, or "sweated," he would dry it on large racks in the sun. It was bagged and sold for $1 per bushel. He shipped six to eight bushels at a time across the sound to Elizabeth City. The tea eventually became associated with being poor. The local stigma, along with availability of other teas, brought an end to the yaupon tea market. "There wasn't a thing wrong with the people," an islander remarked, "but it'd make them mad whenever you mentioned yaupon tea."

### HATTERAS VILLAGE

*As long as I live, there will always be a fish house here.* — Michael Peele, Hatteras Village

Hatteras Village, three and a half miles south of Frisco, is the southernmost village on Hatteras Island. The Hatteras-Ocracoke ferry terminal, serving more than a half-million travelers a year, is located at the southern edge of the village, next to the Graveyard of the Atlantic Museum. To get to the ferry terminal, travelers wind through the heart of the village with multiple establishments, including a library, fire department, and the generations-old Burrus Red and White grocery store that displays a proud collection of community photos, marking its place in Hatteras Village history.

When Hatteras is viewed on a map, the village appears like a shark fin, the tip pointing north. The northern tip is accessed by Kohler Road, an area local people call "up the road." Side roads off Kohler lead to important recreational and commercial fishing hubs, such as the Hatteras Marlin Club and marina, Jeffrey's Seafood, and Avon Seafood. "Up the road" is full of historical houses and graveyards. "This area is most special to me," said Leon Scarborough. "Because it's the least changed."

An architectural survey was undertaken in the late 1990s that describes traditional features of old Hatteras homes. They were built low to the ground near the sound. The wood-framed houses had wood or coal stoves, but no fireplaces. They featured cisterns and small outbuildings such as sheds, separate kitchens, and smokehouses. Small outbuildings with ramps are still common and are used as garages or to store nets, tools, and lawn mowers.

The Hatteras Village waterfront has always been buzzing with activity. Today, commercial fishing boats, charter boats, and leisure boats motor along the channel out into the sound and through Hatteras Inlet to the ocean. The busiest route in pre-bridge days was between Hatteras and Engelhard across the sound. Frazier Peele ran the freight boat *Hadeco*, built in Bettie, from Hatteras to the Pamlico Ice and Light Company in Engel-

*Crossing Oregon Inlet*

Hatteras Village, ca. 1956. (Photo by Aycock Brown, Aycock Brown Collection; courtesy of the Outer Banks History Center, State Archives of North Carolina)

hard, on the mainland of Hyde County. The name *Hadeco* was abbreviated from Hatteras Development Company, a Delco-generated ice and electric company that Peele and island entrepreneur Tom Eaton had up and running by 1935. Ice and electricity were real game-changers for far-flung communities like Hatteras. Fish no longer had to be preserved in salt and could be distributed to mainland markets iced and fresh via freight boats like the *Hadeco*. Island homes eventually got wired for electricity, which made oil lanterns a relic of the past.

Frazier Peele could ferry up to four cars on the *Hadeco*. Buddy Swain recalled boarding the *Hadeco* in Engelhard in 1949 with his family. "Getting the truck on the boat was a feat," he recalled, as they had to navigate a temporary ramp made out of two planks balanced on stacked blocks of wood. That day Pamlico Sound was so rough that his grandmother, a Hatteras Islander, got violently seasick, losing her false teeth in a slop jar kept in the *Hadeco* cabin. Waves crashed over the bow, soaking their truck and all its contents. "Upon arrival at Hatteras," Swain wrote in the *Island Free Press*, "Grandmom put her false teeth back in and vowed never to cross the sound again."

Thanks to Hatteras Inlet affording watermen access to the ocean and sound, Hatteras Village is home to a vibrant community of commercial and recreational fishermen. Throughout the 1980s, Hatteras was the center of the gray trout fishery, and to more efficiently catch trout and other species local fishermen perfected the "drop net" method of fishing, whereby a gill net is set and retrieved from a large reel fixed to the stern of boats. Fishermen also set crab pots, fish pound nets, fish with hook and line for sharks and reef fish, and patrol the shores with dories and seine nets. An ever-growing list of regulations and restrictions has made it harder for fishermen to switch from fishery to fishery, but many hang in there and figure out new ways to adapt.

"The commercial fishing industry is being corralled up," said Michael Peele, equating fishermen with the livestock that once ran free on the island.

Fishermen, as well as hunters, did enjoy more freedom back in the day, partly because society had a different worldview. The sea was a workplace, and anything that swam was fair game. Even dolphins and porpoises were considered little more than big fish.

Harvesting bottlenose dolphins today is unthinkable. Yet a "porpoise" factory operated on Hatteras until the late 1920s. According to a New York Aquarium report, Hatteras was the "only point in North America where a porpoise fishery has ever been regularly conducted." Hatteras fishermen, nicknamed porpoise oilers, took to the surf in dories and intercepted schools of migrating dolphins with heavy drag seines. The outline of a brick kiln, part of a factory that rendered dolphin blubber into oil, is visible by air on the sound side of Hatteras at Durant's Point. The most valuable grade of oil, known as "porpoise jaw oil," was used as a lubricant in delicate instruments and coveted by makers of watches and chronometers. Oil was shipped via freight boat to Nye Lubricants in New Bedford, Massachusetts. "We used to get a thousand dollars a barrel for that," said Damon Gray, former member of a Hatteras porpoise crew.

Times changed as the market for porpoise oil declined and the scientific interest in cetacean behavior increased. The New York Aquarium hired Hatteras fishermen to capture and retain the "lively rangers of the open ocean" for transport to their facility. The animals were loaded in wooden tanks aboard the *Hamlet*, a bugeye freight boat captained by Dozier Burrus of Hatteras Village. The vessel sailed across Pamlico Sound and up the Great Dismal Swamp canal to Norfolk, where the animals were loaded on a steamer for New York. Although the endeavor had mixed results, with several dolphins dying en route, it represented an early shift in American attitudes toward marine mammals.

"When you know you're on the edge, in contact with something that is grander or more wild than you, and that you have a little bit of mastery

*Crossing Oregon Inlet*

Captain Ethelbert Dozier Burrus at the helm of his bugeye, the *Hamlet*, ca. 1915. When "Captain Dozier" retired from the West Indies trade and large schooners, he carried freight on his bugeye with his son, Almy Dole Burrus, between Hatteras Village and local ports such as Elizabeth City and Wilmington. (Photo by Dixie Burrus Browning, part of Maurice L. Burrus Collection)

of it," mused Ernie Foster, "it's very affirming." Foster was talking about the lure of sportfishing, the appeal that compels people to hire a captain to take them offshore to catch the big one. Ernie carries forth his father's charter boat business begun in 1937, taking people out on one of the three vintage round-stern *Albatross* vessels. The fleet can be visited at Oden's Dock across the street from Sonny's Restaurant.

Ernie's father, Ernal Foster, was a pioneer in the charter boat fishery on Hatteras Island. His father had returned to the village during the Great Depression because he knew he could "get something to eat and a place to sleep." He wondered if there was business to be had during the off-months when commercial fishing was slow. So he procured lumber and hired Milton Willis in the Down East community of Marshallberg to build the *Albatross*. "I didn't have enough money to pay him," Ernal Foster said. "The man said, 'Well, I trust you.' So I towed my boat home."

The charter fishing industry grew in the 1950s, particularly with the ad-

The *Albatross II*, one of the Hatteras Village signature charter boat *Albatross* fleet, blends the old-style boat tradition with generations of knowledge and experience, reminding visitors and residents alike of Hatteras's long-standing role as a true fishing village. (Photo by Lynne Foster)

vent of marlin fishing. Captain Foster landed a 475-pound marlin in 1951 on a light linen line and put a customer on a world-record 810-pounder ten years later. By 1953, three Core Sound–style round-stern vessels comprised the *Albatross* fleet, and business was booming for Ernal Foster. Hatteras village was becoming renowned as the marlin capital of the world, and the Hatteras Marlin Club and Tournament was established at this time. In 1958, a couple on the *Albatross II* stunned the fishing world and began a new philosophy of sport when they caught, and released, a marlin. Today, amid dozens of state-of-the-art fiberglass charter boats, the *Albatross* boats shine like vintage gems on the Hatteras waterfront, still in the game.

The Outer Banks, jutting some thirty miles into the Atlantic with turbulent currents and quickly changing weather, was an integral part of the national weather network. A U.S. Weather Bureau station, commissioned for use on Hatteras Island on January 1, 1902, today functions as a museum and welcome center. During World War II, Hatteras native Lucy Stowe became the first woman to work at the station, tracking storms for thirty-seven years. She described the early years, checking air temperature, moisture, wind speed, and other indicators, sending reports "all across the country" as part of a weather forecasting network. The station flew flags to warn locals

*Crossing Oregon Inlet*

U.S. Weather Bureau Office, early 1800s.
(Photo by unnamed photographer, Carol Cronk Cole Collection; courtesy
of the Outer Banks History Center, State Archives of North Carolina)

of upcoming fronts, thunderstorms, tornadoes, and hurricanes. They also spread news by word of mouth and radio, and airplanes dropped sealed tubes to fishing vessels with warnings enclosed. Stowe, who also happened to be the first woman in North Carolina to land a blue marlin, had many opportunities to transfer to Charleston and other areas. She chose to stay in Hatteras Village, however, because she liked "the beach, fishing, and not many people."

The beautifully restored weather station and welcome center is located in the heart of the village at 57190 Kohler Road, next to the Red and White grocery store. The Red and White is worth a visit as well. Established in 1866 by Caleb and Alonzo Stowe after they were freed from prison during the Civil War, the store sold pigs, calico, ammunition, and assorted groceries delivered by freight boat from Washington, North Carolina. Allen Burrus, who owns the store today, told *Our State* magazine that the oaks were "bleeding trees," as that was where his grandfather hung pigs and bled them for butchering. A historical marker across the street marks the "first attempt at reunification," when Hatteras residents accepted federal law; this is not sur-

"It's all about fishing together" at Day at the Docks, Hatteras Village.
(Photo by Lynne Foster)

prising, as anti-secessionists elected Hatteras preacher Charles Henry Foster as congressman to represent the state in Washington, D.C. His authority was rejected, David Stick explained, as the powers that be questioned the "de facto jurisdiction" of a "sand-bar recently captured by the United States Navy."

Weather still defines life on the Outer Banks. The Day at the Docks festival, held along Oden's Dock each September, is a celebration of the community's spirit and resilience in the face of Hurricane Isabel, as well as the importance of the Hatteras working waterfront. Day at the Docks organizers have brought in fishermen from Alaska to Maine, rekindling ties among watermen and providing a forum to discuss shared issues and emerging opportunities in the seafood industry. Musicians, poets, and storytellers are added to the mix, as well as kids' fishing contests, net-hanging races, and a "Seafood Throwdown" chef's competition. At day's end is the solemn and poignant Blessing of the Fleet ceremony. Dozens of commercial vessels converge offshore in Pamlico Sound. A local preacher offers the blessing, heard over every ship's radio. From fisherman Michael Peele's traditional shad boat, a wreath is tossed into the water in memory of fishermen who have "crossed the bar."

*Crossing Oregon Inlet*

Proud fisherman! (Photo by Natalie Abbassi/The Conservation Fund)

Cleaning fish, an important skill that is taught early on Hatteras Island.
(Photo by Natalie Abbassi/The Conservation Fund)

On Saturday morning, Oct. 1, one of the watermen who participated in the blessing [of the fleet] was saved from certain death by his fellow commercial fisherman. "Tall" Bill Van Druten of Frisco, who has fished commercially out of Hatteras for years on his boat, *Net Results*, paraded into the harbor in Hatteras village, along with 29 other watermen on their boats, for the blessing.

The next morning, Van Druten left the dock early in *Net Results* to go drop-netting for Spanish mackerel in the ocean. Drop-netting is a commercial fishing method that involves setting a net off a large, hydraulic reel. The net stretches behind the boat and is anchored with a buoy. The fisherman waits a time for the "set"—for fish swimming through the net to be trapped in it. Then the net is reeled back in, and the fish are picked out of it.

Van Druten was fishing by himself, but luckily some of his fellow watermen were nearby on the sunny, cool morning. It's customary for the commercial fishermen to talk on the radio while they fish, exchanging information about the catch, the weather, or whatever. A few folks apparently noticed that Van Druten hadn't been on the radio in a while. Jeremy O'Neal was also out fishing, aboard *Miss Megan* with his mate Cory Sisler, and he was within sight of Van Druten's *Net Results*.

O'Neal noticed that the boat seemed to be drifting aimlessly, and when no one could reach Van Druten, the younger captain went to investigate. He and his mate found Van Druten totally wrapped up in the net on the big hydraulic reel. His body had apparently passed through the reel numerous times before the buoy stopped the rotation. Paul Dunn and his mate Latane Saunders on the *Shannon D* also arrived to help.

The Coast Guard was called and a boat was launched from Station Hatteras Inlet with emergency medical personnel aboard. The first responders did not want to move Van Druten, and one of the mates drove *Net Results* back to the Coast Guard Station, where they were met by a medical helicopter. Van Druten was taken first to Outer Banks Hospital and then on to Pitt Memorial Hospital in Greenville, where he remains in the trauma unit in remarkably good condition.

. . . The fact that the terrible accident at sea could well have been fatal and that Van Druten's remarkable rescue came just hours after the blessing of the fleet did not go unnoticed this weekend on the island. His fellow

Fishing is not the only way for people to relate to the saltwater environment of the Outer Banks. Surfing has gone from a localized activity in the 1950s and '60s to a wildly popular and competitive sport in the 1970s and '80s. Hatteras native Jeff Oden, a commercial fisherman, is a seasoned surfer, having taken to the waves as a child since he acquired his first board, a bright red Malibu "pop-out," at age eleven. "Today if you see a car pull up you say oh no," Oden told *Coastal Voices* interviewer Susan West. "Back then you were glad to see somebody." He and his surf-rat buddies followed the waves. "We'd gather our nickels and pennies and throw a few coins in Wayne's gas tank, scud on up to Buxton in his old Falcon if we didn't have a wave down here in Hatteras." His passion for surfing was so great that he took to the ocean shortly after breaking his leg in a car accident while in high school. "My friend was saying just the other day, 'First time I saw you hobbling down with the crutch, you jumped in and paddled out.'"

"The magic is an energy pulse that transforms itself into a wave, then breaks where you can ride it," reflected Carteret County surfing champion David Sledge, who has often competed in the Eastern Surfing Association Mid-Atlantic Regionals on Hatteras. Like many surfers, he coveted the rare solitary experience on the water. He described a winter day on Hatteras near the lighthouse when the water and air temperature were relatively warm due to the positions of the Gulf Stream and the Labrador Current. The water was clear, and he was alone. Or so he thought.

"I was at my standard lineup, just about touching the jetty, and I noticed something real strange." He realized he was bobbing amid in a massive school of skates, relatives of stingrays, on their southern migration. "Millions! I was thinking, don't they sting?" Sledge decided to shrug it off and do what he had come to do. "Every wave I took off on, four or five skates would take off in front of me. That was one of those magical moments."

The south end of Hatteras Village was once a low-lying marshy area with walkways and footbridges made of wooden crates and planks that the locals referred as Sticky Bottom. Chubby Dorris grew up in Sticky Bottom and recalled that "there was always water down in that area. It was all swamp." During the depression the WPA crews came into the village and dug mosquito ditches, and the area has since been built up and drained on other occasions.

Just south of Sticky Bottom, next to the North Carolina ferry terminal to Ocracoke, is the Graveyard of the Atlantic Museum. The building was designed to look like one of the many shipwrecks that have washed ashore on the Outer Banks. Open every day but Sunday, the impressive facility began as a community effort but is now part of the North Carolina Maritime Museum system. The facility's changing exhibits tell the story of North Carolina's maritime history. Experiences of Hatteras Islanders are also documented, including shipwrecks that supplied the island with everything from shoes to bananas, the porpoise fishery, and visceral images of German U-boat attacks that occurred just off the beach during World War II.

Near the entrance to the Graveyard Museum is a black stone monument honoring the Hotel de Afrique, an important Civil War site. The Hotel de Afrique served as a safe haven for hundreds of fugitives fleeing the bonds of slavery. They came from the mainland and Roanoke Island once Union forces conquered nearby Forts Clark and Hatteras during the Battle of Hatteras Inlet, August 28–29, 1861. The defeat of Forts Clark and Hatteras, located within a half-mile of each other and constructed of planks, sand, and marsh mud, represented the first Union victory in the war. Persons who escaped slavery at the Hotel de Afrique, which consisted of a wooden house and nine wooden barracks, helped unload Union supply vessels at Hatteras Inlet in exchange for food and shelter. The Hotel de Afrique preceded the better-known Freedmen's Colony of Roanoke Island. In 2013 the Hotel de Afrique site was included in the National Underground Railroad Network to Freedom, comprised of sites and programs linked to the Underground Railroad.

When boarding the ferry for Ocracoke, look back at Hatteras as you pull away from shore. Notice that the southern spit of the island continues for quite a while past the Graveyard Museum and the paved road, a long spit popular with anglers and sunbathers. As the crow flies, the inlet separating the southern end of Hatteras and the northern end of Ocracoke is not far and was once filled in so that villagers could walk and wade from island to island. But the forceful currents constantly scour, shove, and shift the channels and sloughs, making it necessary for the ferry to carry passengers westward for a distance before circling back to Ocracoke. As always, the movement of tide and sand causes a continuing need for adaptation and change, adding to the unpredictable adventure that is the Outer Banks journey itself.

# 6

# Crossing Hatteras Inlet

To get to Ocracoke requires an investment of time: the time covering the road miles it takes to get to one of three departing ferries and the time on the ferry. For those who visit from urban areas with multiple lanes of traffic, you will start to slow down when you hit the two lanes that lead to all three ferries, whether Cedar Island, Swan Quarter, or Hatteras. Then you may have to wait in a ferry line — and of course when you get on the ferry, you lose control of movement and must be patient until the slow voyage is over.

On the ferry, if you pay attention, you will see some of what island living is about. You may see delivery trucks and other service vehicles that bring support to our home, like yours. You may see families on their way to doctor's appointments or island students on their way home from a sports event. You get to feel and smell the salty breezes coming right off the water, follow hungry sea gulls as they ride the air currents waiting for you to throw food crumbs their way, and ramble the decks as you start searching the horizon for first glimpses of Ocracoke. This investment of time can be a suitable introduction to our island.

When you get here, most of what we have to offer can be found without cars, since our village of about 1,000 residents is spread over a square mile. Within this setting, however, you can immerse yourself in history and culture; sleep, eat, and shop in family-owned-and-operated businesses; and get lost in stretches of water and sand, from sound to sea, pondering all the life out here on the edge of the world. Islands will do that to you — and send you back home with something special tucked into your heart and mind.

ALTON BALLANCE, OCRACOKE

Crossing Hatteras Inlet. (Photo by Baxter Miller)

## CROSSROADS OF THE OUTER BANKS
## NATIONAL SCENIC BYWAY

*They are friendly, unhurried, and welcome visitors to the island.*
*— Sam Jones, island entrepreneur*

The southern tip of Hatteras Island and the northern tip of Ocracoke are "so close and yet so far," in sight of one another but separated by more than an hour by ferry. The forty-minute route across Hatteras Inlet filled in with shoals in 2015, so ferry captains had to forge a new, sixty-plus-minute route farther into Pamlico Sound. The passage across Hatteras Inlet is lovely, even in rough weather. The experience of cruising along the wild southern spit of Hatteras Island, watching the distinct surf line of Hatteras Inlet to the east, zigzagging west into the wide Pamlico, and arcing southeast to slide into the ferry terminal at the northern tip of Ocracoke Island gives travelers context for where they are.

Once the ferry lands at Ocracoke, the village is still twelve miles to the south. The next ferry terminal to Cedar Island or Swan Quarter is fourteen miles away on the far southwest side of the village. Travelers disembarking at the Hatteras-Ocracoke ferry terminal immediately find themselves on the uninhabited north end of the island. Heading south on Highway 12 to Ocracoke Village, the road takes travelers, residents, and delivery trucks through wild expanses of open beach, dense thickets of pines, sandhills, dune grass, and salt marsh and across several creeks with intriguing names such as Try Yard Creek, Old Quawk's Creek, Shad Hole Creek, and Molasses Creek.

When viewed from offshore, the village of Ocracoke presents an astonishingly low profile. Miles and miles of open beach give a hint of what those early settlers might have seen with only sand and sea to welcome them. Today, travelers get to experience that same sea-sand line from the two-lane road that threads through the dunes, literally at the water's edge, allowing all who travel this most scenic roadway time to appreciate the closeness of the ocean and the fragility of living on this sandbar.

The road to the village bisects the entirety of the island. When the wind and tide are high, the ocean and sound can appear shockingly close in places. Several ocean and sound access points are available with parking. These are marked and numbered according to milepost. Ocracoke's beaches were ranked as the best in the United States by international expert "Dr. Beach" in 2007, and both Ocracoke and Hatteras beaches have been listed in the top ten many times. Dr. Beach ranks beaches according to cleanliness, safety, and the extent to which the beach is undeveloped and pristine. Ocracoke's beaches fit the bill, and one can walk the shore for miles without seeing another person. Ocracoke's Pony Pen is located about six and a half miles from the Hatteras Inlet ferry terminal on the west side of Highway 12. The fenced-in pasture has a viewing stand and boardwalk for visitors to observe Ocracoke's famous horses, descended from free-range herds that once roamed the entire island. The origins of North Carolina's barrier island horses are often debated, with many believing the horses are descendants of Spanish mustangs belonging to early explorers. Others question this theory, maintaining that yeoman farmers settling the banks brought livestock — including horses — onto the banks from the mainland. Regardless, they are a beautiful part of Ocracoke's history.

All free-range animals were required to be penned upon the establishment of the Cape Hatteras National Seashore in 1953. Ocracoke Boy Scout Troop 290, led by Scoutmaster Marvin Howard, assumed care of the horses in 1954 and began the nation's only mounted scout troop. The boys tamed

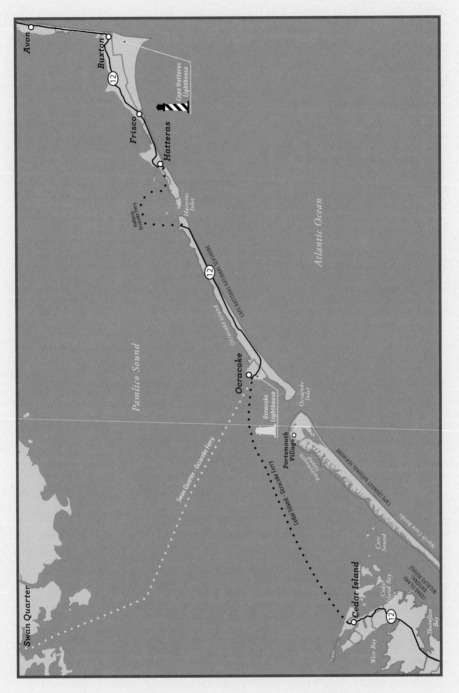

OCRACOKE

the horses and rode, in full uniform, in many events, including the Pirate Jamboree held on Hatteras. Islander Wayne Teeter, who often expressed regret for dropping out of school in the ninth grade, because he "should have quit in the seventh," was a mounted scout in the 1950s and cared for a horse named Beauty. Rudy Austin, who runs a private ferry service to Portsmouth, was also a mounted scout and is depicted in an oft-reproduced photo astride his rearing horse à la the Lone Ranger and Trigger. The National Park Service took responsibility for the horses in the 1960s and cares for them today.

The National Park Service manages a 136-site RV and tent campground on Ocracoke, located on the ocean side of Highway 12 (4352 Irvin Garrish Highway) two miles north of Ocracoke Village. Across from the campground on the sound side of Highway 12 is an unpaved access point to Pamlico Sound. The campground is open from late April to late October. Bathhouse facilities, as well as grills, are available. Campers are advised that no shade can be found, and biting insects—including marsh-bred mosquitoes and no-see-ums—are sometimes waiting for them.

Ramp 72, closest to the village across from Howard's Pub, leads to South Point. If open, it is a true island experience requiring a beach access permit and a four-wheel drive vehicle. South Point at sunrise or sunset is a powerful experience and well worth planning for. People on foot can experience South Point too, but it poses a long, difficult walk over more than a mile of sand to reach the ocean. All other ramps on Ocracoke provide easy access to the sea.

## OCRACOKE

*We have the cleanest water left in the United States.* — *Wayne Teeter, Ocracoke*

Ocracoke Village is comprised of 775 acres. Within those acres is an incredibly rich community of old salts, newcomers, artists, writers, fishermen, carpenters, musicians, and educators. Retirees with nationally—or internationally—recognized credentials have found their way to the island to quietly contribute to the texture of Ocracoke's cultural fabric. Hispanics working at island restaurants, hotels, and shops have been adopted as a part of the community, their children making up a third of the school population.

In island fashion, Ocracoke is thick with stories, rumors, and day-to-day ups and downs, as a whisper can get amplified in small places. No community loves a good story any more than Ocracoke, and locals can tell a tale with great expression. Yet the island is also a place of supreme solitude, especially in the off-season. Ocracoke has long been sought out by poets, nature lovers, and the tenderhearted in search of a little space for soul-searching. Ocracoke seems to give people just what they're looking for.

The village embraces visitors all at once. Driving in from the north, the first sight is the iconic restaurant Howard's Pub, and from that point on you are in the thick of the village. From the Cedar Island/Swan Quarter ferry terminal in Ocracoke, drivers often have to pause to let a family of mallards cross the road. This is a good thing because the ferry puts visitors right in the heart of "down town" at Silver Lake, and driving fast is not an option.

Village houses, restaurants, shops, and government facilities wrap around Silver Lake, once called Cockle Creek or "the ditch" until it was dredged and deepened in 1931 and again ten years later. Silver Lake provides safe anchorage for transient sailors and fishermen; docks along the shore are full of boats for fishing, parasailing, kayaking, day trips to Portsmouth Island, and sailing, including the skipjack *Wilma Lee*, available for sunset and educational charters.

The north side of Silver Lake, where the ferry terminal sits, was known as the Creek neighborhood and the south side was the Point neighborhood. For years villagers living in these areas were called Creekers and Pointers. "Up Trent" refers to a wooded area northeast of the village. Behind the Creek neighborhood down British Cemetery Road is a neighborhood that was once low-lying and marshy until WPA workers started ditching and draining in the 1930s. "I had to lay big old Pepsi crates from the door to get to the road," recalled Nathaniel "Nat" Jackson.

Ocracoke's Back Road, looping from British Cemetery Road back to Highway 12, accesses many side lanes and private homes and "off-the-main-drag" businesses such as coffee shops, bookstores, B&Bs, and restaurants. From Back Road via Sunset Drive or Middle Road, visitors can find the Oyster Creek section of the island, home of newer residences as well as fishing camps. Yes, it is possible to get delightfully lost on Ocracoke.

The main landmark and focal point for the island community is the stark white Ocracoke Lighthouse. Just seventy-five feet tall (about a third the size of the Cape Hatteras light), the Ocracoke Lighthouse is quite visible, thanks to careful foresight and community planning that has kept development on a relatively low profile. The white tower is striking against deep green cedar trees and other foliage, making a picture-perfect scene. Standing since 1823, the Ocracoke Light burns a stationary, nonblinking beam. The 8,000-candlepower light, once fueled by oil, is now automated and lit by a bulb that can be held in one hand. According to the National Park Service, Ocracoke is home to the second-oldest operating lighthouse in

*Crossing Hatteras Inlet*

the nation. The light station is accessed via Lighthouse Road (not water-side Silver Lake Road, as some newcomers assume) and is not open for climbing.

Ocracoke was originally called Pilot Town for good reason. The south end of the island, along with the north end of Portsmouth Island, was the gateway to Ocracoke Inlet, a key shipping point in colonial history. The earliest colonial inhabitants were mariners charged with piloting vessels en route to mainland ports or with "lightering" cargo from large schooners to smaller freight boats that could better navigate the shallow waters of Pamlico Sound. Many of these early pilots and boatmen, according to David Cecelski in his classic work *The Waterman's Song*, were enslaved or free blacks known for their maritime skills.

Ocracoke is replete with legends, stories, and mysteries. Storyteller Philip Howard, owner of the Village Craftsman gallery, is prolific in his blog and newsletter writings, offering historical tidbits and entrancing stories about his home community. His gallery is located at the end of Howard Street, an enchanting and mysterious dirt lane lined with shade trees, traditional homes, and graveyards. It's no wonder Philip Howard was inspired to start a ghost and historic walking tour, as his very surroundings are ripe for storytelling.

One of the most famous stories is about Edward Teach, a.k.a. Blackbeard the Pirate, who met his end at Ocracoke. Piracy became prevalent off the North Carolina coast in the early 1700s, reaching its heyday with the exploits of Teach, who enjoyed the seclusion of the islands, estuaries, and rivers. Blackbeard's fleet was responsible for the capture of twenty-five ships between 1716 and 1718. In autumn of 1718, according to David Stick, after receiving a pardon from the royal governor Charles Eden in Bath, Teach "found" a French ship and was reputed to have shared the booty with Governor Eden.

Outraged Carolinians turned to Virginia governor Alexander Spotswood, and he responded by dispatching two British warships. Robert Maynard's crew engaged Teach's crew in a vicious battle in Ocracoke Inlet on November 22, 1718. Maynard and crew subsequently killed Blackbeard, cut off his head, and put it on the bowsprit of their vessel. Legend has it that Blackbeard's body swam around the warship several times before sinking. The death of Blackbeard marked the end of piracy's short-lived golden age in North Carolina.

Today "Teaches Hole" is a prime fishing slough along the shore of the island just to the south of Ocracoke Inlet. A beautiful way to visit the water body from land is to visit Springer's Point Nature Preserve and walk the Jim

A small cemetery, enclosed by an unpainted, cedar picket fence, lies in the middle of the Springer's Point Nature Preserve on Ocracoke Island.

Ikey D was buried there in the 1960s. For years, no tombstone marked the spot.

In September 1977, another body was laid to rest beside Ikey D. His tombstone reads: "Samuel G. Jones, July 31, 1893–September 27, 1977, I shall pass this way but once. Any good therefore that I can do let me do it now for I shall not pass this way again." His footstone reads: "SAM, When Morning gilds the Skies I'll Be Looking Home to You. In Loving Memory From Your Many Friends."

By all accounts, Sam was a colorful character. Born in Swan Quarter, the principal town in the county of Hyde, in coastal North Carolina, Sam was only thirteen years old when he quit school and left his hometown to seek his fortune.

Sam soon found his way to Norfolk, Virginia. There he secured work at Berkley Machine Works and Foundry. He was industrious, enterprising, creative, and endowed with a strong entrepreneurial spirit. In 1919, when he was just 26 years old, Sam purchased Berkley Machine Works. Shortly thereafter, he invented a stoker for coal-fired steam locomotives, a product that proved to be in great demand. As a result, he soon found himself a wealthy man.

In his mid-twenties, Sam married Mary Ruth Kelly, daughter of Neva May Howard and a Maryland mariner, Captain William Kelly. Neva May was the daughter of Captain George Gregory Howard of Ocracoke Island. Captain George, great-great-grandson of William Howard, Sr., colonial owner of Ocracoke, and a seafaring man (he owned several coastal schooners), lived in a large, two-story house on Howard Street.

According to Sam's own account, he had visited Ocracoke island "as a boy on the Fourth of July which was a big occasion," and prided himself "as one of the old-timey square dancers." After his marriage he began making regular visits to Ocracoke in the early 1930s and soon fell in love with the island and its people. He would often speak of the "easy-going solitude and unique flavor" of Ocracoke Island and the simple folk who lived there. Over the next several decades he would have a significant impact on the life and economy of this isolated barrier island and small village.

Sam Jones and his beloved Ikey D outside Berkley Manor, Ocracoke, 1956.
(Photo by Aycock Brown, Aycock Brown Collection; courtesy of the
Outer Banks History Center, State Archives of North Carolina)

In 1941, Sam purchased more than fifty acres of maritime forest at Springer's Point on Pamlico Sound. This Point was the site of the earliest settlement on Ocracoke, and several dilapidated structures still stood, including an old house, a stable, a jail or storage shed, and a round brick well. Although Sam made use of some of the lumber for projects elsewhere in the village, he never developed the Point, preferring instead to allow the live oaks, cedars, and other vegetation to reclaim the area.

In about 1951, he began construction of the first of four large structures in the village, all of which reflected his unique architectural style: Colonial Revival combined with distinctive shingled towers and numerous dormers. One wag or wit from Hatteras Island remarked that Sam Jones had "shingled Ocracoke."

By the mid-1950s, construction had begun on the second of Sam's palatial residences, Berkley Castle, halfway around the harbor. As with Berkley

The infamous Sam Jones, owner and builder of the Castle and
the Berkley Manor. His horse often attended his get-togethers.
(Photo by Aycock Brown, Aycock Brown Collection; courtesy of the
Outer Banks History Center, State Archives of North Carolina)

Manor, the Castle was built entirely by island carpenters according to the
same style. There is no evidence that Sam ever employed the services of an
architect. Nor did he have blueprints. More often than not, he would simply
stand on the property with his work crew and tell them what he wanted.
Sometimes he would make sketches on the back of an envelope, or draw de-
signs in the sand.

After completion of the first stage of construction, the Castle became
Sam's guesthouse, while the Manor was used mostly for storage. When he
brought friends, clients, business partners, employees, and politicians to
Ocracoke for hunting and fishing trips he would nearly always lodge them
in the Castle. These trips often included lavish parties with music provided
by local performers. It was not uncommon for Sam to require women to
wear ankle-length colonial-style dresses, which he personally selected from

*Crossing Hatteras Inlet*

his well-stocked closets. At times, he would even bring professional square dancers down from Virginia to entertain his guests in the eighteen feet by sixty feet ballroom designed expressly for that purpose. During daylight hours 15–20 people could sometimes be seen playing croquet on the well-kept lawn in front of the Castle.

For years, he had occasionally brought his favorite horse, Ikey D, into the parlor to stand around the organ and enjoy sing-alongs with his family and friends. Needless to say, Sam's wives were less than enthusiastic about this arrangement.

Sam Jones died in September of 1977, after suffering complications from an automobile accident. He was 84 years old. As he had wished, he was laid to rest at Springer's Point, beside Ikey D. Family and friends gathered to bid him adieu, just as they had gathered years before when Sam made arrangements with the local Assembly of God preacher to conduct a funeral service for Ikey D.

Source: Philip Howard, *Ocracoke Newsletter*, January 21, 2011

Stephenson Nature Trail. Springer's Point is made up of 120 acres of pristine maritime forest purchased by the Coastal Land Trust for the public's enjoyment. In the middle of the preserve is a small fenced graveyard containing the remains of island entrepreneur and eccentric Sam Jones and his beloved horse Ikey D.

The village's financial fortunes declined once Hatteras Inlet opened in 1846, as ships no longer preferred Ocracoke Inlet. Thanks to federal jobs associated with two lifesaving stations and the lighthouse, however, and economic benefits from entrepreneurs like Sam Jones and Stanley Wahab, the island survived. Tourism, increasing with road and ferry improvements in the 1960s, has been the key factor saving Ocracoke from the fate of its sister island community of Portsmouth.

By the early 1970s, Ocracoke's economy was booming and Portsmouth had become uninhabited. With ferry access from three directions — Cedar Island to the south, Swan Quarter to the west, and Hatteras to the north — Ocracoke has become a true crossroads. Islanders today are greatly dependent on revenue from visitors, yet they strive to maintain the integrity of their culture and a strong sense of community.

About a third of Ocracoke's permanent population are direct descen-

### MUZEL BRYANT, OCRACOKE'S OLDEST RESIDENT

On Ocracoke, Muzel Bryant, granddaughter of slaves, was the last person connected to this past. Her ancestors had moved to Ocracoke after the Civil War, working in the maritime trades. Her parents worked at the Doxsee clam factory, among other pursuits, and raised thirteen children on the island.

Muzel Bryant and her siblings were unable to attend the Ocracoke School during segregation, but teachers and students stayed after school to educate them in math and reading. Their father, Leonard Bryant, served as sexton of the United Methodist church in the 1940s and 1950s. The Bryant family took their seat in the rear of the church, according to the racial boundaries of the times. Leonard "always wore a white coat and greeted the members cordially," an islander recalled. He also "showed visitors to their seats, passed out the hymnals, and attended to the bell ringing."

All but two of Muzel Bryant's siblings moved off the island. "Miss Muze" stayed on Ocracoke, working as domestic help. She and her sister helped raise Kenny Ballance and his siblings, and Kenny in turn took care of her until her death in 2008 at age 103. "When she first moved here," recalled Kenny, "she wouldn't eat at the table with us. She always thought she had to wait until we were finished. I broke that up one day when a friend was visiting. I told her that my friend refused to eat unless she sat with us." When Muzel Bryant turned 100 years old, the whole island turned out to help her celebrate.

dants of the island's early settlers. The surnames of native Ocracokers include Ballance, Garrish, Gaskill, Howard, and O'Neal. These old island families are woven into the village fabric, reflecting generations of extended family cohesion and interdependency. To newcomers, this might translate into clannishness, but to islanders, it is simply a meaningful and lasting kin-based foundation that has sustained the community for centuries.

Ocracoke, like Portsmouth and other important inlet communities, had African American families living in its midst, whether as slaves or free blacks. Unlike mainland areas that harbored large plantations and great numbers of slaves, maritime North Carolina valued black laborers for their boating and navigational skills; as such, according to David Cecelski, coastal slaves had more leeway to come and go. In the post–Civil War years, the black popu-

Muzel Belle
Bryant at age 100.
(Photo by Scott Taylor)

lation of Ocracoke and Portsmouth declined, but some families continued their island life.

Today Ocracoke School has grown, in large part due to the influx of Hispanic families associated with the service industry. But education on the island has a long history and was key in exposing children to the wider world. The first public school was built on the island in 1917, but two years later Hyde County closed it for lack of funds. "My parents decided then that it was time for us to go away to school," recalled a villager. Several children were sent to a private Methodist school in Misenheimer, North Carolina, or to Washington to the Collegiate Institute. Others attended St. Paul's Episcopal school in Beaufort.

"They thought we islanders had a very distinct accent and we thought *they* did," Fanny Pearl Fulcher said, describing attending school near Charlotte at age eleven. She was interviewed by the National Park Service in 1974.

"I heard some of the girls say, 'Let's go down to the branch.' I had no idea what a branch was except a branch off a tree." Another student returned home to Ocracoke and felt like "the sky was lowered."

By the 1940s Ocracoke had a school that served students through twelfth grade. Alice Rondthaler and her husband accepted teaching positions, moving to Ocracoke in 1948. "It was a wonderful place to teach," she reported. She described Ocracoke children as "bright and eager to learn," fascinated that the "same Atlantic Ocean where they played and enjoyed life was the one that brought the early English expeditions to Carolina." She found that the islanders in general had a "great deal of talent in dramatics and music." When the school had concerts, the "adults joined in. It was a small community."

The Ocracoke School held community square dances two nights a week in the 1940s and '50s. "Ocracoke was noted for square dancing," recalled a villager. People came from Hatteras Island or sailed from Washington, North Carolina. "They'd come over on the bugeye sailboats. They always had plenty of corn liquor with them." Dances were held at the Pamlico Inn, the Spanish Casino, and the old Doxsee clam factory and hunting lodge complex. Old-timey fiddlers and their bands held court. Favorite tunes included "Turkey in the Straw," "Soldier's Joy," and "Under the Double Eagle." The Graveyard Band played dances and parties from the 1920s to the 1950s.

### A Musical Island

"You Ain't Heard Nothing Yet," reads the inscription on musician Edgar Howard's grave, located across the lane from the Village Craftsman gallery on Howard Street. Edgar Howard was a vaudeville musician in New York City in the 1920s and 1930s, playing banjo and sharing the stage with the likes of Al Jolson and Gene Autry. According to Philip Howard, Edgar Howard and his brother Walter had a successful jug band called The Five Harmaniacs. Later Edgar Howard and Ocracoke guitarist Maurice (pronounced "Morris") Ballance played together. They were recorded by ethnomusicologist Karen Helms for Smithsonian Folkways in 1977, contributing four tracks to an album called *Between the Sound and the Sea: Music of the North Carolina Outer Banks*.

Ocracoke's creative spirit and musical talents are alive and well today. The band Molasses Creek has delighted audiences on the island and worldwide with their theatrical, high-energy performances. They were featured on the popular radio program *Prairie Home Companion* and appeared in the

## ROY PARSONS, OCRACOKE'S RENAISSANCE MAN

Roy loved his home of Ocracoke, and he was always ready to tell a story about growing up here. His music career started at fourteen with a Sears & Roebuck guitar he ordered, and I'm told his broadcast career began by singing into the stove flue at "Clemmie's Ice Cream Parlor" with the sound coming out the top of the chimney.

Like many of the young men on Ocracoke in the 1930s and '40s, Roy traveled up north looking for work and adventure. On his first day in New York City, still just a teen-ager, Roy found a room to rent in a boarding house and paid the landlady $2. He left his clothes, shaving stuff, and civil service papers in the room and told the landlady he was going out to eat, and she said the door would be open when he returned.

"I never did find that place again," Roy said. He even got help from the police, but still no luck. "All the houses looked the same, and they're all painted the same color. Woulda taken me five weeks to knock on all those

The colorful and delightful musician, storyteller, and craftsman Roy Parsons.
(Photo by Sundae Horn)

doors and ask, 'Do I live here?'" Somehow he came out of that on his feet, met some musicians, and traveled all over the northeast and mid-Atlantic playing music and finding new adventures, including a stint with "The Barney & Bailey Circus" (as he called it) at Madison Square Garden.

In between music gigs he worked on dredges around Philadelphia, and eventually returned to Ocracoke to work for the legendary Sam Jones at the Castle, and for Col. Egan at the Berkley Center. He cooked, as well as taking care of maintenance and repairs on these two historic Ocracoke landmarks. About this time Roy fell for his lifelong companion, Elizabeth, at Williams Bros. store where she worked. I was told by Della that he came in "looking like Clark Gable in that blue suit. Elizabeth handed him that hot-dog, their hands touched, and it was true love."

Roy built them a home from material salvaged from the old Navy base, and they have lived and worked there ever since their marriage in 1950.

Roy wasn't born with much, didn't have much education, but he certainly made the most of what he had. He was a self-taught man, and an excellent carpenter and craftsman, auto mechanic, cook, entertainer, husband, and father. He was never afraid to learn something new, even taking up the saxophone at the age of 80. He was always the best-dressed man at our shows in a beautiful cowboy shirt, boots, string tie, and fancy belt buckle. We worked together for over 10 years performing in Ocrafolk Opry shows. He was a masterful yodeler, he knew exactly how to get the most out of a story, and his comic timing was perfect. He always enjoyed meeting and talking with the audience after a show, and they loved it too.

He once said, "You gotta grab a hold of life if you want life to hold on to you."

Source: Eulogy by Gary Mitchell, reprinted in *Island Free Press*, September 17, 2007

movie *Nights in Rodanthe*. Band founder Gary Mitchell was instrumental in starting the Deepwater Theater and Music Hall on School Road. The Ocrafolk Opry is held there weekly all summer long, showcasing island musicians. Roy Parsons was a favorite guest star until he passed away in 2007 at age eighty-six.

The Ocrafolk Music and Storytelling Festival is another great venue to enjoy local and national talents. Organized by the nonprofit Ocracoke Alive! the multistage venue takes place on the first weekend in June. A highlight of the festival is the old-time community square dance, with Philip Howard as caller. Up-to-date information can be found at www.ocracokealive.org.

## Getting Around

Before roads and bridges, the easiest route for Ocracokers traveling to the mainland was a half-day mailboat ride to Atlantic, where they could catch a midday bus to Morehead City. Otherwise they could ride nine hours on a freight boat to Washington, North Carolina. Traveling north to Norfolk was more arduous, involving thirteen miles of sand tracks just to get to the north end of Ocracoke Island. A private ferry took people across the inlet to Hatteras. The Manteo-Hatteras Bus Line, a bus service run by the three Midgett brothers from Rodanthe, would take travelers the length of Hatteras Island, across Oregon Inlet via ferry, and up to Manteo. "It was like going on a safari across a desert to get to Manteo," remarked Earl O'Neal.

In 1938, an enterprising Ocracoke resident began a taxi service from the village to Hatteras Inlet, navigating sand paths in a station wagon. The ferry, run by Hatteras resident Frazier Peele, began in 1950 as a passenger ferry and expanded to a four-car operation by the time the state bought his business in 1957. "The ferry consisted of taking a boat, putting a platform on it, taking boards for a ramp and running the car up on the boat," an islander recalled. "We just ran the car off in shallow water, and off we went; there were no docks or anything."

## The Mailboat Aleta

Captains Elmo Fulcher and George O'Neal took turns running the mailboat *Aleta*, a "work horse" vessel that plied Pamlico Sound between Ocracoke and Atlantic twice a day, every day, for almost fifteen years. Alternating weeks, O'Neal or Fulcher would depart Ocracoke at 6:30 A.M. and arrive in Atlantic around 10:30 A.M., navigating by pocketwatch when the fog was thick. There they would meet the mail truck, as well as a passenger bus, that arrived in Atlantic from Morehead City. After loading, the *Aleta* would depart Atlantic at 1:00 P.M., returning to Ocracoke by 5:00 P.M.

The *Aleta* carried as many as sixty passengers, who piled into the cabin or onto the bow, stern, and top deck. It also carried freight, including groceries, packages, and fish. "Why only last week I carried three sheep to Atlantic from Ocracoke," Captain O'Neal told the *News and Observer* in 1948.

The arrival of the mailboat was the big event of the day, as residents gathered around the dock to see who or what was arriving. Sometimes let-

The *Aleta*, Jack's Dock, Ocracoke. (Photo from the Katherine Steger Collection, Core Sound Waterfowl Museum and Heritage Center)

ters were read out loud by recipients to neighbors gathered at the landing. Mailboats were, according to Ocracoke writer Pat Garber, "central to coastal communication."

When the *Aleta* was retired from the postal service, Elmo Fulcher bought out George O'Neal's share and turned the craft into a commercial fishing boat, harvesting shrimp in Pamlico Sound for many years. The *Aleta* came to rest on the bottom of South River in Carteret County.

The *Dolphin*, run by Ainslee O'Neal, was the last mailboat to operate between Ocracoke and Atlantic, until the waterborne route was discontinued in 1964.

### Standing Guard

Since the 1700s, Ocracoke Inlet was strategic to a wide range of shipping and military campaigns, including its defense during the colonial period, the War of 1812, the Civil War, and World War II. A Navy advance amphibious training base was established on the island during World War II. "Tactical cover and deception" efforts, which have only recently come to light, were deployed by Navy Beach Jumpers to simulate the sounds and appearance of battle to throw off the enemy. They also scanned the waters off Ocracoke Island to detect activities of German submarines. Thanks to the efforts of

*Crossing Hatteras Inlet*

Cedar Hammock Coast Guard Station (originally a lifesaving
station) on Ocracoke's north end, washed away in October 1955.
(Photo from the Alice Rondthaler Collection, Ocracoke Preservation Society)

Ocracoke historian Earl O'Neal, a monument commemorates these efforts
at Loop Shack Hill, just near the northern village boundary on the sound
side of Highway 12.

Lifesaving has had a long history on Ocracoke, from the Lifesaving
Service stations established at Hatteras and Ocracoke Inlets to the Coast
Guard station that was decommissioned in 1996. Ocracoke has had its
share of wrecks, including the famous "ghost ship" *Carroll A. Deering*, a five-
masted, coal-hauling schooner that went aground on the shoals near Hatteras Inlet in 1921. Rescuers found a table set in the galley, food ready to
serve, but no people onboard—just a cat. As Bland Simpson pointed out in
his book *Ghost Ship of Diamond Shoals*, the mystery of the *Deering* has never
been solved.

When I was a small boy, I used to sit at night and listen to the older people tell of the shipwrecks along the coast of North Carolina, especially around Cape Hatteras and Ocracoke Island were I was born. "God help the sailors on a night like this!" was, and is to this day, a household saying in our section of the country.

Old Arcadia Williams, who has been dead these many years, is responsible for the tale I'm about to tell. We will call her "Kade" as that was her nickname. Kade "slept out." What I mean by that is she didn't sleep at home by herself, but always slept at some neighbor's house. Kade's people had been dead for years and she was all alone and afraid to sleep at home for fear, as she said, of being "taken with the miseries" and dying without anyone knowing about it.

"It was in the fall of the year," she began, drawing the big cuspidor a little closer so as to get a better range for her spitting. "It was in October, a heavy Northeaster had been blowing for two days and getting worse by the hour. It never blew any harder nor rained any more since Noah's Ark. It blew that big oak down, Clarissa," she said, turning to my grandmother,

> that stood to the eastward of our smokehouse, and those two red cedars that stood between our house and old Kit Neal's place. Young'uns, I thought every gust of wind would be the last, as that old house of ours wasn't any too strong. It kept up for eight solid hours.
>
> Along about two o'clock that night Father Jack who had lain down upstairs, had a nightmare. Young'uns, he almost scared all hands of us to death. Brother Wid pulled him out of bed and sister Beck threw a pitcher of water in his face. During all this time, mind you, the wind and rain was roaring so loud we could hardly hear each other talk. Finally we brought him out of his fit and he told us his dream. He said he had dreamed of going down to the sea and beholding a terrible disaster with hundreds of people washed upon the sand and that he had picked up an infant only to discover it was drowned.

"While we were listening to this story," continued Kade,

literally hair on end and mouth agape, there came a knocking at the door, and when brother Wid opened the door there stood as fine a figure of a drowned man as ever I laid eyes on. Before anyone had a chance to speak to him, he turned loose the door knob and pitched head foremost onto the floor, landing about two feet from where I was sitting on a stool in the corner of the fireplace. The men folk managed to get him over by the fire and thaw him out. It was fully a half hour before he was able to speak.

He told us that he had just washed ashore from a steamer that had struck the beach about five miles away and he believed everybody aboard was drowned. Upon reaching the beach, he had seen a dim light in the distance and had walked toward it until reaching the woods where he lost sight of it. He had groped around in the dark until he spied the light in our window. He said the steamer had sprung a leak after rounding Cape Hatteras and the captain had run her ashore in a futile effort to save the passengers and crew. Her name was the steamboat *Home* bound from New York to Charleston with about 130 passengers aboard.

"While this man was telling his story," Kade continued,

someone in my family sneaked out of the house and gave the alarm that a steamer was ashore. It wasn't very long before everybody knew about it and the whole population of the Island turned out. Men began to run by with lanterns and torches, screaming "Wreck on the beach" and "Vessel ashore."

All the men folk went down to the wreck that night. It happened about five miles up the beach at a spot called the "Hammock." As soon as the men arrived at the scene they started to pull the drowned from the water. My father said that the last thing he found was a drowned child, the same as he had seen in his dream that very night.

The following day was a sad day for this Island as well as for the survivors. The menfolk had worked from four o'clock that morning until sundown. Every piece of canvas was used to sew up the dead in for burial, as well as all the bed quilts that were donated by the people here on the Island. Most of the dead could not be identified and were buried just as they had been washed ashore with their clothing and jewelry on.

Having now finished her story, Kade removed the toothbrush from her mouth, fired one parting shot at the spittoon, toddled over to the window, looked out into the darkness, and said in a voice almost inaudible, "God help the sailors on a night like this."

Source: Walter Howard, 1952; reprinted in *Ocracoke Newsletter* (Philip Howard), October 12, 2004

### *Fishing: A Living Heritage*

Before tourism became the economic mainstay of Ocracoke Island, most families relied on commercial fishing, especially after World War II. In recent years, fishing has become more of a part-time occupation for islanders, who supplement their income with other pursuits. Still, the seafood industry is central to the character and identity of Ocracoke. When fishermen joined together and, with the help of neighbors and partners, secured the last remaining fish house on the island, they reaffirmed their commitment to their fishing heritage with the entire community's support. The fishermen's can-do spirit is evident at the annual Ocracoke Working Watermen's Association Oyster Roast fundraiser held at the fish house each December.

"You see all sorts of amazing stuff on the water," said Morty Gaskill, one of Ocracoke's younger fishermen. He was sitting at a small wooden table in the Watermen's Exhibit located in the Community Square where visitors can learn about pound nets, beach seines, and other ways fishermen get seafood to consumers. "Just the other day I saw little sea turtles playing and darting everywhere underwater in the grass flats," he told the handful of people exploring the exhibit. "You feel a lot more connected to the earth than you would in a desk job, because you see what the earth has produced." Morty explained that fishermen have a vested interest in not depleting the very resources that sustain their livelihood. "You have to have an idea of what you need to do so it'll still be there."

Rex O'Neal of Ocracoke was also on hand to share a tale. Rex is the second-youngest of eleven boys and was the first "hospital born baby" in his family. He's spent most of his life commercial fishing and building houses on the island. He especially loves flounder gigging, a traditional fishery that

*Crossing Hatteras Inlet*

Ocracoke's community-owned fish house serves local fishermen year-round.
(Photo by Dylan Ray)

involves poling a skiff along shallow shoals at night while shining a lantern or flashlight in search of the round, flat fish. Once spotted, the flounder is "gigged" with a pronged spear. Rex likes to joke that he has nine lives, having survived being stranded on an island for four days, a small plane crash, and falling overboard at night while flounder fishing by himself. When he fell overboard, it was 1:30 in the morning.

"The tide was screaming out the inlet," he recalled. His motorized skiff was still running, making tight circles dangerously near him. "Had my boots and oilskins on, they were heavy, and I was swallowing water—every time I popped back up here the boat came!" He managed to kick off his boots and drift away from the boat. To his great relief he realized he was holding a flashlight. "I started shaking and flashing the light." After a bit other fishermen began returning to the island after a night of flounder gigging, and one noticed his boat "still going around like a wild thing" and his flashing light. He plucked an exhausted and extremely lucky Rex O'Neal from the water. They had seen his light and picked him up. "That was one of my nine lives," he added. "I'm down to about one or two left!"

Rex O'Neal, claiming he never had a great relationship with teachers, was a little nervous the first time he was recruited to carry a half-dozen teachers out on his boat to fish crab pots, gill nets, and pound nets. The teachers were taking the "Salty Dogs" course offered by the North Carolina Center for the Advancement of Teaching. The week would involve guest lectures about fisheries management and ecology, readings about life as a fisherman, and best of all, fishing excursions with Ocracoke watermen to learn how to fish a net, clean the fish, and even prepare the catch for supper. Alton Ballance, a former teacher at Ocracoke School, was instrumental in transforming the old Coast Guard building into a state-of-the-art educational center. He explained that Salty Dogs was the most popular seminar.

"Teachers love it," Alton said. "They love talking to Rex and the other fishermen, putting themselves in their white fishing boots, and learning what it takes to get fish from the sea to the consumer's plate." The goal of the seminars is to inspire teachers from all over North Carolina to think in new ways, learn new things, and share what they learn with their students.

"I am very interested in how people make a living fishing," a teacher from the mainland told a reporter for North Carolina Sea Grant's *Coastwatch* magazine. "I always had taken seafood for granted. I never realized how hard the fishermen work and all the regulations that they have to follow."

Since the end of World War II and the new opportunities and challenges it left behind, Ocracoke has adapted, but not without sacrifice. "The road. That's what changed all of Ocracoke," said a villager. The state ferry system ushered in tourists "from all parts and sites" and brought a hectic pace to the island. "The major impact on this village is when they put the road in the '50s, and the ferry systems started from here to the Atlantic and then Cedar Island. The State took over Hatteras Inlet, and the people really started coming in. I'm not going to say it's all for the better. I know everybody is probably better off financially but nobody has time now to do any visiting. They never have time to do anything but work."

Yet few islanders would argue that tourism has not benefited the community. An Ocracoker reflected that if it had not been for the employment opportunities from tourism, and the highway and ferries that brought visitors to the island, Ocracoke could have gone the way of Portsmouth Island and become an abandoned town.

Ocracoke is an overwhelming step back in time for first-time visitors

Charlie "Mac," the driver of the Ocracoke-Hatteras mail truck, boards the Hatteras Inlet ferry at the northernmost tip of Ocracoke Island. He has come through ten miles of sand dunes and beach to cross from Ocracoke Village to the ferry. (Photo by Martha McMillan Roberts, Standard Oil [New Jersey] Collection, SONJ 80682, Archives and Special Collections, University of Louisville, http://louisville.edu/library/archives)

coming into the creek on the ferries from Swan Quarter and Cedar Island, a mix of old traditions and community spirit infused with a steady flow of visitors from around the world. Ocracoke residents are civic-minded, staying as engaged as possible with county government, forming numerous nonprofit associations, and holding community meetings about local issues on a regular basis. Ocracoke has two newspapers, the *Ocracoke Observer* and the online *Ocracoke Current*, and a community radio station, wovv. Islanders work diligently to balance the economic benefits of the tourist season with the quiet, community atmosphere of the winter. During a 2010 community meeting, the question was asked, "Is Ocracoke a community or an enterprise?" to which an islander replied, "Both. Depends on the season."

All in all, Ocracokers have a creative spirit and willingness to adapt.

## FIELD OF DREAMS IS A REALITY

Pinch yourself, you're not dreaming. That really is baseball on Ocracoke!

Over 200 people came out to the *first ever* home baseball game March 27, 2015, on the brand new ball field at the brand new Ocracoke Community Park. That's a pretty good percentage of our little island's population. What if 20 percent of the residents of New York City came out for a Yankees game? There'd be no room for all of them in the bleachers. That's what happened on Ocracoke, too! It was standing room only at the baseball game.

Vince O'Neal, head coach of the high school baseball team *and* president of the Ocracoke Youth Center, which owns the new park, was chosen to throw out the first pitch. Garick Kalna is on the OYC board and helped make the dream come true. Still, he said, "I never imagined that it would feel this good to stand up here and see a baseball game. The field is beautiful. So many people came out for the game, so many people helped make it happen."

Thanks to broad community support and dedicated leadership, Ocracoke Community Park now, for the first time, provides Ocracoke's youth with year-round activities. (Photo by Melinda Fodrie Sutton)

*Crossing Hatteras Inlet*

The Ocracoke Youth Center board has been working for three years to build this field of dreams. Their efforts have been supported by grass roots organizing and fundraising, including the Ocracoke 5K/10K race and a golf cart raffle ($19,230!), and generous grants from Ocracoke's occupancy tax board and the Outer Banks Community Foundation. The Burrus family that sold them the property is owner-financing it; without their cooperation, it never could've happened. Darren Burrus has donated about $100,000 worth of labor to get the field built, Vince said. Other fundraisers are planned for the fall.

Coming soon to the Ocracoke Community Park: filling in the sandy area behind the bleachers with gravel, building two batting cages, installing permanent and roomier bleachers with handicapped seating, adding a flag pole, and opening a concessions stand. Eventually, there will be nature trails around the perimeter of the park that connect with trails at the bordering NPS and NC Coastal Land Trust properties.

Source: Sundae Horn, *Ocracoke Current*, March 27, 2015

They accept the challenges and welcome all who want to be a part of their community for a day, a week, a summer, or a lifetime. The people of Ocracoke, true to their past, make the best of changes as they come.

### PORTSMOUTH

*Core Banks, the loneliest coastline in the entire United States.* — Sam Jones, Ocracoke

Gliding and weaving across Ocracoke Inlet in a shallow-draft skiff, skimming along sloughs and banking the edge of ever-changing shoals, presents a lesson on the importance of local knowledge. Rudy Austin, owner of Portsmouth Island Boat Tours, knows "the bottom." The ruddy-faced, white-bearded Ocracoke native has the invisible underwater landscape etched in his mind, every channel, lump, and shoal; Rudy could navigate to Portsmouth blindfolded.

The Austin family has deep roots in Ocracoke and Portsmouth. Rudy's father, Junius Austin, regularly carried provisions from Ocracoke to Portsmouth, until the last two inhabitants, Elma Dixon and Marion Gray Babb, decided it was time to move to the mainland in 1971. Today, Rudy and his brother Donald make that crossing several times a day, bringing visitors, students, teachers, and locals to the well-kept, peaceful, amazingly quiet, uninhabited village. The Austins' connection to Portsmouth and their knowledge of its ways and people is profound.

Once adventurers from Ocracoke step foot on the shores of Portsmouth Island, they have crossed county lines—from Hyde to Carteret—and have entered Cape Lookout National Seashore Park. The historical village of Portsmouth sits on the northern point of Core Banks, which runs south for about fifty-six miles to Cape Lookout, broken up by Ophelia Inlet and New Drum Inlet. Cape Lookout National Seashore is comprised entirely of wild, uninhabited barrier islands. This is where nature takes its course without beachfront houses lining the shore and falling into the sea during storms. This is where sand is free to drift and migrate with the wind and tide and no one is trying to hold the ocean at bay.

The lonely stretch of banks between Portsmouth and Cape Lookout was used primarily for livestock and fishing camps in the early twentieth century. Place names include the Evergreens, Three Hats, High Hills, and the Pilentaries. A Portsmouth Islander said, "It must have been little communities that was up there at the time, and they named it this that and the other. First thing that came across their mind I guess." According to researcher Roger Payne, the "Pilentaries is a set of marsh islands named after a medicinal nettle plant."

For a day visit, the quickest access is via passenger ferry from Ocracoke. Visitors can also journey to Portsmouth from the south by way of four-wheel-drive vehicles along a seventeen-mile beach path. This route originates at the Long Point Cabins across Core Sound from the Down East community of Atlantic. Traveling from Long Point across the swash and plains takes time, but the experience gives visitors a much deeper understanding of how barrier islands live, breathe, and move.

Today the village is a walk back in time. Visitors are free to roam the lanes and ponder what sort of lives people led on Portsmouth. The National Park Service staffs the village with volunteers during the summer months to greet visitors. Interpretive exhibits in many of the structures provide a brief history of this seafaring village. The Friends of Portsmouth Island continues to be an important connection between the community and the park service in caring for the history and future of Portsmouth.

## Portsmouth Village:
## Ocracoke's Sister Town

*I cannot think of Portsmouth as a forsaken ghost town. Portsmouth*
*is an island with a soul! —Dorothy Byrun Bedwell*

The village of Portsmouth, tucked safely on the sound side of Portsmouth Island with vast plains between it and the ocean, became part of Cape Lookout National Seashore just a few years after the residents left the island in 1971. People sold their property to the federal government but were granted lifetime leases to their houses. The park service undertook major cleanup and restoration efforts and continues to maintain the remarkably pristine village today.

People with connections to the windswept village of Portsmouth bristle at the term "ghost town." The village has been abandoned since the 1970s, although the houses, church, post office, lifesaving station, school, and cemeteries are still intact. But "ghost town" implies forgotten and forsaken, and Portsmouth is anything but.

In 1989, the Friends of Portsmouth Island was organized to promote and encourage the preservation of village structures, sites, furnishings, and history. The Friends, with the help of the National Park Service and many volunteers, hold a Portsmouth Island homecoming on the island during even-numbered years, drawing hundreds of descendants to the village for singing, storytelling, and rekindling family connections.

Portsmouth, like Ocracoke, began in the mid-1700s as a pilot town and "lightering" site where cargo was off-loaded onto smaller boats for transport to inland ports. The village flourished with maritime trade, and by 1810, Portsmouth was the second-largest settlement on the Outer Banks. This same period saw Cape Lookout and Shackleford Banks become inhabited by seasonal fishing settlements and, eventually, year-round villages like Diamond City, Mullet Pond, and Wade's Shore.

As an official commodity inspection port, Portsmouth became the region's largest town, populated with merchants, inspectors, crewmen, tavern owners, and others associated with the booming business of transatlantic shipping. According to David Stick, an astonishing 1,400 vessels passed through Ocracoke Inlet in a single year during 1836–37. The growing number of sick or quarantined seamen coming to port compelled the federal government to build a marine hospital at Portsmouth in 1846. That very year, a storm opened Hatteras and Oregon Inlets, reducing the importance of Ocracoke Inlet and sending the population of Portsmouth on a downward

## DR. DUDLEY, PORTSMOUTH'S CONTROVERSIAL PHYSICIAN

The marine hospital established in 1847 on Portsmouth was one of only five in the country. Its mission was to serve sick or quarantined seamen suffering from dysentery, smallpox, venereal disease, and other illnesses. The fifty-by-ninety-foot, two-story building had twelve rooms and seven fireplaces. It was staffed by a doctor, a nurse, and three slaves.

One physician was especially memorable to islanders: Dr. Samuel Dudley. In fact, Doctor's Creek in Portsmouth was named after Dr. Dudley, who tended to seamen as well as villagers. Dr. Dudley was controversial, however. Sarah Olson, park historian, wrote that Dudley had initially "arrived at Portsmouth in search of a teaching position, and soon set himself up as the town doctor."

Many villagers "thought him a quack," particularly after a smallpox outbreak when he avoided patients for fear of contracting the disease and ignored a legal order to remove the sick from town boundaries. Olson said that the sick and dead were "finally removed only after several inhabitants of the town threatened to burn down Dudley's residence."

Nonetheless, Dr. Dudley went on to serve more than one term as the island's official surgeon. Levin Fulcher told folklorist Connie Mason about a Portsmouth man's request to have seven Ds carved in his coffin. The Ds stood for Dear Devil, Do Decently Damn Doctor Dudley.

spiral. By the post–Civil War period, almost all boat traffic had switched from Ocracoke Inlet to Hatteras Inlet. The marine hospital closed and was converted into a Weather Bureau station.

Once ship traffic began using the newly cut inlets to the north, the thriving port town became a sleepy fishing village. The community was somewhat buoyed, however, by the establishment of a lifesaving station in 1894. The old marine hospital building, which had become a weather station, was slated to become the new lifesaving station; islanders, according to a park historian, burned it down to ensure that a new building would be constructed.

Portsmouth Islanders recalled the days of prohibition when the Outer Banks were used by bootleggers and rumrunners; Coast Guard "rum chasers" patrolled inlets in search of contraband liquor and would sometimes insist that fishermen remove their nets to prove they had nothing to hide. Yet, according to an islander, the Coast Guardsmen also traded spark plugs and gasoline to fishermen for quarts of whiskey. The *Messenger of Peace* that wrecked off Portsmouth was full of whiskey; news got out, and "the next day, you could go anywhere on Portsmouth to a bunch of bushes and kick it, and a fifth of whiskey would fly out," said Cecil Gilgo. "There was more drunks on Portsmouth then there ever was in one place at one time."

The community of Portsmouth was divided into three distinct neighborhoods. The village proper was on the north end, containing houses, the Methodist church, the schoolhouse, the lifesaving station, a gristmill, a fish house, the post office, and community stores. The middle community was less than a half-mile south and consisted of houses, the village's only dipping vat used to de-tick livestock, a couple of stores, and a Primitive Baptist church that was destroyed by a storm in 1913. Sheep Island, about a half-mile from the middle neighborhood, was separated by a creek and connected by small bridges. Sheep Island got its name from a large hill where sheep and cattle would congregate during storms.

Oral histories from Portsmouth descendants emphasize how attached people were to their neighborhoods, all of which were within a fifteen minute walk. A man named Dave Salter who lived on Sheep Island courted Portsmouth villager Jonesie Roberts for fifty years. "They both died single, he having refused to live down the banks, and she having refused to live up the banks," recalled an islander.

The sand roads and bridges in Portsmouth were maintained by neighbors who would assemble on a designated day when repairs were in order. Portsmouth residents had at least five bridges to keep up: three "down the banks," the "little bridge" up the banks, and the "big bridge" midway in the village. "Everyone would help one another," a resident recalled. "They never charged when they helped one another — we never charged nobody a penny for doing anything."

Portsmouth Islanders were thrifty and made good use of materials at hand. Ashes from the woodstove were used to clean iron pots and pans. Women made soap from meat scraps and lye, boiling skins and lye in a pig pot, or "hamboard"; they cut bars of soap into squares once the mixture cooled in a flat pan. Light rolls were "made up every night, put in the pan to cook next morning." Fish was preserved in barrels full of salt. "They'd put a rock down to keep them under." Before it was cooked, the fish had to be soaked in fresh water overnight to remove the salt. Women also sewed and

Henry Pigott and Lum Gaskill bring the mail into the village. Lum Gaskill
held the mail carrier contract from Ocracoke from 1968 to 1971.
(Photo courtesy of Cape Lookout National Seashore)

washed for Coast Guardsmen for pay. Laundry was done by heating water in lard cans and using a scrub board.

Blowing sand was a constant in the lives of villagers; a woman recalled getting blasted with such force that her legs bled. Many residents tossed oyster and clam shells beneath their houses as a sort of foundation against the blowing sand. "The reason they put the shells under the house was to keep the wind from lashing the sand from under the house and making big holes," reflected a resident.

"We didn't know anything about a law," reported a man who grew up on Portsmouth. "There were no fights, no drunks, no trouble—we were just free people." Villagers were not, however, immune to county, state, and federal laws and would travel to the mainland to attend to such issues. A favorite story involved the case of Portsmouth resident and Civil War veteran "Uncle Sam" Tolson, who made a trip to New Bern on an oyster schooner only to be arrested when he was mistaken for Lincoln assassin John Wilkes Booth. Members of the Wallace family, who ran a menhaden plant on Portsmouth, "went to New Bern court to testify who (Sam Tolson) was," recalled a villager, as the accusers were threatening "to cut his head off."

Lizzie Pigott, descended from Portsmouth Island slaves and one of the few African Americans who lived on Portsmouth in the twentieth century, cut hair for villagers. When folks heard her playing the accordion on her porch, they knew she was open for business. Her brother Henry Pigott had the job of meeting the mailboat every day. He'd pole a skiff just offshore to a channel and wait for the *Aleta* to give him a sack of letters and packages, or some passengers. Henry and Lizzie were among seven siblings, but most moved off-island for work opportunities. Their grandmother Rosa Abbott had been a healer and midwife on the island.

One Portsmouth native recalled his mother taking time to read to a black neighbor who did not have the benefit of an education. "Just about every evening he would walk from his house up to my mother's home and she would read novels to him. And when she was a reading we weren't allowed to fool around—we'd sit in a chair and be quiet or else go to bed, our choice."

### From Porch to Porch

All islanders enjoyed the simple act of visiting, spending evenings with relatives and neighbors to talk and sometimes sing. Listening to the older folks was educational for children. "When we were children Papa and Mama would carry us with them visiting for the night—we weren't allowed to open our mouths or say a word," recalled a former Portsmouth resident. "We paid attention to those old folks talking—it was interesting too, the old folks talking."

Portsmouth Island had a rich tradition of storytelling. "Never let this be told," warned a Coast Guard station keeper in reference to an event that became a favorite story. The keeper was known for his strictness but would sneak out of the station at night and visit his wife's bedroom. A man on night watch, having been told not to descend the stairs, noticed the keeper slip away. With help from his fellow guardsmen, he climbed out of the tower on a rope made from bedsheets. The crew crept to the keeper's house, loaded the Lyle gun—used to shoot a line out to distressed ships—and stuffed it with a catalog. When they lit the fuse and shot the gun toward the bedroom window, "every leaf separated and they were afire!" The keeper ran out with his pants off, but the men beat him back to the station.

Ghost stories were another favorite topic, and the windswept landscape of Portsmouth Island lent itself to the tradition. Along the path toward Sheep Island was a clump of haunted bushes. "There was the most ghosts seen there," laughed an islander who recalled that "everybody on Sheep Island" was scared to pass. Foxfire, or a ball of light hovering over the ground, was taken to be a jack-o'-lantern by children, and their parents advised them to turn their pockets "wrong side out [and] they'd go some other direction." Parents told the children to say, "Feet, take care of this body," and run.

### Making a Living

Portsmouth Islanders found work as hunting guides in the early twentieth century, and some worked at nearby hunting clubs or lodges, catering to well-heeled businessmen in search of sport. Ten miles south of Portsmouth Village was the Pilentary Club of Core Banks. The club was owned by the Mott family, who hailed from Bouckville, New York. Franklin D. Roosevelt was once a guest of the Motts at the Pilentary. Portsmouth villager Joe Abbott, who was kin to Lizzie and Henry Pigott, walked to the club every day to cook and clean for guests. He was also known to entertain them with his singing abilities. The Pilentary Club was destroyed in the '33 Storm, as were numerous others, bringing to a close the heyday of the gentlemen's salty getaway.

Portsmouth fishermen had the best reputation in the markets of New Bern, Washington, and Greenville, particularly for oysters and mullet. Huge oyster rocks on the sound side of Portsmouth made the oyster fishery especially important in the fall and winter months. One year, Sarah Olson writes, the keeper of the Portsmouth Lifesaving Station reported "that the entire male population of the town was 'out oystering'" Freight boats and fish buy boats would transport fish and oysters from Portsmouth to inland port markets.

In 1919 Charles Wallace and Will Webb built a menhaden fish oil plant on Portsmouth. Portsmouth was the chosen location because, according to an islander, "the fish were on the eastern beach." The wooden factory had a well; an "elevator" that "dropped down in the boat, right in the fish" to convey the catch out; and a "great big brick dryer chimney." Two of the menhaden vessels were the *Alliance* and the *Gaskill*. Eight to twenty-five men worked the factory. When boats came in ready to unload, the factory boss would blow the whistle, and islanders knew it was time for work. The factory ran for about eight years then shut down due to "shallow water — the channel filled up, and the boats couldn't get through."

### Dancing, Learning, and Praying

Music was an important part of village life, in both church and family. "Every home had an organ," according to a Portsmouth resident, because pedal pump organs "were only $35 a piece from Sears and Roebucks." Square dances were popular, usually held at "any house that was available that evening." Jesse Babb, a Coast Guardsman, played fiddle, and sometimes Roby Fulcher from Atlantic played fiddle when he was stationed at Portsmouth. Ivy Scott from Harkers Island and Thomas Rose played twin fiddles at Portsmouth dances when they were fishing in the area. Edna Earle played the guitar. Dances were also held at the old marine hospital after it had closed, and islander Sam Tolson would arrive with his "dancing slippers" in his pocket "so he wouldn't get them muddy."

In the early years Portsmouth children were educated at an academy. The two-story building was located in the center of the village next to a pond referred to as Academy Pond by former residents. A man recalled a fellow student who temporarily escaped the wrath of a teacher by seeking refuge in the pond. "We had a boy that was pretty rough," he told an oral historian. The teacher was preparing to punish him, when the boy ran outside and jumped into the middle of the pond. It was in the dead of winter. "He took his hands and threw them up and said, 'Come on in Miss Linda. The water's fine!'"

Music was always part of life on Portsmouth.
(Photo from the Marian Gray Babb Family Collection)

The Academy Pond school was destroyed in a storm around 1916 and was replaced by a new school located between Sheep Island and Portsmouth: "They tried to build it fair, in the center," said a villager. "The Sheep Island children were coming to this school, too." Islanders recalled that school went through seventh and, later, eleventh grade. To graduate, students had to travel to Beaufort to pass an exam. Teachers were recruited from nearby communities such as Ocracoke and Atlantic or from inland towns. The Portsmouth school closed in 1943, and by 1956, according to Sarah Olson, there were "no children at all living in the town."

Portsmouth once had two churches: a Primitive Baptist church located in the middle community, and a Methodist Episcopal church near the head of Doctor's Creek in the village proper. Both were destroyed in a 1913 storm, and the Methodist church was rebuilt by 1915. The Primitive Baptist church, which had met about once every three months and served a small congregation of Sheep Islanders, was never rebuilt. Instead, members sailed to Cedar Island to attend the Primitive Baptist church there. "The people would come to Cedar Island Saturday afternoon and stay Saturday night," an islander recalled. "They lived their religion, those Primitive Baptists."

For many years the Methodist church on Portsmouth served the villagers' needs, from regular worship services to weddings and funerals. A "large crowd of people would come from the south of the island for church

*Crossing Hatteras Inlet*

and Sunday school," an islander explained, "the girls carrying parasols and wearing white dresses." Sunday school was held in the afternoon, and young people would gather afterward for a square dance and stewed chicken. But the congregation got smaller and smaller as the twentieth century unfolded. By 1956 Portsmouth residents were "described as too feeble to attend regular church services," Sarah Olson found. So a "minister from Sea Level, North Carolina, visited their homes approximately once a month."

Portsmouth villagers were isolated yet not alone, as their survival depended on their connections to Ocracoke and the mainland communities of Atlantic, Cedar Island, and Beaufort. They engaged in trade with farmers and merchants, who kept island households and the Coast Guard station stocked with supplies. Freight boats delivered goods, and Portsmouth Islanders would meet the boats in shallow-draft skiffs to offload the supplies. "They didn't have any docks," said a villager. "The storms were so bad, they would tear them off."

Portsmouth Islanders also maintained their kinship to other communities through worship, family connections, fishing, and recreation. Portsmouth Islanders sailed to Ocracoke regularly to attend square dances, sometimes held in the Coast Guard station. After each bad storm, more would move to Ocracoke or Down East.

"They didn't leave because of fright," said Lionel Gilgo. "They left because they were tired of cleaning up after the storms."

Challenges for Portsmouth Islanders continued to mount, and opportunities declined with the decommissioning of the Lifesaving Service in 1937, coupled with the Storms of '33 and '44. The one-room school closed in 1943, compelling families with children to move off the island. The post office and general store closed in 1959, making residents more dependent on Ocracoke and leaving only a few families to face the hard realities of isolation. By 1966 when Cape Lookout National Seashore was established, the end of Portsmouth as a community was confirmed with the acquisition of this portion of Core Banks for the newly formed seashore.

Henry Pigott, Marian Gray Babb, and her aunt Elma "Addie" Dixon were determined to stay, but with the death of Henry in 1971, the elderly ladies had no choice but to leave their beloved island home.

### It's Still Home

Jessie Lee Babb Dominique was proud of the fact that she was the last baby born on Portsmouth. Frances Eubanks, who grew up spending summers

## HENRY PIGOTT, FAITHFUL ISLANDER TO THE END

Mr. Pigott was a resourceful man, a requirement of anyone living virtually alone on an island where there is no electricity, no plumbing, and no telephone service.

In one out-building on his property, Mr. Pigott stored boxes of windowpanes, all sizes of nails, and wooden shingles to repair his home. Mr. McNeill, who leased the house after Mr. Pigott died, still has a shopping list Mr. Pigott had prepared. It was for two fly swatters and eight pints of bug spray.

He had a miniature screened out-building called a milk, cool, or dairy house in which he housed the foods requiring refrigeration. Cool air was produced when the wind blew across the pan of water. Every house on Portsmouth used these types of structures to keep foods cool and out of reach of hungry varmints.

Mr. Pigott's and the rest of Portsmouth's fresh water supply came from rainwater collected from their roofs in cisterns. Cisterns were boxes made of wood caulked like a boat to retain the rainwater or in one instance a boiler from a wrecked steam ship was used. Resourcefulness is key to surviving on the banks.

Miss Babb says Mr. Pigott fished for a living. Henry clammed and oystered. He'd get a mess for him and some for us. He always had a garden and grew all kinds of vegetables.

Mr. Pigott also worked for the postal service. Daily he would pole his skiff out to meet the mailboat as it made its way to Ocracoke, then he delivered the mail to the post office.

Mr. Pigott never married. He shared his two-story home with his younger sister, Elizabeth. "They took care of each other," Mr. Salter says. After Lizzie died, Henry was never the same. He was always lonesome for his sister that he loved.

Mr. Pigott died of pneumonia and was buried next to his sister in the family cemetery behind the Dixon-Babb house. One account of his funeral read, "Seventeen men and four women braved a blowing January gale of wind to see he was given a fitting funeral on his native island."

Source: *Carteret News-Times*

## MARIAN'S SONG: ON MY ISLAND HOME

I step back upon the shore,
Back to times and folks before,
Islanders and mailboats days,
Clear the misty haze,
On my Island Home.

From the Church I hear a hymn
Addie plays the pump organ
Lionel opens with a prayer
Henry rings the bell
On my Island Home.

Watermen and Lifesaver
Women knitting net
Hunting guides no nine to five

Marian Gray Babb and Junius Austin discuss the news of the day while friends
listen on Marian's porch, Portsmouth Island. (Photo by Ann Ehringhaus)

Just glad to be alive
On our Island Home.

See Miss Annie's at her post
Filing mail and greeting folks
Whittler's wait her work to end
Catching-up among friends
On my Island Home.

Ocracoke her sister town
Across the bar, right on the sound
Survives and thrives today
But that's not the fate
Of my Island Home.

Portsmouth Town will never die
And will seldom change
No roads, or wells, small sandy lanes
Cisterns caught the rain
On our Island Home.

I visit many sleeping friends
Not so far from my peaceful kin
Candy pulls and Christmas plays
Remembered foreign days
On my Island Home.

Junius comes it's time to go
Back to Beaufort afore it blows
I almost wish it would
Give me one more day
On my Island Home.

Source: Music and words by Connie Mason, *Calico Creek Waltz: More Music of Coastal North Carolina* (River Rise Studios, 1998)

*Crossing Hatteras Inlet*

on Portsmouth with her grandparents, recalled going to Portsmouth with Jessie Lee Babb on her birthday. This small but meaningful birthday gathering turned out to be Jessie Lee's last visit to her beloved home-place.

"We were leaving to go back to the mainland and the boat was waiting for us. Lee turned around and looked and had tears in her eyes, 'I just got to take another look before I leave.'" Frances herself got choked up telling the story. "That was the last time she saw Portsmouth. I can see her standing on Haul Over dock right now, looking back."

Jessie Lee Babb died in an automobile accident on the mainland two days later. Her love for Portsmouth lives on in all who knew her and the old village.

"No one lives there, but I feel like there's a strong presence, something of a closeness to the spirit of the past," Dave Frum was quoted as saying in *Our State* magazine. Frum has long worked as village caretaker for Portsmouth. "You get the sense that important things happened here."

When I was growing up on Ocracoke, I always heard that a few people were still living in Portsmouth Village. My mother would talk about the supplies they used [to] ship to the island from the Community Store where she worked before I was born. As a child I went with my father flounder gigging at night just offshore of the village. We could sometimes see a faint lamp light from the houses where the last remaining residents lived. As a teenager, I finally got to visit the village on a summer day when Raymond Garrish and I decided to launch out on our own in my old wooden 16-foot skiff. We ran aground several times, but finally got there.

By then the remaining three residents were gone. Henry Pigott had died in 1971 and Marian Babb and Elma Dixon left the island the same year. Most of the old houses still had furniture in them.

Soon after that the State of North Carolina purchased the island and deeded it to the federal government to become part of the Cape Lookout National Seashore. I continue to visit this special place with family and friends and teachers who are on Ocracoke for programs through the North Carolina Center for the Advancement of Teaching.

Perhaps my most meaningful moment on Portsmouth happened when my daughter Maddie was about eight years old and we visited the village during Thanksgiving. We explored around the old buildings and paths and eventually landed at the community cemetery near the post office. Standing next to the tombstones of several children, I quickly realized that she was trying to understand death and dying. "Why did they have to die?" she asked. I did my best to explain how difficult living could be in such remote places without easy access to medical care. She was quiet for a while and then said, "Daddy, did Santa Claus visit a place like this?"

Source: Alton Ballance, Connie Mason Oral History
Collection for National Park Service

# 7

# *Crossing North River*

## DOWN EAST

*WELCOME TO DOWN EAST*

The Down East National Scenic Byway spans the communities from North River to the great Pamlico Sound, meandering around the heads of creeks, bays, and salt marshes, following the paths of Native Americans and early colonists. The aroma of fresh salt air as you approach the byway alerts and heightens the senses and, for us, tells us we're home.

Communities here are rooted in relationships formed on the shore and the fishing grounds of Core Sound, seeing people through hard times and good times. We are dependent on one another because being on the water instills that kind of camaraderie. This is what has held Down East together for generations: our understanding of the water and our dependence on it, and on each other. We hope everyone visiting our area will feel that sense of sharing.

Down East is a place where neighbors welcome folks home with a mess of fresh fish. Here we willingly share what we have and the things that are important to us, trusting that the same simple gifts of trust and friendship will be returned.

It is in our character to welcome you here, and we do, in hopes that you will learn to respect our natural resources and appreciate the traditions of our communities that have held us together for generations.

JONATHAN ROBINSON, ATLANTIC

Crossing North River. (Photo by Baxter Miller)

## THE SOUTHERN REGION OF THE OUTER
## BANKS NATIONAL SCENIC BYWAY

*I just inhaled the good salt air at North River Bridge.*
*— Elizabeth Pigott Peeler, Gloucester native*

Down East begins with the pungent smell of salt marsh at the North River Bridge, the geographic and cultural divide between the thirteen Down East communities and the rest of the world. From side to side, the road is a 360-degree expanse of marsh and shoreline cut with tidal creeks and ragged peat banks and dotted with white egrets, ibises, and blue herons, providing the perfect entrance to a world apart. Here, depending on the season, you can find a workboat in the distance, a clammer close to shore, or an oyster-tonger working in a hard, cold nor'easter. A closer look tells even more. The black needle rush and spartina cordgrass bend with the weight of periwinkle snails grazing along the blades. Tiny herds of sand fiddlers leave skitter marks along the sandy shore, and a stray loon may be slightly bobbing and feeding in waters just south of the bridge. In a winter freeze, the marsh is frothed with frost, and ice fringes the shore.

Before it washed away in a storm, a handmade sign on the eastern side of the bridge read, "Welcome to 'the original' Down East." On the eastern bank of North River is the community of Bettie, and some thirty miles farther is the ferry terminal at Cedar Island, where passengers and vehicles embark for Ocracoke. The drive from Bettie to Cedar Island takes about fifty minutes, but visitors need to take the time to meander off the main highway and catch a glimpse of the living maritime heritage of Down East.

The region makes up about half of Carteret County's landmass, yet Down East's 6,000 souls represent a fraction of the county's 68,000 residents. Technically part of the mainland, Down East is a peninsula made of smaller peninsulas. Down East communities were once settlements that emerged on the high ground between marshes. Small bridges spanning creeks still define community boundaries.

Before roads and bridges began linking villages in the 1920s, these communities depended on boats, and everything on land was completely oriented toward the water. The family vehicle was a skiff, and people sailed to Beaufort to take care of business or to find a doctor. They'd sail home on prevailing southwest winds, headed "down sound" or "down east," giving reason to the region's name found on no maps: Down East.

People who live Down East are often called Core Sounders, especially by Hatteras and Ocracoke Islanders, whose families have, for generations, fished and hunted together and married back and forth. The shallow, grassy estuary of Core Sound has sustained inhabitants for generations, as a source of food and livelihood and a shared heritage of maritime living. Many folks still call the sound-facing side of their house the front, echoing back to days of skiffs along their shore connecting them to everything beyond.

"I chose to stay Down East at a lesser economic rate and a higher quality of life," reflected ferry captain Dennis Chadwick of Straits. "I've got some friends that live in Atlanta that made a lot of money, but at the expense of not smelling saltwater or hearing the surf pounding on Cape Lookout at night."

The names Core Sound and Core Banks come from the Coree Indians, who inhabited the region until the arrival of colonial-era settlers in the late 1600s. The Coree had temporary camps on the barrier islands and permanent settlements on Harkers Island and other sites Down East, particularly Cedar Island. Like the Hatterask, Pamplico, Neusiok, and other Iroquoian-

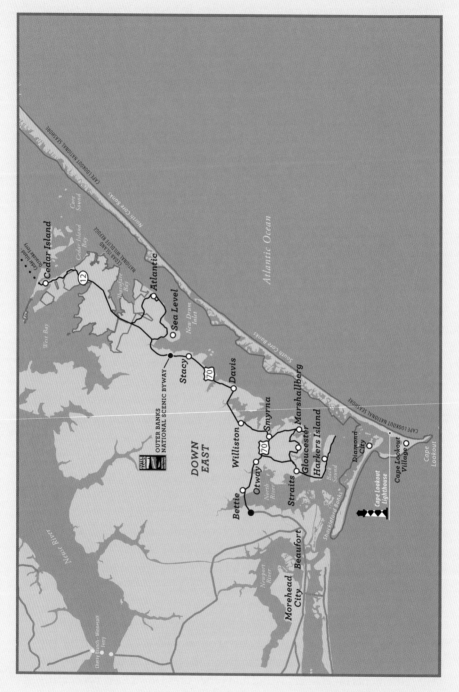

DOWN EAST

or Algonquin-speaking peoples of eastern North Carolina, the Coree were weakened by warfare, disease, and starvation following European contact. The eastern plain tribes of North Carolina made their last stand in the Tuscarora Indian War of 1711–15.

Lyrical place names and artifacts are all that are left to remind us of the earliest inhabitants. The Coree shell mounds, containing oyster shells, animal bones, pottery shards, tools, and arrowheads, are common along the shores of Down East. The first roads of the 1920s and '30s were built from the great Coree shell midden piled at the east end of Harkers Island. As the piles were loaded onto barges, pottery shards, weapons, and even an Indian skeleton were found in the midden. These oyster shell roads caused many tires to go flat before the shells were ground down into hash by traffic.

Carteret County is named for Sir George Carteret, one of several English lord proprietors who oversaw colonial provinces and allocated land grants. The first English settlements on the mainland of Core Sound, as the region was then known, were located in the Straits, Gloucester, and Marshallberg areas. A handful of families established large pine plantations for timber, turpentine, and tar used in shipbuilding. They lived along the Straits, a key waterway for shipping from the port of Beaufort to New Bern.

Today, residents can identify sites that were former saltworks, brickyards, tar kilns, and colonial-era boatworks. Cannonballs, bullets, ballast stones, and grinding or mill stones have been fished out of creeks and mud banks. Remnants of try works — old brick kilns, metal pots, tools, shackles, and harpoons — tell the story of whalers who established camps on Shackleford Banks.

Communities Down East have been periodically uprooted by storms and other hardships. Families have been scattered in times of scarce fish, compelling men to search for distant jobs. Some have gone north to work tugboat and dredge-boat jobs; others have traveled as far south as Cortez on the Gulf Coast of Florida, where families migrated by train in search of mullet.

Communities have also been connected, historically and practically, by mailboat, freight boat, fish buy boat, and family work skiff. They remain bound by family ties, common identity, and a shared resiliency. People from deep-rooted families are linked by a shared past, and all Down East residents are connected through schools, churches, fire departments, and neighborhood events like fish fries, homecomings, and pig pickings.

Down East is a place where the native brogue can be heard at gas pumps and ball fields, where a fisherman and a fisheries scientist live side by side, and where gravestones are as natural in yards as swing sets. Family ties are traced when someone asks, "Who are your people?" Here, "whose" you are determines "who" you are. People "from off" who move Down East are called "dingbatters" by natives, a term that can be used endearingly or not, depending on the context of the story. Whether native or not, folks share a love for a place replete with quiet communities, expansive estuaries, and the smell of marsh and pine.

As the southern link to Ocracoke and the Outer Banks, Down East's well-worn route follows the same path of yesterday's oyster shell roads and Indian trails. Landmarks and tourist attractions are few, but the maritime heritage of this region is evident in every glance. Workboats still grace little creeks, and small harbors are busy with fishermen preparing for the next trip, hoping to bring fresh shrimp, fish, or crabs to the dock. Boatbuilders and decoy carvers advertise their wares with small yard signs or hand-painted shingles. Experiencing Down East is as much about what you do *not* see as what you do. It is, and proudly so, a place and time apart.

### BETTIE

*Ruth, get the collards and mullets ready. . . . I'm coming home!* — Clarence Salter, Bettie

Bettie prides itself in being the "Gateway to the Original Down East." Serving as the southern entrance to the Outer Banks National Scenic Byway, Bettie was once called Woodville and Simpson. "Bettie" was chosen in 1903 upon the establishment of the community's first post office, named after a woman who handled the mail.

Bettie has long been a farming community, although fishing and boatbuilding added to the economy as well. A community school once operated here, and family-owned stores provided locals with provisions. Situated between North River and Wards Creek, Bettie was self-sufficient and even had a restaurant and fishing pier on the causeway of the North River Bridge in the 1950s and '60s.

Many families ran truck farms, growing sweet potatoes, Irish potatoes (often pronounced "ar'sh" or "ice" potatoes by locals), cabbage, onions, and watermelon. Buyers purchased entire fields of produce, loading trucks that hauled vegetables to northern markets. Migrant workers stayed on the larger farms in labor camps during picking season.

Bettie remains a community lined with farmland, rich black dirt growing strawberries in the spring and collards in the fall, as well as sweet potatoes, corn, and soybeans. Today fewer farmers work the fields, but Bettie is still geared toward growing things.

Brightly colored flags draw customers to Simpson's Greenhouse and Berry Patch during the growing season. The farm is run by George and Sandra Simpson. George's father was one of the largest producers Down East. Sandra runs the produce barn, equipped with a kitchen for baking pies, breads, and other treats. Nanny's tomato pies and strawberry pies cannot be beat.

### OTWAY

*When I was a young boy the old folks put shrimp in the garden as a fertilizer.*
— O. C. Lawrence, Otway

Otway is hard to miss, as it comprises one of the busiest crossroads and centers of commerce Down East, with a gym, a county library, a pizza take-out, a pharmacy, gas pumps, auto repair shops, and a Dollar General. Otway has been a crossroads community and center of commerce since the first gristmill was built on Dill's Point eons ago. The community sprawls along the east side of Ward's Creek and is named for famed nineteenth-century privateer Otway Burns, who once plied the waters of the Straits and kept a house in Beaufort and Swansboro.

The people of Otway are always proud to share their connection to North Carolina's famous privateer. His ship, the *Snap Dragon*, was equipped at Elijah Pigott's boatworks on the Straits as a ship of war in the early 1800s. With the *Snap Dragon* and its skillful crew, Burns plundered around $4 million from America's enemies on the open sea, making him a wealthy man and the most successful privateer in American history. Otway Burns died in 1850 and was buried in the Old Burying Grounds in Beaufort, with one of the cannons from the *Snap Dragon* fixed upon his tomb.

The community of Otway has an agricultural heart and a history of participating in truck farming. Sterling Hancock's father was a farmer. He helped his father pile potatoes into a large mound. "Bulrushes," or marsh grass, were cut with their tractor mower and were used to cover the potatoes. Then the whole potato "bank" was covered in dirt for insulation. "You had a door that you'd go in, and get them whenever you wanted to," Sterling Hancock recalled.

A striking figure in Otway's business history is Oliver "Ol" Lewis, an early twentieth-century mover and shaker. Lewis sported a white Stetson hat and a tobacco-stained beard. He ran a general store and filling station, a farm, and a fish house. He was one of the first to truck fish and produce to distant markets, buying sweet potatoes and mullets from locals. "He owned a bank on Front Street in Beaufort; lost it during the Depression," said Sterling Hancock. Lewis also owned the first automobile in Otway, a Model-T. "He didn't know how to drive it. He got in it and he took off and went right through the back of his garage," chuckled Mr. Hancock. "And he was hollering at it, 'Whoa! Whoa!'"

Decatur (pronounced "De-KATE-er") Gillikin is an Otway legend, as stories attest to his superhuman strength. Born in 1821, he was known throughout eastern North Carolina as the "Samson of Carteret County." People say he was a giant of a man at six feet, six inches tall and 260 pounds. Decatur demonstrated his strength in numerous wrestling matches against sailors docked in the area. A favorite story of Down East's own "Fish House Liar," Sonny Williamson, has Decatur sailing to Beaufort to trade. One day the sheriff confiscated his skiff for nonpayment of taxes. It took six men to get the skiff out of the water and padlock it to the courthouse steps. After discovering what happened, Decatur snapped the padlock, dragged the skiff through town to the water, and sailed home to Otway. From that day on, Sonny Williamson claimed, Decatur Gillikin would make it a practice to drag his skiff through the streets of Beaufort, piling groceries and supplies into it like a shopping cart before sailing home.

### STRAITS

*The first piece of equipment I ever drove was an Allis-Chalmers tractor.*
— *Dennis Chadwick, Straits*

Straits is named for the body of water it borders between Harkers Island and the Gloucester–Straits communities. It was once the primary waterway from Beaufort Inlet to Pamlico Sound before the intracoastal waterway was dug in the 1930s. Sailing ships, menhaden vessels, mailboats, freight boats, and fishing boats plied the waters of the Straits regularly. Today, small trawlers and channel net skiffs are frequently seen fishing there. Visitors can find a popular public access point for recreational fishing and kayaking in the community of Straits on the north side of the Harkers Island bridge.

Straits is a residential community made up of quiet, tucked-away neighborhoods, but travelers can experience the heartbeat of the community by stopping at the brightly painted Chadwick Brothers Bait and Tackle store at 1604 Harkers Island Road. The store is owned and operated by Lillie Chad-

Down East provides an excellent place to explore and experience untouched beauty, quietly and peacefully. (Photo by Lillie Miller)

wick Miller, whose ancestors helped settle the community in the early 1700s. Miller's grandfather Ira Chadwick started the store in 1941 with his brother. The Chadwicks wisely built the store to coincide with the construction of the bridge to Harkers Island. For generations they have served motorists, visitors, and locals alike. Today the store owners follow the tradition of providing a front porch swing and chairs and invite visitors and locals to stop and chat with the family.

Settled around 1700, Straits is one of the oldest communities in the region. Samuel Chadwick was a Yankee whaler who sailed to the Core Sound area from Falmouth, Massachusetts, and bought 130 acres in 1725 along Whitehurst Creek. As a shore-based whaler (as opposed to the Nantucket whalers, who lived shipboard for years at a time), Chadwick spent the spring months camped out at Cape Lookout hunting right whales with several other crews. After the whaling season, he'd return to his home in Straits, where he and his wife, Mary, attended the Straits church.

The Straits church began with a colonial-era Anglican congregation in 1750 but became Methodist after the American Revolution. According to a church history titled "Lest We Forget," 1778 marked the official establishment of the Straits Methodist Church congregation. In 1809, the Straits Tabernacle Church, as it was then known, constructed a new building with local pine and plaster made from "burnt oyster shells." Church lore recalls a Reverend Starr who prayed that if a ship were to wreck, "send her to these shores" and let "her cargo be food," as his flock was near starving during the War of 1812. Within a week, the story goes, a ship "laden with flour was cast on the beach on Core Banks."

In 1860, the Straits church was the only Methodist church established Down East. "People came in boatloads from Harkers Island and Shackleford Banks" to worship together. A Shackleford Banks congregation under the Straits church charge met in a schoolhouse on the banks, and it was the "responsibility of the Banks people to come to Straits on Saturday afternoon and get the preacher when it was his appointed time to preach at the Banks." Near the turn of the century, Straits preachers began to hold camp meetings in the summer on Shackleford Banks that would last several days. The present-day church, Straits United Methodist, was built in 1891, and the picturesque place of worship can be found at 311 Straits Road, Gloucester.

### GLOUCESTER

*We walked from Gloucester to Marshallberg to the show on Saturday night.*
— *Eloise Nelson Pigott, Gloucester*

Gloucester, tucked between the communities of Straits and Marshallberg, is truly "off the path" and almost hidden, although at one time it served as the central hub when the ferry to Harkers Island docked there. Once known as Up Straits, Gloucester was renamed by Josephus Pigott when the post office was established in 1910. "Captain Joe" ran the schooners *Charmer I* and *Charmer II* to the West Indies and New England from his homeport on the Straits. He suggested the name Gloucester after his favorite port in Massachusetts. Pigott also ran a general store, later run by his children Bill and Florence Pigott.

At Railway Landing, Lloyd Pigott operates Straits Railway, a traditional boat repair business founded by his grandfather and namesake. Pigott has two rails and a mechanized wench used to pull trawlers and other boats out of the water for bottom repair and painting. Straits Railway is the last of its kind Down East and makes for an interesting visit for those seeking to understand more about this region's close connection to the water.

Gloucester was an important business and transportation link, serving as the gateway to Harkers Island via a private ferry before the opening of the Harkers Island bridge in 1941. A favorite story from the ferry days tells of Oliver Chadwick, who ran the ferry between Gloucester and Harkers Island. The original ferry was small, about twenty feet wide and forty feet long. "It ran so regularly that when our clock stopped, we set it by the ferry," recalled Erma Hansen. She also remembered the day when a circus was ferried from Gloucester to Harkers Island. The circus arrived at the dock in trucks too large or heavy to be ferried all together. "It took forever to get the elephants out, one at a time," she remembered. "Each elephant tested every board on the dock before crossing it."

The Gloucester Community Center, a humble building in the shade of tall pines, can be found at the corner of Pigott and Ferry Dock Roads. The club is the site of two events that infuse the sleepy community with hundreds of people each year. The oldest event, the Gloucester Community Club Chicken Barbecue, began in a potato-grading shed that was on-site in 1955. The chicken barbecue is now held twice each summer, and proceeds go toward the Woodrow and Mary Dudley Price Memorial Scholarship for a graduating high school senior. Woodrow Price, former managing editor of the *Raleigh News and Observer*, lived in Gloucester with his wife, Mary Dudley, and was an avid outdoorsman. Mary Dudley Price, a journalist in her own right, volunteered with North Carolina State's seafood laboratory and contributed to Joyce Taylor's cookbook *Mariner's Menu*.

The chicken barbecue is quite the cultural event, as a crew of "chicken flippers" meet at the barbeque pit and light massive amounts of charcoal, placing some 260 chicken halves on racks and "dobbing" them with secret sauce. When the crew chief decides it's time, two men cross their arms, grab each end of the rack, and flip the chickens, walking down the pit until each rack is turned. The women of the Gloucester Community Center spend the afternoon making slaw and baked beans and plating a dazzling array of pies, cakes, and cookies. When the crowds show up to eat, the members form a serving line, chatting and joking with friends and neighbors far and wide, almost all of them repeat customers season after season.

The Gloucester Mardi Gras is another annual event at the Community Club. It was started in 1992 by Gloucester boatbuilder and musician Bryan Blake as a way to bring a little color to a gray February day. Modeled after the rural Mardi Gras celebrations of southwest Louisiana, this is a true community effort. The ingredients for the gumbos and twenty-one turkeys (to be deep-fried, Cajun style) are donated. A children's king and queen march is a highlight of the day. There is also a "Fool's Procession" that takes to the streets of Gloucester complete with musicians, people in costumes, and

Children dance while the Lost Girls Band plays at Gloucester Mardi Gras, 2016. (Photo by J. J. Burgess)

makeshift "krewes." Gloucester Mardi Gras is held at the community center on the Saturday of President's Day weekend or the Saturday before Fat Tuesday, whichever comes first.

The official Gloucester Mardi Gras live recording tells the tale:

> Once upon a February, deep amid the shivering pines and frosted marshes of Down East, a single speck of glitter fell from the sky and landed on a picnic table in Gloucester, North Carolina. All the people gathered around, wondering what to make of it. As folks ruminated, a boatbuilder broke out a fiddle and started a crazy little tune. An accordion sang out, and a fisherman on the fringe found himself shuffling his white rubber boots. Wishing her neighbors full bellies, a young mother showed up with butter and a sack of flour. So a welder from Marshallberg fetched his black iron pan and started making a roux. Around and around and around he stirred, and twenty years later he looked up to find the Gloucester Mardi Gras going full bore. What is this mysterious Cajun spell brought by a single sparkle in the dead of winter? Each February people far and wide gather at the Gloucester Community Club under sheets of rain, salty winds—even drifts of rare coastal snow—a motley krewe dancing on the end of winter's long tail. Gumbos bubbling, turkeys

*Crossing North River*

frying, little kings and queens spinning in an orbit of beads. . . .
Here's to twenty years of a little place and time touched by a way-
ward speck of something shiny.

## HARKERS ISLAND

*A bright spot of earth, the place of my birth . . . twisted oaks and my kinfolks.*
— Sonny Davis, Harkers Island

Crossing the Straits on the Earl C. Davis Bridge, travelers can look across
the water and see Beaufort to the west and wild Browns Island to the east.
The bridge leads to Harkers Island and is named for Benjamin Franklin's
first cousin Ebenezer Harker. Ebenezer moved into the area from Boston in
1730 and purchased what was then known as Craney Island.

Harkers Island is about five miles long and runs west to east. The island's
main road is called Island Road or "the front road" by locals. It traces the
south-facing shoreline looking across Back Sound to Shackleford Banks
and Cape Lookout and meanders past stands of twisted live oak trees with
canopies shaped by southwest winds. Drawings of the wind-shaped oaks are
found on the cover of the Harkers Island United Methodist Women's cookbook *Island Born and Bred* and on Joel Hancock's history of the Harkers
Island Mormon faith, *Strengthened by the Storm*. Hancock writes that the live
oaks not only endure salty tempests better than other trees but are "made
greener and fuller by the storm itself."

Indeed, the story of Harkers Island is a compelling one of remaking
a life and community in the wake of catastrophe, of mass exodus and pioneering a new land. Long-established island families of the Willis, Guthrie,
Lewis, Yeomans, Rose, and Hancock clans are directly descended from
nineteenth-century Ca'e Bankers (pronounced "Ca'e" Bankers, short for
"Cape Bankers"). Ca'e Bankers lived, hunted whales, and fished off Core
and Shackleford Banks until storms of 1896 and 1899 ravaged their home-
steads and drove them to higher, safer ground. Some went to Marshallberg;
others, to the Promise Land of Morehead City or Salter Path on Bogue
Banks. But many floated what was left of their houses and belongings across
Back Sound to nearby Harkers Island, where they bought land for a dollar
an acre.

Joel Hancock, a third-generation descendant, wrote, "Houses were torn
down board by board, loaded on skiffs, transported across the water, and
then hastily rebuilt." Other houses were "left intact, laid upon dories, and
floated across."

Ca'e Bankers flourished in their new surroundings on Harkers Island, living in kin-based neighborhoods and continuing with their trade of fishing and boatbuilding. The population of the island quadrupled between 1899 and 1903, but the thick groves of cedars, oaks, pines, maples, and yaupon bushes remained intact, with settlers staying close to the south shore in sight of their homeland and close to their fishing grounds.

Their collective identity as Ca'e Bankers was only made stronger after they were compelled to leave the banks. Although natives of Shackleford have long since passed away, many Harkers Islanders had grandparents, if not parents, who were born in Diamond City, the largest community on Shackleford Banks. The story of the bankers' exodus is told with great reverence by islanders, underscoring a deep and abiding attachment to place. "Some [islanders] feel a 'hankering' now and then to go back to the Banks, not as tourists go to the beach to frolic, but to stay for days — even weeks — at a time, living off nature's abundance, relishing the isolation, the primitiveness; stirring memories remaining only in the blood," wrote Josiah Bailey. He added that islanders return to Shackleford in order to "tend the totems over their sacred ground, and in so doing, to renew their spirit."

An ongoing Harkers Island tradition is riding to Shell Point sometime during the day, usually early morning or late afternoon, to watch the "Light (of Cape Lookout) come around." This pilgrimage seems to quietly reaffirm the connection of Ca'e Bankers to Shackleford Banks and Cape Lookout. No one knows who started this tradition, but it is a daily ritual not to be broken. Newborn babies are sometimes carried to Shell Point before they're taken to their own home. Others at life's end make that final ride on their way to the family cemetery. The Shell Point ritual is a reflection of islanders' deep connection to their Ca'e Banks roots.

Harkers Islanders are renowned for their tightness as a community. Sarah Page, who taught first grade on Harkers Island, learned this lesson on her first day. "Not only did I have thirty-one little students sitting there patiently waiting for me, but most of the mothers came to school with their children that day," she recalled. "I have since learned that that was sort of a custom [for] the first graders. . . . [Mothers] had their chairs lined-up around the classroom."

Harkers Island is best known for its strong, family-based tradition of wooden boatbuilding. Devine Guthrie built lapstrake whaling dories on Shackleford Banks and continued his craft on Harkers Island, building skiffs in his backyard. His son Stacy learned beside him, as did other island builders of the mid-twentieth century, including Brady Lewis, who perfected the famed "flare bow" design and the Rose Brothers with their workboats and party boats.

Harkers Island boatbuilders have a distinctive ability to create functional works of beauty for both commercial and recreational purposes without written plans. Like the musician who plays by ear as opposed to written music, these builders work by the "rack of the eye," creating vessels that are perfectly trim, true, and seaworthy. A "Harkers Island boat is one of the best boats that's ever been built in this country," according to builder Calvin Rose, brother to James and Earl of Rose Brothers boatbuilding fame. "I guess it's the type of material, the design of the boat that we put in it, and then we put ourselves in that boat. When that boat is finished, what's in *us* is in that boat, and I think that's what makes our boats one of the best boats built."

"After everyone had left Diamond City and Shackleford Banks around 1900, the fishing crews had to be reestablished," recalled islander David Yeomans. "Some of the crews went over to Cape Lookout and built shanties, one for sleeping and cooking, and one for storing the fish." Like the boatbuilding trade, commercial fishing not only took root on Harkers Island; it flourished. Once an ice plant was built in Beaufort in the 1920s, island fishermen began selling bluefish and mackerel to a Beaufort fish house, and soon the village had its own fish houses. The first fish house on Harkers Island was established in 1929 by H. B. Hunter, who dealt primarily in clams and mullet. By the late 1950s, over a dozen fish and scallop houses operated on the island.

The last fish house on the island closed in 2009. This is a striking fact, considering that a great number of islanders have been employed in the seafood industry at one time or another. Post–World War II job opportunities at nearby Marine Corps Air Station Cherry Point, however, compelled many full-time fishermen to seek the security and regular paycheck of a government job, fishing part-time when the mullet were running or the shrimp were thick.

A young man recalled his start in channel netting, a unique way of shrimping invented by Harkers Island fishermen. Boats are anchored on specific "sets," areas of prime shrimping near channels and sloughs. "That was my main job, staying on the boat to hold the set when I was ten years old. [The captain] gave me half a share." A Marshallberg fisherman recalled holding a set one day as a boy, only to be knocked overboard by the oar of a

Jamie, Burgess, and Houston Lewis, Harkers Island boatbuilders.
(Photo courtesy of the Lewis Family)

### BOATBUILDING, THE ISLAND WAY

The Lewis family personifies that mix of art and work that is the Harkers Island boatbuilding tradition.

"As far as plans, we ain't ever done that," said James Lewis, Jamie's son, who explained the family business as his father worked on a hunting skiff in the shadow of a 41-foot Goliath, also put together without drafts. "I grew up in it. Daddy grew up in it. It's just something we know how to do" (Jonathan Cox, *News & Observer*, July 17, 2007).

Burgess Lewis (1913–97) learned his life skills of fishing and boatbuilding along the shores of Harkers Island. Working with Brady Lewis and the other foundation-builders of Harkers Island design, Burgess Lewis developed a style all his own that is still talked about around the harbors and marinas of Carteret County and beyond. His graceful balance of length to width can be seen even at a distance.

His legacy does not end there but continues to live in the work and lives of his sons, Jamie, Houston, Paulie, and Stevie, all masterful in their own right as boatbuilders, model makers, and boatyard workers. This legacy continues today and will carry forth in the next generation.

Lewis Brothers Boatworks is where brothers Houston and Jamie Lewis have established their own reputation for finely crafted boats since 1954. Today, that operation continues with Jamie, his son James, and his son Dereck and serves as a daily working reminder of an island tradition and a family business that has contributed to the cultural integrity and economic stability of this community for almost sixty years. Their reputation for quality is grounded in their inherited sense of design and style, and their generations-old knowledge of how a boat handles in the water and holds itself in the wind and tide is unmatched even on Harkers Island. "This has just been a way to make a living," is what Jamie Lewis will tell you, but his boats say much more.

2016 North Carolina Heritage Award recipients James, Houston, and Jamie Lewis. "I am especially excited and proud for Daddy to receive this award as a culmination of a lifetime of hard work and true craftsmanship," said Jamie's son. "[He] taught me almost everything I know about boatbuilding." Jamie simply flashed a shy smile and said, "I don't know how come they picked us." (Photo by Rodrigo Dorfmann, from the NC Heritage Awards Program)

In a very honest and quiet way, their unspoken commitment to this tradition is evident in every boat, and that commitment has supported this business for three, almost four, generations. For them, there is no boasting of numbers sold or who bought them broadcast in slick ads found in high-cost magazines; for Lewis Brothers Boatworks, the tradition it stands for and the well-earned reputation the Lewis family has established will provide. That's all they have ever needed.

competing crew. Today, fewer crews mean less competition, but fishermen still work sets named long ago by their predecessors, such as the Gold Mine, Locust Tree, Turkle Rock, and Rip.

"The tide went out and the twentieth century rushed in," said Irvin Guthrie about the '33 Storm that punched an inlet between Cape Lookout and Shackleford. From that day forward, Harkers Island became a popular jumping-off point for sportfishermen seeking easy access to the ocean.

Harkers Island was home to several well-known charter boat captains who could put anglers on schools of blues, mackerel, trout, and drum. Fishermen's Inn, Grayson's, Cape Lookout Motel & Restaurant, Calico Jack's, and Mrs. Harker's Lodge were family-owned businesses that emerged to provide a clean room and a hot breakfast for fishermen who came to fish at Cape Lookout. Some of those weekenders have returned as full- and part-time residents in their retirement, fishing the waters at Cape Lookout every chance they get.

The most famous charter captain was Stacy W. Davis, who commissioned Brady Lewis to build the *Leona*. Captain Stacy trained his sons to follow in his footsteps, including Sonny Davis, who hired the Rose Brothers to build the party boat *Captain Stacy*. Jimmy "Woo Woo" Harker worked out of his grandmother's legendary Harker's Lodge on Shell Point before he became captain of the *Carolina Princess* in Morehead City. "Any day you make it back to the dock," Woo Woo Harker was fond of saying, "is a good day on the water."

No discussion of Harkers Island would be complete without mention of the central role music, both sacred and secular, has played in the lives of islanders. "We didn't have a thing to do on a Saturday night but walk up and down the road and sing," an islander told folklorist Amy Davis. "We didn't have cars, so we just walked back and forth to church . . . [to] school, we just

Early visitors to Harkers Island stayed with the legendary Mrs. Gladys Harker at her lodge on Shell Point, 1948. (Photo courtesy of the State Archives of North Carolina)

sang on the way." They sang church hymns, "old love songs," and popular songs heard on the radio. "And we would just sing whatever part anybody could do until we would make trios."

Harkers Island musicians have enjoyed regional and national exposure. These include the Coastal Playboys of the 1950s and 1960s, who had their own radio show on WBMA in Beaufort. The Huckleberry Mudflap of the 1960s made well-known recordings, including the hit song "Blue Surf." Country star Kathy Mattea's hit "Eighteen Wheels and a Dozen Roses" was written by Harkers Islanders Gene Nelson and Paul Nelson, who now make their home in Nashville. Music was part of everything that happened on Harkers Island, from school plays to church choirs and family gatherings.

"I guess the Lord has just blessed us," said a Harkers Islander, reflecting on why the community harbored such musical talent in singing and instrument playing. Singing, according to a local woman, was a family pastime

Folklorist Jean Ritchie interviews Harkers Island fiddler Ivey Scott, summer 1951. (Photo by George Pickow)

### IVEY SCOTT AND THE BOOZE YACHT

Ivey Scott, legendary fiddle player from the mid-1900s, made famous the ballad "The Booze Yacht," a true story from the days of prohibition and rum-runners. A yacht named the *Adventure* was riding low in the water just off-shore of Cape Lookout. The crew of the *Adventure* saw the Coast Guard coming their way and tried to flee but instead ran aground on a shoal. To lighten the load, the crew of the *Adventure* started throwing burlap sacks full of liquor overboard. After hundreds of bags were discarded, the boat rose up and they made their escape. The next day crews were fishing off Shackleford Banks and caught floating bottles in their nets. They agreed to keep the news to themselves and planned to return the next day to look for more; but one of them drank too much, and by morning the story was all over the island.

Ivey Scott's ballad is set to the tune of "The Sidewalks of New York." The "Beehive" is a nickname for the East'ard, a now-defunct store on the island where fishermen gathered daily, and "King Lock stoppers" was the brand name of a type of bottle cork. "G's," of course, is money.

> Down around the Beehive, Harkers Island retreat
> Every night and morning, the fishermen would meet
> One day there came a rounder, a rushing by the door
> Said "Boys let's go to Cape Lookout,
> there's a booze yacht run ashore."
> That's when lots of rounders, for miles and miles around
> Kept their gas boats busy, cruising through Core Sound
> Some of them were happy, and some of them were sore
> But King Lock stoppers stood ace high
> when the booze yacht run ashore.

> (Chorus)

> This way, that way, to the Cape they run
> The coming of the *Adventure*, put fishing on the bum
> Some folks lost religion, and back-slid by the score
> King Lock stoppers stood ace high when the booze yacht run ashore.

> Things have changed since those times, some are up in their G's
> While others they are down and out, but most feel just like me
> Some would part with all they got, and some a little bit more
> To see another time like that, when the booze yacht run ashore.

> Source: *Island Born and Bred: A Collection of Harkers Island Food, Fun, Fact, and Fiction* (Harkers Island United Methodist Women, 1987)

largely cultivated in one of the island's eight churches. She noted, "Even the children, if you were out on the boat, sitting in the car, or whatever, loved to sing." She recalled that her sister, on her deathbed, joined her family in song, "singing her part" of the harmony of a favorite hymn. Oral histories gathered from Beaufort residents tell of "that crowd from Harkers Island a singin' on their way home in their sail skiffs."

At the "end of the road" on the eastern point of Harkers Island lies the product of a vision that was a long time coming. The Core Sound Waterfowl Museum and Heritage Center had humble beginnings as the dream of a small group of decoy carvers. Under the leadership of a dedicated board

James Allen Rose surrounded by his work and his memories on Harkers Island.
(Photo by Charles Zug, *NC Folklore Journal*, North Carolina Folklore Society)

### JAMES ALLEN ROSE'S FIRST GUITAR

One of the island's most beloved musicians, storytellers, and craftsmen was James Allen Rose, who passed away in 2013. Rose, recipient of the North Carolina Heritage Award, kept a modest workshop on the east end of the island, where he made some 3,000 model boats in his lifetime. He enjoyed visitors stopping by to admire his work. "He always made time for me, even when I arrived unannounced," said folklorist Amy Davis. "We'd sit on his porch and play music together." Rose, who enjoyed touring as guitarist for the Coastal Playboys, told Connie Mason about receiving his first guitar on the mailboat.

> Mom used to get a little catalog from Lancaster Seed Company. On the back of it, they had a picture of a beginner's guitar. And the offer was, if I would sell four dollars worth of seeds, and send that four dollars, I could receive that very fine, beginner's guitar.
>
> I rode a rusty old bicycle all over Harkers Island until I had sold

four dollars worth of seed at five cents a pack. Now the post office was down along the shore then, and out on the dock was the *Pet* mailboat. After school I wouldn't ride the bus, so I could go down along the shore way, just to check and see if my guitar was there yet. "Mr. Floyd, is there a package in there for me?" And finally, he said, "Yeah, here's something, right here."

I half ran home, laid it on the table, me and mom opened the box. She said, "Here's your guitar." I went to work, putting the strings on it and everything, but I didn't know what to do with the thing. I took it over to Uncle and he tuned it. He said, "I'll draw you a diagram of where to put your fingers on the chords. " He said, "Now, you practice. Put your fingers on those dots." I took it home, and I tried it. I started humming along with it. After a little while, Mom said, "Maybe you should take that outside!"

Source: James Allen Rose interview, Connie Mason
Oral History Collection for National Park Service

and staff, the dream grew into today's 20,000-square-foot, state-of-the-art facility. Located on land managed by the National Park Service and operating in partnership with the Cape Lookout National Seashore Visitor Center and ferry service, the Core Sound Waterfowl Museum and Heritage Center is a repository of Down East's cultural treasures, memories, living traditions, oral histories, and educational programs. More than a museum, the center serves all of eastern Carteret County as a meeting place and a sacred place, as weddings, funerals, and down home gospel singing take place there. The Willow Pond hiking trail provides a contemplative journey through maritime forest, waterfowl habitat, and wild coastline.

Exhibits at the Core Sound museum range from decoy carving and hunt clubs to boatbuilding and fishing. Traveling exhibitions, environmental education learning centers, a library, an oral history repository, and a demonstration area for carvers, boatbuilders, and quilters find a home at the museum. The entire second floor of the museum is dedicated to community-designed exhibits from Cedar Island to Bettie. Events throughout the year attract locals and visitors alike and almost always involve Down East cooking of traditional coastal dishes such as stewed shrimp, scallop fritters, duck with rutabagas, and light rolls. Waterfowl Weekend, held in conjunction with the

Setting decoys on a trot line, Core Sound. (Photo from the Doily Earl Fulcher Jr. Collection, Core Sound Waterfowl Museum and Heritage Center)

Core Sound Decoy Carvers Guild's Decoy Festival on the first weekend of December, is the largest event of all, with thousands of visitors meeting world-renowned carvers, artists, authors, and musicians.

Today, Harkers Island is the most developed community Down East, with a growing population of retirees and part-time homeowners. In recent years, many see progress as a double-edged sword, but it was welcomed in the early 1900s. Earl C. Davis, namesake of the Harkers Island bridge, was an educated, self-made man whose interests extended far beyond the island. The bridge, phone lines, an electric cooperative, a movie theater, and a community water system were all the results of his hard work and political astuteness. Foretelling a real estate boom and rise in property values, Earl Davis had the foresight to subdivide his family property into affordable lots for islanders, allowing fishermen, boatbuilders, and young families to "pay as they could," providing a way for what would be the last generation to own property on the island. Today, many sons and daughters of the island's original families remain on Harkers Island thanks to "Mr. Earl."

*Crossing North River*

# CAPE LOOKOUT NATIONAL SEASHORE

WASHINGTON (AP)—*President Johnson signed a bill at a White House ceremony today and the seventh national seashore park came into existence—the 58-mile Cape Lookout, N.C., National Seashore. Johnson, who described the new park as a "wild and beautiful shoreline," said there has been important progress in conservation but the real challenge lies ahead. —*High Point Enterprise, *March 10, 1966*

And quite a challenge it has been. Some fifty years later, Cape Lookout National Seashore remains Carteret County's most valuable natural and cultural resource, home to Cape Lookout Lighthouse, the Shackleford horses, Portsmouth Village, and fifty-five miles of ever-changing, never-to-be-developed barrier islands.

"The chancel rail of Carteret" is how Shackleford native and writer Gretchen Guthrie Guthrie described this ribbon of sand that inspires all who have ever experienced this pristine treasure. A look from space reaffirms her description, with the image of an old church altar, the perfect metaphor for this narrow, sacred, spiritual protector. As visitors sometimes learn and the locals already know, these sandbanks have had a tight hold, measured in generations for those whose "crowd came from off the Banks."

Thanks to their national park status, Core and Shackleford Banks have been allowed to continue serving as a natural barrier island system, absorbing the energy of the ocean and protecting the mainland from the daily pounding of surf. They are Down East's much-needed buffer from the sea. Although the system still functions as it always has, the constant give-and-take of sand and sea moves the islands ever closer to the mainland.

On the park's ocean side, the dunes and grasses seem endless. It is the literal edge, calling fishermen in the fall and seashell collectors in the spring to gather from the waves. On the sound side, the creeks and marshes provide the perfect resting place for migrating ducks and geese, giving hunters a chance to carry on the rich waterfowling traditions of Core Sound. In summer, the islands are a family's paradise where shallow, calmer waters are well suited for clamming and swimming.

Far beyond what is visible along this unspoiled landscape are the stories of the people who once lived here, the bankers who lived and died on what is now a national treasure. These accounts are more than stories or a history lesson; these men and women and their experiences shaped an enduring culture, the salty backbone of a tribe who remain tied forever to this marshy, weathered land, a subtle testament to the fact that though Down East may change, its soul remains the same.

## History

The Cape Lookout National Seashore Park was initially designated a state park in 1959. On March 10, 1966, President Lyndon B. Johnson, with the support of coastal leaders and state legislators, signed a bill establishing the 30,000-acre, fifty-six-mile-long park spanning from Ocracoke Inlet to Beaufort Inlet.

Authorizing a national park was the easy part. Acquiring the land claimed by nonlocal hunt clubs, developers, and locals with ancestral ties to Diamond City and other settlements proved more difficult. By 1976, the park was officially established and included the previously disputed "Cape Lookout Village" area between the lighthouse and the Coast Guard station. This section contained several private houses, built by fishermen, servicemen, and sportsmen. Those who could prove that they owned property in the Cape Lookout Village area on January 1, 1966, were granted twenty-five-year leases. Lease agreements were also negotiated with camp owners northward along Core Banks.

Similar struggles took place north of the lighthouse with prominent upstate hunt club owners and developers along Core Banks, resulting in lawsuits that dragged on for almost a decade. Condemnation proceedings to overcome squatter's rights, Supreme Court rulings, disputed land values, and special legislation were all part of obtaining Core Banks in its entirety.

Acquiring the Portsmouth Island acreage on the north end of Core Banks proved to be less controversial than obtaining the Cape Lookout and Shackleford areas. A historic leasing program for the homes and structures and an immediate commitment from the National Park Service to preserve them was implemented. All of those leases have been completed, and the entire village is now under National Park Service care.

Land acquisition of Shackleford Banks came to an emotional end in 1985. Of some sixty camps, only a handful of claimants had clear deeds, and only two would ultimately obtain a twenty-five-year lease on their property. In his book *Hope for a Good Season*, Carmine Prioli noted, "Most . . . faced the prospect of eviction from land that had been an important part of their lives for many years." In the summer of 1985 the federal government sent notice that all unauthorized structures, livestock, animals, and personal property had to be removed from Shackleford Banks by midnight on December 31 of that year. Whether out of spite, resignation, or both, all cabins were burned, including the two that had secured leases. The Cape Lookout National Seashore Visitor Center on Harkers Island, then a small facility, burned to the ground as well. The story is well known among Down Easters.

The violence and bitterness surrounding Cape Lookout National Seashore's formation was part of the massive change and cultural upheaval taking place during this period. All of the banks communities were increasingly pulled into modern life with the development of bridges, roads, and a ferry system, all of which brought in new people who threatened the only way of life banker communities had ever known. While a few visionaries applauded the coming of the "progress" the park service promised, most islanders felt helpless in stopping the loss of family lands necessary for the formation of the national seashore. A generation later, their sense of loss has yet to fully heal.

Today, a somewhat peaceful coexistence has emerged between locals and park managers, although disagreements continue to flare up, and many question the priorities reflected in the National Park Service's decision making. However, work continues in building bridges of understanding between the community and the park service, and most agree that, in the long run, the establishment of the park has protected the banks held sacred by many.

### Shackleford Banks

*There is something akin to reverence in their voices as they talk of Diamond City ... when Diamond City was something more than just a name.*
*— David Stick, Outer Banks historian*

Named for John Shackleford, who purchased the land in 1713, Shackleford Banks is the southernmost portion of the Cape Lookout National Seashore. Uninhabited for more than 100 years, the pristine, nine-mile-long barrier island has a rich cultural history. The temporary "whaler's huts" mentioned in eighteenth-century surveys grew into permanent settlements by the mid-nineteenth century. Before devastating storms struck at the turn of the twentieth century, Shackleford Banks had a much larger population than Harkers Island.

Diamond City, named after the black-and-white diamonds painted on the lighthouse, was the largest of the historical settlements of Shackleford, located on the eastern end near Cape Lookout. Moving west, smaller settlements included Bell's Island, Sam Windsor's Lump, and Wades Shore. Geographer Roger Payne explained that a "lump" is a local term used along the southern Outer Banks and refers to a "small island, hummock, or a high portion of ground or even a shoal." An oral history excerpt captures a fading manner of banks speech: "I was born on a lump which was betwixt Shackleford and Cape Lookout Banks."

Sam Windsor's Lump was "where the only black family on Shackleford Banks lived and where the dipping station was," according to an ancestor of Shackleford villagers. A dipping station, or vat, was where livestock was submersed in a toxic mixture to remove disease-bearing ticks; this was required as part of the government's effort to eradicate cattle ticks.

Orlandah Phillips, born in 1900, had a grandfather born on Shackleford. "In those days Shackleford was known as Ca'e Banks and people lived in hamlets along its entire length. . . . They lived at the head of these creeks, each of which had six to eight feet of water, deep enough for [sail] boats to enter and leave."

Early homesites were of the "story and a jump" style of architecture common throughout coastal North Carolina near the turn of the century. Houses were typically built of salvaged materials and were moveable if the need arose. A. A. Willis, writing in *The Mailboat* journal, described Shackleford houses as perfectly adapted to the environment: house timbers were fastened with wooden pegs, and porpoise or shark hide served as door hinges. Families used cisterns or shallow wells for water and kerosene lanterns for light. Early settlers made whale oil lanterns out of conch shells or wooden skiff bailers. Mattresses were filled with seaweed, and the passing days were marked with a calendar made of corks strung on a rope.

THE WHALE FISHERY  Diamond City is best known as a whaling village, although Ca'e Bankers fished a variety of species throughout the year. Whales were hunted off Shackleford and Cape Lookout since the mid-1700s. The south-facing beach of Shackleford enabled fishermen to intercept right whales close to shore as they migrated north each spring. Unlike New England whaling operations that took to the sea in large vessels, the North Carolina crews launched small, double-ended rowboats from the beach.

According to an 1887 government fisheries report, men formed six-man crews and established lookouts and "camps among the sandhills." Orlandah Phillips, whose family lived on Shackleford, offered a detailed description of the whale hunt.

"When a whale was sighted, the six men in each crew would jump into their boats and the whale belonged to whichever crew got to it first." The crew rowed boats that were "twenty-one feet in length, five feet wide, and built of three-quarter-inch juniper." Each boat was "lap streak design because it was less likely to leak [and] had ribs made out of cedar roots, stripped." While four men rowed, "a man would stand in the head with the shackle iron and lance, and the captain steered from the stern."

When the six men approached the leviathan, the lance man would wait for the right moment, then pierce the whale with a harpoon or "shackle iron." "They'd aim for the lungs and cut the lights, causing the whale to bleed to death," Phillips explained. "They knew the whale was dying when it began to spout blood." By the late 1800s, crews were using a whaling gun, which fired "bomb lances," explosive projectiles designed with "rubber feathers" to guide the missile. Historians Marcus and Sallie Simpson explained that "these bombs exploded deep within the whale's body, thus ending the hunt quickly and often at a safer distance."

Towing the whale back to the beach for butchering was no easy task; several crews worked together, getting the whale as close to the beach as possible. To make sure the whale did not drift away at high tide, the men secured the carcass with ropes and anchors. At camp, almost everyone in the community joined the process of cutting and rendering down the whale, hauling fifty-gallon kettles, bricks for the cook fires, firewood, knives, and scrapers to the site.

The men climbed the dead whale and began butchering it with cutting spades, peeling off the blubber and cutting it into brick-sized chunks for the try pot. A villager named Billy Hancock had the job of cutting the "whale-bone," or baleen, out of the whale's mouth. "He wore a suit of oilskins, fitted tight so there was hardly a piece of him that wasn't covered," David Stick wrote. Then he'd "take his axe and go into the whale's mouth," disappearing from view, only to emerge with a "piece of mouth bone with him."

Sammy Willis, who lived on Shackleford as a boy, said the people "weren't concerned about taking a bath, but it'd be weeks a getting that thing cut up." Whale oil and baleen (used to make corsets, collar stays, and buggy whips) were "sold at auction to the highest bidder," according to Simpson and Simpson in their *Whaling on the North Carolina Coast*. Each crewman received a share of the profits, and the owner of each try pot was given five gallons of oil. In the 1880s, about four whales per season were killed and processed.

The height of the shore-based whale fishery on Shackleford ran from the end of the Civil War until the turn of the century. Fishermen continued to set up camps and lookouts after Diamond City was abandoned. The Simpsons note that the "last shore crew for whaling at Cape Lookout was disbanded when a fire destroyed most of its gear in 1917."

Shackleford fishermen liked to name things. They named sandhills, grassy shoals, and favorite fishing sloughs. They named their kin-based fishing crews like sports teams. Josephus Willis, for example, was captain of the Red Oar crew, named for their brightly painted oars.

Shackleford whalers also had the unusual tradition of naming whales that were especially notable. The names they gave contain hints about who threw the harpoon, where it was killed, or under what conditions. There were the Big Sunday and the Cold Sunday whales, the John Rose and Tom Martin whales, the Little Children and—that dry humor shining through—the Haint Bin Named Yit whales. The Little Children whale was so named because "the boats that chased and killed it were manned mostly by young boys, as the older members of the whaling crews were preoccupied elsewhere."

The most famous and destructive whale was named the Mayflower, a reference to its massive size, and was conquered by the Red Oar crew and an African American crewman. When the Shackleford whalers took to their lapstreak pilot boats, the whale turned on them. "She stove one boat, knocked her to pieces!" said Allen Moore, whose grandfather was a whaler. The Red Oar crew, alarmed at the ferocity of the whale, went into hot pursuit. Sam Windsor, a black fisherman who lived on Shackleford's Sam Windsor's Lump, held the exalted position of harpooner. He stood ready at the bow, waiting for the whale to surface.

"That whale, she's a danger to us," said Captain Josephus. "Sam, you're about 225 pounds of nothing but muscle. We've got to kill that whale!" The crew "saw the darkening coming out on the water." Sam Windsor threw the lance and made a direct hit, piercing its lungs. He "saw how big it was" and said, "Trouble. Trouble right here." The whale dived and then "come up a fighting. She headed to the bar. She tore everything up.... Ran about a mile straight in shore spouting blood."

"My grandmother," recalled a Shackleford descendant, "said that the whale bellowed like a calf. The bellow was so loud she felt the vibrations of it clear over at the lighthouse." The Mayflower yielded 700 pounds of baleen and forty barrels of oil. Its complete skeleton hangs today in the North Carolina Museum of Natural Sciences.

Ca'e Banks women knitted socks, hats, sweaters, and gloves from wool collected on branches from wandering herds of sheep. They sewed clothes for the family and made sunbonnets. After a breakfast of light rolls and molasses, according to A. A. Willis, the "men would have to sit on the beach and look out for whales and fish." The midday meal was called dinner and was the biggest meal of the day. "Everybody had a good appetite [and] when it come to dinner time they wanted a big dinner — fish and collards and ducks or whatever."

Children addressed adults as "Aunt" or "Uncle" out of respect, regardless of actual kin ties, and a woman was often identified by her first name plus her husband's first name, such as "Mary Wes, Annie Randolph, Emma Seward, Het Bob." Children were sometimes identified by their mother's or father's name plus their name.

Storytelling was a popular pastime on Shackleford Banks. According to Ca'e Banks legend, a boy named Sal's Mart had a mother named Porpoise Sal, who washed ashore from a shipwreck. As recounted in *The Heritage of Carteret County*, Diamond City villagers saw the mysterious woman talking to porpoises, which "seemed to understand what she had to say." At the time, a porpoise factory operated at Cape Lookout, and Porpoise Sal "told the people of the Banks community that God had sent her to tell them to stop killing the porpoises." She lived at Diamond City for a few months before vanishing, while her son continued to live at the banks.

Ca'e Bankers were very much connected to the mainland. Whalers sold barrels of oil and other whale products to traders in Morehead City. Fishermen depended on buy boats from Morehead City and Beaufort to purchase their catch and, in the nineteenth century, traded salted fish for corn, which was ground at a mill in Straits. Banks stores were stocked by freight boats from the mainland, and islanders sometimes traveled to Beaufort or Morehead to go shopping.

### Diamond City

Diamond City, also called Lookout Woods, was located at the mouth of the Ditch or Drain, the low cut between Shackleford and Cape Lookout. Although the '33 Storm opened it into a full-blown inlet, banks dwellers in the nineteenth century merely had to wade across it during high tide. The land on which Diamond City sat is completely eroded away today.

"At Diamond City there was three stores and them three stores didn't sell anything but powder and shot, coffee and sugar and flour," recalled Alan

Moore. "There was no pickles over in the stores, [and] no music of any kind, unless it was John Linden with an old tin pan and Tommy Noe with a fiddle."

School was held during summer months in a small building that doubled as a church. David Stick found that Diamond City villagers were open to a variety of church services and revivals over the years, including Baptist, Methodist, Mormon, and Pentecostal. Church met about once a month, as preachers came from the mainland and rotated among area churches.

SAN CIRIACO HURRICANE OF 1899  Nothing is permanent on a barrier island, including Ca'e Banks settlements that grew throughout the nineteenth century yet were completely abandoned by 1904. A series of hurricanes racked the banks in the late 1800s, but the San Ciriaco storm of 1899 — packing 140-mile-per-hour winds — was the worst. Having wreaked havoc in Puerto Rico and surrounding islands, the storm crossed the southern Outer Banks on August 17 and left a broad swath of devastation.

"The wind blew from the Northeast at first and brought in tides from that," said a Ca'e Banker, describing a familiar pattern. "Then . . . the wind shifted to the Southwest and again blew as hard or harder than before." The shift in wind and tide proved devastating to Shackleford Banks. "The waters came together—the waters from the ocean and the waters from the sound met." Houses were flooded and washed off their foundations. Gardens were destroyed and trees were uprooted. Wells became contaminated with saltwater. Fishing gear was obliterated and creeks filled with sand. Cows, pigs, horses, and chickens drowned.

"The aftermath was a truly ghastly scene," Jay Barnes emphasized in *North Carolina's Hurricane History*, "as battered caskets and bones lay scattered, unearthed by the hurricane's menacing storm surge."

Harkers Islander Joel Hancock noted that Mormon missionaries arrived at Diamond City and Harkers Island "just after the first storm and right before the second one." The second storm was a hurricane that hit the coast on Halloween the same year. Not as severe as the San Ciriaco, it was devastating all the same, given the lack of protective trees and dunes. During this "cracking time" of dislocation and change, when many destitute bankers sought a new life, the Mormon missionaries were welcomed, and numerous people embraced the new denomination.

The great storms of 1899 marked the beginning of the end for Shackleford communities. Families packed their worldly belongings, including houses if still standing, and floated all that was left across the sound to Harkers Island or Marshallberg or west to Salter Path or what would become known as the Promise Land neighborhood of Morehead City. By 1901, according to Joel Hancock, Diamond City "was a ghost town," and Harkers Island grew from a handful of people to almost 200 families in the space of two years.

## Cape Lookout

*When I was born, Mama brought me home to*
*Cape Lookout, and this has been my home ever since.*
*—David Yeomans, Cape Lookout and Harkers Island*

Cape Lookout is the fishhook-shaped tip of Core Banks. The name likely came from the use of the cape as a mariner's lookout. Early settlers built camps on the beach, and "older men would watch for whales from high sand dunes," according to geographer Robert Payne. The cape's sandhills, long eroded away, ranged from twenty-five to sixty feet in height and included a great one near the whaling community of Diamond City.

The bight of the cape's hook has served as one of the best harbors on the Atlantic Coast, sheltering colonial-era sailing vessels to modern vessels today. The barb of the hook is called Wreck Point, underscoring the cape's reputation as both a harbor of refuge and a spit pointing to dangerous nearby shoals.

Unlike Portsmouth and Diamond City, the settlement at Cape Lookout in the nineteenth century was more of a seasonal fishing camp and lifesaving station than a year-round village. The Cape Lookout Lighthouse and keeper's quarters were first built in 1812, and a lifesaving station was operating by 1888. An 1861 survey found "a few inhabitants" near the lighthouse, and an 1890 Lifesaving Service map includes "shanties" that were probably seasonal fish camps. According to park historian Tommy Jones, a visiting journalist counted around eighty residents at Cape Lookout in the early 1900s, "enough to warrant establishment of a one-room school house." Jones suggests that the increase was due to a small migration of mainlanders, mainly from Down East Carteret County, to take advantage of a booming commercial mullet fishery.

By the 1920s, the people of Cape Lookout and Shackleford had moved their homes and families to higher ground. According to records from that time, Cape Lookout was described as "one of the lonesomest places in the country," but the people there did not think so. Their hearts—and their work—remained on the banks, even after they were forced to leave by the lack of fresh water and storm tides. Fishing camps left behind at the Cape and along Shackleford allowed people living on Harkers Island to fish, hunt, and tend livestock along Core Banks and Shackleford for decades, retaining strong ties to the banks. Commercial fishermen continued to ply the waters around the banks for their living. After the Storm of '33 broke open the inlet at Cape Lookout, Barden's Inlet gave the growing number of motorized workboats easy access to the ocean for fishermen in the region.

The jetty at the hook of Cape Lookout is very popular among recreational fishermen. The history of the jetty goes back to 1915, when the Army Corps of Engineers began preparations for a coaling station and harbor of refuge at Cape Lookout, launching the jetty and shoreline stabilization project. A resident recalled the building of a breakwater at the cape, which involved the train delivery of fifty cars of stone per day for three years. The great granite stones, transported from an upstate quarry, were shipped across the water from Morehead City and loaded onto a rail track that was laid across the sands of the cape to the point.

GUARDING THE COAST  Cape Lookout has been instrumental in guarding the coast, including what may have been, according to David Stick, the only fort built in North Carolina during the American Revolution. The precise location of Fort Hancock, built from trees from the cape woods, remains a mystery, but it was northwest of the present lighthouse. Active for two years (1779–80), the fort was an effective safeguard against British raids but apparently never engaged in battle.

The 163-foot Cape Lookout Lighthouse, strikingly visible with its black-and-white diamond design, was built in 1859, replacing a smaller, wooden-shingled lighthouse that had operated since 1812. Visitors climbing the 203 steps to the top balcony can marvel at the thought of the lighthouse keepers who made the same climb carrying two five-gallon buckets of whale oil or kerosene. Officers fulfilled this and other tasks on a daily basis, including one of the few female keepers, Charlotte Ann Mason, who served Cape Lookout Light from 1872 to 1875. Upon reaching the top of the tower, the keeper filled the lamp with oil and lit the wick, located inside the Fresnel lens. The lens, which required regular polishing, was made of glass plates and looked like a giant pinecone. It was large enough for the keeper to stand inside to attend the lamp.

Orlandah Phillips shared a family story of two young girls (one of whom was his grandmother) who lived at the light with their father, the keeper. "On stormy nights it wasn't uncommon for birds to break their necks and wings against the lighthouse," he said. The girls would "gather up the dead birds from along the platform that encircled the top of the lighthouse." They would then "put the birds on forks, and roast them over the burning wick."

Lighthouse keepers and assistant keepers typically lived on-site with their families in keeper's quarters near the tower. Family members often assisted in the day-to-day operations and kept gardens and livestock. In-residence keepers were no longer needed when the light became automated in 1950.

Three lifesaving stations were built along Core Banks: at Portsmouth, Core Banks, and Cape Lookout, each five miles apart. The Cape Lookout Lifesaving Station was established in December 1887, one of the last to be commissioned along the North Carolina coast in response to frequent shipwrecks along the treacherous coastline. The active season for the lifesaving station crew was fall through spring. The station keeper stayed year-round, however, and had a nearby house for his family. Park historian Tommy Jones noted that the crew was made up of Carteret County men, making it easy for them to spend off-duty months closer to home.

The heroic rescue of the three-masted schooner *Sarah D. J. Rawson* in February 1905 earned Keeper William Gaskill and his crew a gold medal of honor. The vessel, loaded with lumber, ran aground on the outer point of Cape Lookout shoals in gale-force winds, and one man was swept overboard. The Cape Lookout lifesaving crew, all sick with influenza, spied the distressed ship nine miles from the station. According to the official report, they sailed and rowed toward the vessel but found it in a "seething mass of breakers" and wreckage, compelling them to anchor nearby until morning. At 11:00 A.M., they managed to get a line to the six-man crew and hauled them, one by one, to the safety of the rescue boat.

The lifesaving crew provided emergency support to the residents and fishermen of Cape Lookout, particularly after Shackleford Banks was abandoned at the turn of the century. Crewmen assisted fishermen in distress, provided medical transport to Beaufort or Harkers Island, and provided telephone communication to Beaufort. Tommy Jones reported that the crew even prepared the dead and built coffins when needed. Their official duties included clearing lumber and other debris after storms and reporting washed-ashore items to the Treasury Department's Wreck Commission.

When the Lifesaving Service was joined with the Revenue-Cutter Service to form the U.S. Coast Guard in 1915, a new station was built at Cape Lookout. During World War II, the Navy occupied the station after having it moved to a new location at the cape, thanks to the help of house-mover Denard Davis and his mule. The U.S. Coast Guard operated at the cape until the station was decommissioned in 1982.

CAPE LOOKOUT AT MIDCENTURY World War II brought a renewed military presence to Cape Lookout and Core Banks as U.S. Coast Guard stations (former lifesaving stations) and Army bases protected the mainland. With those bases came much-needed work for local people (both military and civilian) and new surnames for the communities as servicemen from all over the country married local girls.

After the war, the U.S. Coast Guard station at Cape Lookout remained the favored assignment for all those Down East draftees who joined the Coast Guard in hopes of coming home to serve at Cape Lookout, Fort Macon, Ocracoke, or Hatteras. USCG Station Cape Lookout remained active until 1982, when it was combined with USCG Station Fort Macon, leaving behind decades of proud memories of Cape Lookout. Today the National Park Service plans to restore the station as a house museum dedicated to that rich military history.

By the late 1940s, life changed all along North Carolina's coast, including Down East Carteret County. Postwar prosperity allowed locals to expand family fishing camps to summer family cabins so that another generation of Ca'e Bankers could retain their connection to their ancestors' home-place. By the 1960s, wooden frame cabins were clumped together by families and friends, in the long tradition of "squatter's rights," and small yards were fenced to keep the free-roaming livestock at a distance. Summers meant "going to the Banks" every possible minute for the local people to spend their evenings and weekends clamming, cooking together, and riding up and down the beach in old rusty trucks. It really was "the best of times" for those descendants who had been forced off by storms just a generation before to be able to return often (sometimes daily) to their homeland.

At the cape, summer camps were made from recycled military structures and fishing camps from Lookout Woods. Here a growing number of families from the mainland gathered often to retain their connections to this place. A dance hall was built from a converted home, and musicians came by boat to provide entertainment for summer residents. A favorite destination over the years was Sally and Les Moore's store, affectionately known to this day as Sallie and Les', which provided snacks, bait, and a fishing report for all who came. They were the last to leave in 1978, a sad day for the couple and everyone who loved them and the history they lived in that little store.

Today the camps on Shackleford are gone, but twenty structures remain on Cape Lookout as the Cape Lookout Village Historic District. Cape Lookout Lighthouse, the 1907 keeper's quarters, the lifesaving station, Sally and Les's store, and other homes and structures bear witness to the men, women, and children who made a life there.

## MARSHALLBERG

*Katie will be the sixth generation to live on this piece of land.*
— *Harriet Hill, Marshallberg*

Marshallberg, located on the peninsula where Core Sound and the Straits meet, has a long and rich history of commercial fishing, boatbuilding, farming, education, and church life. Families have lived there for generations. Many of the two-story homes with wraparound porches were built by Curt Davis, known as a "fine house carpenter," high praise from a community of boatbuilders. One of Davis's descendants recalled that "he'd walk to neighboring communities to work, even to the ferry at Gloucester to get to Harkers Island. He'd be gone a week at the time."

Marshallberg was known as Deep Hole Point in pre–Civil War days, named for an immense hole dredged in Sleepy Creek. The heavy, wet earth was loaded on scows and transported to the east end of Bogue Banks, where it was used to build the ramparts of Fort Macon, which was being built from 1828 to 1834. Deep Hole Point became Marshallberg upon the establishment of the post office, in honor of the area's longtime mailboat captain Matt Marshall.

As the twentieth century unfolded, Marshallberg grew. The busy, thriving community had two tomato canning companies, fish houses, a crab processing facility, several stores, the Lyric movie theater, a school that went through the sixth grade, and even an academy of higher learning. The community produced countless schoolteachers, as well as five doctors.

Dr. Laurie Moore was from Marshallberg. He was well loved and took care of his patients whether they could pay or not. The epitaph on his grave in the Victoria Cemetery says, "Our Generous and Kind Beloved Physician." Joel Hancock recalls seeing Dr. Moore for his college physical. "He was puffing on a cigarette and said, 'Don't ever start these things.' He'd say, 'If you got money pay Edna, if not just go on.'"

Mildon Willis and Sons Boatworks, established in 1910, operated on the

Beaufort, N.C., April 29, [1902] yesterday was a typical spring day and one made auspicious by the speech of North Carolina's Educational Governor on the last day of the commencement exercises of Graham Academy, Marshallberg, N.C. Some 2,000 people from Morehead City, Beaufort, and the interior of Carteret County east of Beaufort, assembled on the spacious grounds surrounding the academy building. The refinement, beauty, and intelligence of the section were well represented. Governor Aycock's speech, delivered from the piazza of the dormitory building, electrified them. It came straight and hot from a heart warm in the cause of education, from a mind trained to the great need of proper citizenship.

The trip down the sound from Beaufort was made on the naphtha-fueled launch "Kitty Waters." Quite a contingent from Morehead City and Beaufort accompanied the Governor and party aboard the launch and in sharpies.

Marshallberg is a small town ten miles east of Beaufort, on Core Sound, noted for a homogenous people, an excellent preparatory school, large crab and oyster industries, and last, but not least, the fact that the vicinity is absolutely free from malaria. The school was organized in the fall of 1887, by the Rev. W. Q. A. Graham of the Methodist Episcopal Church (North). During its thirteen years' existence aided by the church, its power and influence has been far-reaching. During the present regime the school has prospered beyond the expectancy of its fondest friends. The enrollment the past school term was 120 pupils, coming from five States—North Carolina, Virginia, New Jersey, New York, and Ohio.

Relating to the industries there I am advised that some two thousand people are employed in these and that during the season the shipment of crabs will average fifteen hundred dozen daily. Marshallberg is favored with a daily mail and passenger service by naphtha-fueled boat and numerous are the sharpies that touch her dock.

Our Methodist, Baptist, and Episcopal folk down this way are thoroughly in earnest in this matter of education and if certain other sections don't get a move on 'em the county of Carteret will lead them in the educational procession that is moving on.

Source: C. J. Rivenbark, "Speeches on Education that Stir
Men's Souls," *Raleigh News & Observer*, April 29, 1902

banks of Marshallberg harbor, building and repairing boats ranging from small skiffs to large oceangoing vessels. The world-famous *Albatross* charter boat fleet of Hatteras Island was built by Mildon Willis—just one example of how far-flung coastal communities were linked despite the lack of roads.

Jarrett Bay Boatworks is known far and wide as a top manufacturer of recreational fishing vessels. Established in Williston, Jarrett Bay Boatworks moved to Marshallberg on Mildon Willis's former boathouse site. Owner Randy Ramsey named two Marshallberg builders as major influences. Myron "Ace" Harris was a pioneer of charter boat fishing, and he and his son Buddy built a charter boat each winter in Marshallberg. Randy Ramsey said, "Captain Ace's boats performed well in the ocean, were efficient, and set the bar for charter boats along the Carolina coast for many years." Boatbuilder Ray Davis was a Marshallberg icon, known for launching works of beauty on the banks of Sleepy Creek. "Throughout our years in Marshallberg, Ray would visit almost daily, riding his bike and taking time to offer a helping hand or kind word," Ramsey remembered. "He was a fine man with a sharing nature that helped me learn what I know today about the boatbuilding business." The Davis family tradition is carried on by Ray's grandson Gary Davis, who is part of the Jarrett Bay team on Core Creek.

Claude Brown was known as the "last pioneer" of Marshallberg. He kept livestock on Brown's Island, procured much of his own food, and fished his nets right up until the day he died in 1998. He named his boat the *Miss Belle* after his wife. He was one of the first, along with Myron Harris, to run party boats out of Marshallberg harbor. He was an ace baseball player who also had a reputation as a horseman, leading the seasonal "pony penning" on Core Banks. He tamed wild horses by riding them into deep water.

"Uncle Claude could make it if you put him in a sandspur patch," reflected his nephew Julian Brown. "Old heads" like his Uncle Claude represented a fading ethos. They valued hard work, knew everybody's name in the neighborhood, and paid their debts. Most of all, they valued independence and made a living peddling vegetables, seafood, and meat they butchered themselves. Julian Brown related the time he told his grandfather he had gotten a job teaching school in Engelhard. "I've signed a contract," he told the old man. His grandfather didn't reply. After a bit, the younger man said, "Granddaddy, you don't act like you're too happy with my decision."

"Well son," his grandfather responded, "You must not think much of your life when you start selling it off by the hour."

*Preacher, I know there's a God. When you got a boat in the water and you've got to*
*make a decision, you know there's someone helping you.* — Kenny Lewis, Smyrna

"Where there is a crossroads, there is the beginning of civilization," began a 1927 *Beaufort News* article about Smyrna. "Smyrna is a gathering point. Here have gathered the things which mean most in the well-ordered life of any community." The article was written in a prosperous time, as Down East roads had recently been paved, Smyrna School had been expanded to accommodate consolidation, and a country doctor had set up home and shop across the road from the school. Truck farms were growing, with their Irish potato crop in the spring and sweet potatoes in the fall, selling to northern buyers who bought produce by the truckload. Fish and produce could now be transported with ease, thanks to newly graveled roads and wooden bridges.

Smyrna was an epicenter of boatbuilding until the early 1900s. Smyrna builders were known for turning out large wooden sharpies, used as freight boats or to harvest oysters. A sawmill and marine railway operated in the community. Smyrna resident Van Sellers remembers working at the railways as a young man. "Lige Piner would come by and poke me with his cane — he'd say, 'You better get going, I have other boats I've got to pull up here!'" Dances were held at Piner's railway on weekends.

Dr. Joshua Judson "Shake It" Davis, who had been the only permanent physician on Hatteras Island at the turn of the century, moved to Carteret County in 1910 on a sailing schooner to find better educational opportunities for his twelve children. "He sailed here on his Hatteras-built schooner *Maggie E. Davis*," said his grandson John Davis. "I have a model of it that I built." After practicing medicine for more than a decade in Beaufort, he moved to Smyrna in 1922, opening his practice as well as a pharmacy where he made his own medicines. "He was always dressed in a suit with a white shirt and a bow tie," Davis recalled. "He always wore a hat." Down East people nicknamed him "Dr. Shake It," mimicking the instructions he gave with each bottle of medicine: "Shake it before you take it."

Just south of Smyrna is a collection of houses with a community name not found on maps: Tusk. More of a neighborhood than a community, Tusk is a "clump of houses and a cemetery" that remains a quiet hammock of working families and retirees, surrounded by marshes, creeks, woods, and fields bordering Core Sound.

Today Smyrna remains an important community crossroads with schools, churches, and businesses. For travelers, this intersection is an important link to the main corridor of Highway 70 from the side roads of the byway. Roads from Marshallberg and Gloucester connect back to Highway 70: west leads back to Beaufort, while east threads through more Down East communities and intersects with Highway 12 to the Cedar Island–Ocracoke ferry terminal.

### WILLISTON

*I was born and raised here, and the longest I've been away was two weeks.*
— Thelma Willis, Williston

Just north of Smyrna across Wade Creek is Williston, named after early settler John Williston, the namesake of the Willis clan so prevalent Down East. Before the post office was established and the present name chosen, Williston was called Springfield.

Like Smyrna, Williston was a major boatbuilding center in the early days, turning out graceful sharpie sailboats and broad menhaden steamers. Vessels included the *Regulator* (1882), the *Manteo* (1890), and the *Sickle* (1910). Elmo Wade, famous for his menhaden vessels, was master builder for Willis Brothers Boatworks on the banks of Jarrett Bay. He also built models of his vessels, one of which is included in the Smithsonian's maritime collection.

Julian Guthrie took over where Elmo Wade left off, serving as master builder at Hi-Tide Boatworks at the same site next to Elmer Willis's clam house. The Harkers Island native built workboats, yachts, head boats, charter boats, and sharpie sail skiffs from the 1950s to the 1970s. Recognized for his craftsmanship, he was awarded the prestigious North Carolina Heritage Award in 1993.

Willis Brothers Seafood, also known as the clam house, was owned and operated by Elmer "Clam King" Willis of Williston. "He was the sole producer of every clam that Heinz Soup Company used," Elmer's daughter Nancy Lewis said about her father. Today the concrete-block clam house is falling down in disrepair on a thin piece of land between Highway 70 and Jarrett Bay. It's hard to believe that the site was once a bustling hub of commerce from the 1930s to the 1970s, with tractor trailers tearing up the road with countless loads of clams and scallops. Willis bought shellfish from local fishermen. As demand grew, he also had clams and scallops trucked in from out of state for processing.

"The big clams were used for chowder, and the little ones were shipped to Cleveland, Ohio," explained Nancy Lewis. "Did you know Cleveland,

Ohio, was the clambake capital of the world?" Her father had an uncanny business sense, expanding his sales and expediting the process with inventions, such as a scallop-shucking machine, for which he obtained patents.

Margaret Daniels, who grew up in Williston, recalled shucking scallops for the Clam King. "You'd go in six o'clock every morning, and you would clean and package and shuck scallops until two o'clock the next morning," she said. The shucking machine had rollers that would "roll the gut off of them." She worked with women who would "take their BC Powder in their Co-cola and off they go again!"

Elmer Willis held massive clambake fundraisers to help with community projects such as purchasing high school band uniforms or an elementary school lunchroom expansion. The scale of these events was captured by a *News and Observer* journalist in 1954, who counted 32,500 clams, 580 pounds of chicken, 1,000 carrots, 8 bushels of sweet potatoes, 400 pounds of Irish potatoes, and 200 pounds of onions. "All items," the article stated, "were distributed and tied in individual cheesecloth bags to make a total of 700 servings." Willis was politically astute, attracting politicians of all sorts to his annual clambake, including at least three governors who made the trip all the way from Raleigh to the clam house in Williston. The Clam King, after all, had called.

"We were raised by a community," reflected Margaret Daniels, one of a pack of youngsters who roamed the shoreline of Williston. She recalled a preacher's wife whom "no one liked" and a prank the kids pulled on her one Halloween. "She had this little bitty car," she chuckled. "That night, we got a block and tackle and the boys climbed up the pine tree and we blocked and tackled that thing up that pine tree about twenty feet in the air." On the school bus the next day, they got a clear look at the dangling vehicle. After school they were met by parents and neighbors. "Half of Williston was waiting for us and made us get that car out of that tree." She added, "It was harder to come down than it was to go up."

### DAVIS

*Tell me of a place more perfect and I'll say it isn't true. — Ira Leon Willis, Davis*

Midway between Bettie and Cedar Island is Davis, the geographical center of Down East. It is also known as Davis Shore, a name harking back to the days of boat travel, and people who live in Davis call themselves Davis Shoremen, no matter what their age or gender. They also say they live *on* Davis Shore, not *in* Davis Shore, another maritime holdover.

"We are pure Core Sounders," said Elizabeth Salter Ritchey. "We love it and we thank God every day for giving us the opportunity to live where we live."

Davis has three churches, all of them Baptist: the First Baptist Church, the Davis First Baptist Church, and the Free Will Baptist Church. Lifelong resident Milton Styron, whose twin brother was a preacher, was once asked why all three churches in the community were Baptist.

"The reasons are deep," he said. "We don't have enough time to do that topic justice."

Davis residents cheerfully explain that their community is divided into the "up the road" section and the "down the road" section, one populated by Democrats and the other by Republicans. "In my church," a local recalled, "the Republicans literally sat on the right of the aisle and the Democrats on the left—which was considerably less populated!"

Davis crossroads, where Highway 70 turns sharply north toward the Cedar Island ferry terminal, has its own tradition. The corner gets "decorated" under the cover of darkness each Halloween in a tradition that has long served as a rite of passage for Davis teenagers. The morning after Halloween, residents wake to find the corner bedecked with a "haunted" outhouse and other assorted junk, including rusted cars, old crab pots, closed-to-fishing signs, and other "found" items.

On the other corner is Davis Shore Provisions, built in 1942 as Johnny Davis's Store. Davis Shore Provisions carries Down East–themed gifts, local artisan works, home-baked goods, crab pot Christmas trees, and decoys from local carvers. The restoration of this important icon from Davis's community history was a welcome effort for the community, helping residents and visitors alike to appreciate the history it represents.

Davis is a jumping-off point to Cape Lookout National Seashore's Great Island Camp on south Core Banks. Davis Shore Ferry and Cape Lookout Cabins and Camps transport passengers and four-wheel-drive vehicles across Core Sound to the seashore. The camp is made up of twenty primitive cabins managed by the National Park Service (reservations can be made at www.recreation.gov). The cabins are equipped with generators and propane tanks for basic amenities such as hot water, refrigeration, gas stoves, and flush toilets. Camping on Core Banks is an unforgettable experience of watching beautiful sunrises, endless beach wandering, first-class surf fishing, clamming, and birding.

Davis Shore has been welcoming visitors to Core Sound since the early 1900s. This community was once the center of waterfowling traditions along

## DAVIS SHORE CHRISTMAS

Davis Shore's annual Christmas celebration has revived the tradition of holiday gatherings, sing-alongs, prayer, and the lighting of the community corner Christmas tree. Davis residents have a flair for pageantry, and their Christmas celebration is no exception. Crab pot Christmas trees are hung from every light pole, lighting up the main road in spectacular fashion. Garlands of holly hang on every house, and churches open their doors, revealing a banquet of sweets and hot cider. Even Santa and Mrs. Santa show up in an old-timey, holly-bedecked wagon pulled by a mule.

After a church service, participants take part in a recessional to the community corner for the lighting of the tree. Davis Shoreman Ed Pond explained that this is a long-standing tradition for the community. "Villagers have walked on dark Christmastime roads for more than a hundred years. Some rode in Christmas Wreath festooned wagons." The event serves as both a memorial for those who have passed, and a homecoming for the youth of Davis. Taylor Munden, Ed Pond wrote, a "son of Davis Shore," spoke up during the Christmas recessional. "As a small boy he remembered the smell of juniper and napping in the forepeak of his granddaddy's boat as they shrimped at night on Core Sound."

Core Sound, with more hunting and fishing guides than any other community in the 1930s and 1940s. During that time, Davis Shore hosted the likes of Babe Ruth and Franklin D. Roosevelt, who came to hunt along Core Banks. Frances Murphy, Albert Murphy, and Ammie Willis were well-known guides for sportsmen at the Core Banks Rod and Gun Club. Ammie Paul and Henry Murphy were first-rate decoy carvers as well.

James Styron Fish Company in Davis recently closed its doors. James Styron started the wholesale business in Beaufort and eventually moved it to his home community in Davis. For many years, he operated a bait operation, running two vessels that fished for menhaden in Core Sound. Menhaden is an oily, boney fish used to make fish meal and oil (a rendering plant once operated on Oyster Creek in Davis) or for bait by crabbers and sportfishermen. Davis Shore menhaden crews were known affectionately as the Mosquito Fleet by the larger crews working out of Beaufort.

"Milton Styron was a true fisheries warrior," wrote Pam Morris, in reference to the patriarch of Davis Shore. "Mr. Milton" was a born-and-bred

Early morning sunrise, Core Banks. (Photo by Lillie Miller)

Core Sounder fisherman until his death in 2015. Featured in the documentary *Core.Sounders: Living from the Sea*, by the North Carolina Language and Life Project, Milton Styron did every kind of fishing. He crabbed, fished, shrimped, and even worked as a crewman on the menhaden mosquito fleet. He was a fierce advocate for the industry and attended countless fisheries meetings. At a heated public meeting in Atlantic, Milton Styron famously waved the "jawbone of an ass" to make his point with a biblical reference.

Milton Styron is remembered for his encyclopedic knowledge about fisheries ecology and behavior and his impressive memory of every storm, drought, freeze, and flood that impacted the coast since the '33 Storm. He was also a great storyteller, often holding court in his favorite chair next to his wife, Ruby. His tale about getting attacked by a rabid fox and "putting him out of business" with a brick has become legendary. He mostly liked to talk about fishing.

"Buddy, my twin brother, and I were just six or seven years old, and Granddaddy took us fishing one day—we had the best time!" Milton spoke with a heavy accent and punctuated his stories with heavy pauses. "So the next day, we sat in the swing and cried because they had left us." The moral of the story: he was never left ashore again and spent his whole life on the deck of a fishing boat. "A loaded boat looks the best to me."

Just after daylight the next morning, someone noticed a skiff loaded with people, and it was Mama's brother Carlie, his wife, his little girl, and his neighbor, wife, and their little girl. This neighbor of Carlie's was a very smart woman. She had dry clothes for her family and a big pan of "Davis Shore" lightrolls, all packed in a 50-pound lard can.

The tide had left its mark at the third stair step at our house, and everything was in a big mess. The cow had lived through the storm somehow, and so had the hogs. The fall garden was gone, and there were plenty of drowned chickens.

Sometime during that day, [a group of men] asked Papa to go with them to the Banks' "Old Hunt Club" in search of Paul's parents. . . . Papa's boat, the "Hilton," was the only boat left on the shore. Papa said he didn't see much need of going, but he went.

Papa had carried a small skiff in the hull of the "Hilton," and [they] poled up to the Club House. The folks were all living, but they had had a bad night, and most of the Club House had been destroyed. Late that evening they started back for Davis, and found a lot of concerned people on the shore to welcome them back home.

Source: Mabel Murphy Piner, *Once Upon a Time: Stories of Davis, North Carolina* (Carteret County Historical Society, 2002)

Davis's history includes the compelling story of Davis Ridge, a neighboring community made up of African American families who thrived from the 1860s until 1933. Slave owner Nathan Davis deeded the "Ridge" property to Sutton Davis and other former slaves after the Civil War, whereupon they established themselves as avid fishermen, boatbuilders, and farmers.

Sutton Davis built a fish factory where menhaden "scrap" was dried and marketed as fertilizer. He and his crew built two large fishing schooners, the *Shamrock* and the *Mary Reaves*. By all accounts the blacks and whites of Davis Shore worked together on many fronts and shared a great mutual respect.

But the Davis Ridge community was especially devastated by the '33 Storm. The inhabitants, in fact, had to join hands and wade to higher ground. They ended up settling in Beaufort and began a new life there. Some, like

Miss Lue Lewis picking crabmeat at Luther Lewis and Son Seafood, Davis.
(Photo from the Nancy Willis Lewis Collection, Core Sound
Waterfowl Museum and Heritage Center)

Adrian Davis and Herbert Davis, became top captains in the county's menhaden fleet. Captain David Davis died tragically with his crew upon the sinking of the *Parkins* in Beaufort Inlet during a storm in the winter of 1942.

Davis was the site of an Army camp from 1941 to 1945. Although much was top secret during the World War II period, Davis resident Ed Pond surmises that the camp was a radar base. A 150-foot rotating tower that was in operation, he claimed, was used to track German submarines. Davis Shore families, concerned for the soldiers and their tent encampments, which were frequently invaded by clouds of marsh mosquitoes, offered to house, feed, and do the men's laundry. A former soldier at the camp who not only found a warm welcome but met his future wife in Davis, wrote a letter to Ed Pond many years later emphasizing "the people were so hospitable and kind—indeed some of the finest people I've met."

Luther Lewis and Son Seafood is on the east side of Highway 70 at the foot of the Oyster Creek Bridge. Started as a crab-picking plant by Luther Lewis and his son James Paul in 1962, the company expanded into shrimp, fish, clams, and scallops. In recent years, the company limited itself to crabmeat once again. After a storm damaged their facility and facing a flood of imported crabmeat, the family stopped picking in 1998. The imports undercut domestic prices, and hiring people to pick crabs became less economical.

"So I started making crab cakes," Nancy Lewis said. She explained to her husband, James Paul Lewis, that she could never find a decent crab cake in a restaurant, so she aimed to start her own market. On her first day, as she was mixing up a batch of crabmeat, buyers from a major food distributor stopped in to sample her product. "Three head buyers dressed in their suits—they said, 'What are you doing?' And I said, 'Well, I'm mixing up some crab cakes.' They said, 'Well let us try them.' They put them in their line that day."

## STACY

*I didn't see any reason to leave; everything I wanted was right here.*
—*Roy Hilton Willis, Stacy*

Stacy, formerly Mason Town and Piney Point, is located between Oyster Creek to the south and Nelson Bay to the north. Before canals were cut from Beaufort and Morehead City to the Neuse River, vessels rounded Down East and sailed north along Core Sound en route to the trading port of New Bern. Piney Point was an important landmark halfway from Harkers Island to Cedar Island, before mariners turned west up the Neuse River.

Stacy's western edge borders a massive 57,000-acre pocosin swamp drained a century ago for farmland. The project was a failure until it was taken over in the 1930s by "Miss Georgina" Yeatman, who built a landing strip so she could fly herself in and out of the remote site from her home state of Pennsylvania. Today, Open Grounds Farm, dubbed the largest contiguous farm east of the Mississippi, produces industrial quantities of corn and soybeans.

Stacy is the smallest Down East community, with a population of about 200. Hurricane Isabel damaged almost all of the homes in the community in 2003. The long-term effects of the storm can be seen today, with many of the homes having been elevated or abandoned, but most residents of Stacy have adapted and continue to work and live in the footprint of their ancestors.

Stacy was settled in the midst of some of the best waterfowl hunting

*Crossing North River*

## STACY, MY DADDY'S HOMETOWN

Stacy doesn't have a Macy's
Sidewalks or a stoplight
Hope it never will.
But she's got what can't be taught or bought
The finest folks that ever walked or set a sail.

She's got Pittmans, Robinsons, and Dixons
Hamiltons and Fulchers and some Salters too.
With Masons, Styrons, Gaskills, Willises,
And for goodly measure a dingbatter or two
She's got Nelsons and a lot of Lewises
The finest kind of people I hope you get to know
In Stacy, pretty little Stacy, quiet tiny
Stacy, My Daddy's Hometown.

Cross Mariah Creek, then right, onto Horseshoe Street
Eastward to Piney Pint, what a lovely sight!
Great day looking out at Brit's Bay
Smelling all the salt spray—everything's alright!
Back around going north to "downtown"
Past the church and "bloodfield," and then through the swamp;
You find Masontown, my father's family sacred ground
Looking over Core Sound—where it all began.

Down East strung like little shining pearls,
Founded on marsh mud, hummocks and white sand.
Each place pretty as old lace
Fashioned by our Maker's strong all-knowing hands.

He made Atlantic, Sea Level, Cedar Island,
Hunting Quarters, Straits, Core Banks and Symrna, too.
Otway, Bettie, Marshallberg, Gloucester,
Davis Shore, Williston, Harkers Island, too.

And the people, the finest kind of people I hope you get to know,
In Stacy, pretty little Stacy, quiet tiny
Stacy, my daddy's hometown.

Source: Connie Mason, *Calico Creek Waltz: More Music of
Coastal North Carolina* (River Rise Studios, 1998)

Northern pintail, carved by master carver Mitchell Fulcher of Stacy, is the
signature decoy of the Core Sound Waterfowl Museum and Heritage Center.
(Photo from the Core Sound Waterfowl Museum and Heritage Center Collection)

grounds of the region, with its marshes, hummocks, and sheltered sound
waters. The village sits across from Core Sound's north Core Banks, including Portsmouth Island and the historic hunting lodges of the Pilentary Hunt
Club, the Carteret Rod and Gun Club, and Harbor Island Hunt Club, which
thrived in the 1920s and early 1930s. Hundreds of hunters came to the banks
to experience the sound's winter duck hunting season. This provided important income during the winter for hunting guides and decoy carvers, who
fished during the summer. Making a living was season-dependent.

Stacy is known as the decoy carving capital of Down East. Early carvers
chopped out decoys for utilitarian purposes—first to feed their families and,
later, for hunters visiting from northern metropolitan areas. Stacy's carvers
turned out pintails, redheads, coots, buffleheads, and canvasbacks that reflected their innate understanding of waterfowl and their skills in creating
lifelike ducks of wood to attract migratory birds into the waters of Core
Sound.

"They never did use no sandpaper on the decoy body," said Roy Willis,
a Stacy carver. Willis, using his typical economy of words, described how his
father, Eldon Willis, and his father's partner worked together. "He'd take a

Mr. Homer Fulcher, Stacy, was one of the first to teach decoy carving in Carteret County. He received the North Carolina Heritage Award, along with Julian Hamilton Jr., in 1995. (Photo by Kerry W. Willis)

log and just chop it into the shape of a decoy, give it to Mr. Elmer. Mr. Elmer would put it in a wood vice, take a draw-knife and slick it off with that."

Stacy was home to Mitchell Fulcher, Carteret County's most accomplished carver. Born in 1869, Fulcher was known for his attention to artistic detail in his carvings. He'd draw patterns on shoe box lids and carve wood salvaged from boats with a hatchet, handsaw, and pocketknife. His nephew, Edfred Gaskill, recounted a tale that shows the old carver's sense of humor.

"One of his neighbors came walking through his yard, and he had three decoys sitting on the edge of the porch. He had just painted them. The guy talked to him and then went on to the landing and came back and the decoys were gone. He asked Mitchell, 'What happened to your decoys?' He said, 'Well, the cat came up here and drug one of them off and eat it. The other one, Susie came out here and got him and took him in the house and cooked him. The other one there, a flock of ducks come by and he flew off.'"

Homer Fulcher, known as "Mr. Homer," helped bridge the space be-

Roy Willis's life was Core Sound. He never forgot those childhood years of following his Daddy through the marshes, picking up decoys along the shore, and learning the ways of the water and the fowl that followed the seasons along Core Banks during the '50s and '60s. Those experiences shaped his life. Roy's deep love for hunting began then and there on the waters of Core Sound as he watched his father, Eldon, and his friend Elmer Salter carve working decoys that would later pen their names in the history books of Carteret County. Roy began to carve duck heads as a boy for his father, and as a young man he took Mr. Elmer's place beside his dad as they became known as the first carvers in this area to actually sell their decoys for others to use.

As one of Core Sound's most respected carvers, Roy's place in history had only begun beside his father as a carver of working decoys that sold for $2 each. Roy's influence would grow with the creation of the Core Sound Decoy Carvers Guild in 1986; Roy served as one of its first board mem-

Roy Willis surrounded by kids at the Core Sound Museum, where he introduced thousands of visitors and students to Core Sound decoy carving. (Photo from the Core Sound Waterfowl Museum and Heritage Center Collection)

bers and was named "Featured Carver" in 1990. Roy helped build the Core Sound Decoy Festival into one of the most respected waterfowl festivals in the country.

From that foundation he helped establish and build the Core Sound Waterfowl Museum and Heritage Center in 1992. There he gave countless hours of carving demonstrations for more than twenty years. His passion for talking to anyone who loved hunting and decoys flourished there and across the region as he traveled around eastern North Carolina to festivals and museums to share his beloved decoy carving traditions with all who would listen. Roy became more than a keeper of this heritage. He was a respected voice for preserving this way of life and the place he loved best — Core Sound. His vast knowledge and his passion for these stories, along with his enthusiasm for decoys, could hold the interest of a first-grader or a ninety-year-old.

Roy's way of sharing this Core Sound heritage was his very own. He could relay the history lessons of days gone by with the old-timers or share special hunts of recent seasons with the younger generation. Roy lived this heritage daily for all of his almost eighty years. His knowledge of decoys and their makers, the old hunt clubs, and the stories of the hunters who have come and gone was unmatched.

Roy Willis represented generations of living history. He was a link to Core Sound's past and a vital part of the future through his work with young people and with visitors of all ages, and through his commitment to recording the stories he heard throughout his life.

tween function and art with his interpretation of ducks and shorebirds. His worked ranged from no-nonsense, functional decoys to more artistic mahogany carvings of fish and shorebirds. Recipient of the North Carolina Folk Heritage Award, he and his lifetime friend Julian Hamilton Jr. brought decoy carving to the highest ranks of the state's traditional arts. Homer Fulcher became one of the first in the region to teach classes in carving. He and fellow carver Alvin Harris of Atlantic taught the first carving classes at Sailors Snug Harbor in Sea Level, sharing the craft with retired merchant mariners. His efforts inspired the training that is offered today, ensuring a "next generation" of decoy artisans.

*Fresh jumping mullets and hardy collard greens are why you have never
seen a hungry Core Sounder. — Sonny Williamson, Sea Level*

Just northeast of Stacy is a high-rise bridge over Salter's Creek, leading to
the junction of US 70, which turns east and winds through Sea Level and
Atlantic, and NC 12, which continues straight to Cedar Island. Those who
choose to explore the fishing communities of Sea Level and Atlantic still
have a route to Cedar Island and the ferry landing by way of Old Cedar
Island Road at the north end of Atlantic.

Sea Level lives up to its name, having one of the lowest elevations Down
East. The community was once called Wit, and during colonial times the
whole region from Sea Level to Cedar Island was called Hunting Quarters,
a name derived from the Coree Indians.

Sea Level, like other Down East communities, has struggled to maintain its seafood industry amidst countless changes in regulations, ecology,
and perceptions. Resident Helen Beacham recalled when her grandfather
sold terrapin turtles to Tilman Taylor's fish house, where they'd then get
shipped to New York as a restaurant delicacy. "I remember hearing those
things scratch the bottom of that skiff. . . . I didn't dare put my feet down,"
she laughed.

Jimmy Morris, owner and operator of a clam hatchery in Sea Level
called Millpoint Aquaculture, has adapted to shifting winds, in terms of
both the market and the climate. His facility is located on Core Sound,
directly across from Core Banks. The protective dunes directly across the
sound on Core Banks were leveled by Hurricane Isabel, making his equipment especially vulnerable to ocean overwash that came across the land
during Hurricane Irene.

"Shellfish mariculture has its challenges," he wrote, "especially when
hurricanes flatten your hatchery and nursery." His shoreside hatchery, tanks
now held aloft on large beams, looks like something out of the movie *Water-
world*. Morris, considered an innovator in his field, keeps finding ways to
persevere. He embodies the term "climate resilient."

Despite its location "way Down East" at the edge of Core Sound, Sea
Level has a business center. Sea Level is the only community Down East
with a bank. An extended-care facility with a pharmacy and clinic operates
across the street from the bank and fire department, and a retirement home
serves the needs of the region's elderly.

## SEA LEVEL HOSPITAL

Sea Level Hospital was the first and only hospital ever built Down East. Brothers Alfred, Leslie, William, and Daniel Taylor, who grew up working at their family's fish house and oyster canning plant, ran sailing sharpies and freight boats to mainland port towns. They had the drive and the business sense to expand, eventually developing a regional enterprise and then an international firm. Their West India Fruit and Steamship Company, established in 1934, shipped bananas and other cargo from the West Indies to Norfolk and New Orleans.

"Did you know it was possible to take a train to Cuba?" asked Tom Mann of Marshallberg. He explained that the Taylor brothers' shipping line included a railroad system that involved offloading train cars in South Florida onto a barge destined for Cuba. In Cuba they were loaded back onto a train to pick up bananas, sugar, and other products from plantations. The Taylor brothers bought and ran the Palm Beach Biltmore, a mark of their grand success.

Wanting the best in medical care for their parents and neighbors in isolated Down East, the Taylor brothers built a state-of-the-art medical facility in the remote fishing village of Sea Level in 1953. Doctors and nurses were recruited, and the reputation of Sea Level Hospital spread far and wide. The facility included a school of nursing that laid the groundwork for families of health care workers. The brothers built the Sea Level Inn and restaurant next door to serve families with loved ones in the hospital. The hospital was donated to Duke University in 1969, and in the 1960s and 1970s the facility transitioned to an extended care and nursing home facility. It is now run by a private corporation.

## ATLANTIC

*People speak a brogue in which the words flow out as melodious as any song ever written.* —*Eddie Hill, Atlantic native*

The main corridor of Carteret County's section of the Outer Banks Byway is US Highway 70. One of the first cross-country routes in the United States, Highway 70 stretches 2,300 miles, from Arizona to the Down East community of Atlantic. Accustomed to jokes about being the "ends of the earth," Atlantic folks like to say, "No, we're the beginning!"

Atlantic is a beautiful oak-shaded community. Old homes, winding lanes, and a working harbor give this Core Sound village a sense of timelessness and tradition. Though Atlantic was once a thriving fishing community, its economic pace has slowed considerably in recent years. The welcome sign still proclaims, "Living from the Sea," a reminder of the community's core identity.

Atlantic was Down East's only incorporated town in the early 1900s. Education was important to the villagers, so in 1905 Atlantic's 500 residents voted to tax themselves to fund the construction of a public high school. It was the first high school in Carteret County. Atlantic High School was chosen to be a teacher training course center for the region as well, contributing to the fact that high numbers of teachers have emerged from Down East communities. Before the course was discontinued during the Depression, many completed the requirements and filled teaching jobs across Carteret County and inland.

Larry Earley, a photographer who took an interest in workboats built by Atlantic's Ambrose Fulcher, said, "If there's a beating heart to this changing community, it throbs at Atlantic Harbor, where the white fishing boats are tied up in a long row." John "Buster" Salter, fisherman and ferryman, agrees. "That's what we've done all our lives here," Salter emphasized. "Our fathers and grandfathers and their fathers before them."

Two of the largest seafood operations along the Eastern Seaboard were based in Atlantic, providing incomes for hundreds: Clayton Fulcher Seafood Company and Luther Smith and Son Seafood. One family empire was mainly Democrat, the other Republican; one Methodist, the other Baptist. Despite those differences, both exerted influence in the industry that stretched clear to New England and in the political world from Raleigh to Washington, D.C.

Clayton Fulcher Seafood was established in the 1920s and grew with satellite fish docks in Cedar Island and Harkers Island. It once ran an oyster canning operation and for generations bought fish from the "long haul" crews that worked Core and Pamlico Sounds. The family-run operation included a large ice-making facility and freezer. Before closing in 2007, it was run by Clayton Fulcher's grandsons. Although the company closed its doors, its "cousin" company, Garland Fulcher Seafood of Oriental, North Carolina, continues to serve as a seafood hub.

Luther Smith and Sons Seafood was established by Billy Smith, called a "towering figure in North Carolina's commercial fishing industry" by a reporter. He had tremendous political clout in the region and served on many

Atlantic harbor, generations of hard work, beautiful boats, and "living by the sea."
(Photo by Susan M. Mason)

boards and commissions, always a tireless advocate for the commercial fishing industry. His wife, Janice, was "a spitfire of a woman" who seemed to take care of—or keep up with—at least half the population of Down East. She was instrumental in making the North Carolina Seafood Festival's Blessing of the Fleet the deeply moving event it is today.

Atlantic appeals to retirees, newcomers seeking a quiet refuge, and visitors attracted to the kayaking, fishing, and bird-watching opportunities along the shore. A recently installed "Welcome to Atlantic" sign indicates the pride Atlantic residents have in their village. Neat yards, commercial fishing boats, and shady oaks give Atlantic a weather-worn charm. Some of the sons and daughters of fishermen and storekeepers who moved away have retired back in Atlantic; a few joined in with long-term residents to form a beautification club dedicated to keeping the community the lovely place it has always been.

Elmo Gaskill, native son and retired principal, spearheaded efforts to save the old Hunting Quarters Primitive Baptist Church, founded in Sea Level in 1829 and moved to Atlantic after the Civil War. When the last member of the congregation passed away in 1998, the modest church building began showing signs of neglect. Gaskill recalled attending the church as a child with his grandfather, who had been a deacon for sixty-five years. "Those were long sessions sitting and listening to all those Primitive Baptist preachers," he said. He formed the Friends of Hunting Quarters Primitive Baptist Church in 2006 and quickly raised $10,000 for a new roof, paint, and other improvements, such as repairing the picket fence used to keep live-stock out of the churchyard. Located at 146 Shell Road, the church is open during select hours to visitors.

A true living heritage can be found at Harris Net Shop, located at 141 Old Cedar Island Road in Atlantic. Started in 1970 by Roger Harris, the net-building business is now run by Harris's daughter Heidi Roberts. She manages two full-time jobs, sewing fishing nets and working for the North Carolina ferry service. If you are lucky enough to catch her at the net shop, Heidi will tell you about her family's business. Interviewed by Atlantic-born artist and photographer Susan Mason, Heidi explained that her nets go to far-flung ports in places such as Alaska, Massachusetts, and Florida. Her father helped refine turtle excluder device placement, the round grid required by the federal government to minimize shrimper and sea turtle interactions, in shrimp nets. You can hear Heidi talking about how "making a net is like making a dress" at www.carolinacoastalvoices.com.

People still talk about a hub of economic and social activity at the waterfront store called Winston Hill and Sons (1930s–80s). The general store carried everything from hoop cheese to Sunday suits, sour pickles, and push grass-cutters. Owned by brothers Winston and Roderick Hill, the store ensured that whatever the people of Atlantic needed, they had. Whether packing out boats on Sunday afternoon for a week's fishing or ordering hams for Christmas, the old store was part of every family's daily life.

Elmo Gaskill recalled Sunday nights at Winston Hill's as fishermen gathered to decide who "got what fishing grounds for their upcoming week of long hauling." On Sunday evening, the captains would meet and put the names of hauls, such as Royal Shoal and Barry's Bay, in a hat. The fishermen would draw the name of the area they'd fish that trip. "If you didn't set your nets by eight o'clock or so," Gaskill explained, "then anybody could come along and take that haul."

Jonathan Robinson is as comfortable in chest waders and fishing boots as he is in a suit and tie. He can begin his day in a long-haul boat before dawn and end it arguing a point of law as a member of the county board of commissioners. His Down East accent is so thick that newcomers have trouble understanding him, yet he manages to get his idea across with unsettling passion. Like the great majority of elected officials in Carteret County, he's

"I have about as much Christmas spirit as a rotten sweet potato," Janice Smith said one December while delivering a truckload of gifts throughout the community. Her husband, Billy, the most powerful "fish baron" and political heavyweight Down East has ever seen, was ill with a cold. "There's nothing sicker than a sick man," Janice said with characteristic deadpan delivery. Janice was only seventeen when she married Billy, but the two soon grew their business, Luther Smith and Son Seafood (started by Billy's father), into an empire.

"More than anything else," Janice told journalist Susan West, "crab potting really got us on our feet." The couple hired Marvin Robinson to build their first wooden trawler in 1960, the *Myron Ann*, named after their daughter. By the 1980s they were building steel trawlers, their fleet named after family members. The Smiths helped establish the North Carolina Fisheries Association, now in its sixty-fourth year. Their combined commitment to

Billy and Janice Smith stand in front of their trawler, *William H. Smith*. Built by Tinker Wallace of South River, it was one of the last built in the Luther Smith and Son fleet, ca. 1980s. (Photo from the Janice Smith Collection, Core Sound Waterfowl Museum and Heritage Center)

the fishing industry and the men and women of Down East continues today in their legacy of hard work and unselfish giving of their children and grandchildren, who are actively involved in the fisheries and community efforts. Janice took the helm of Billy's leadership in the community after his untimely death in 1996. Fishing was not only their livelihood, but their lives.

Billy and Janice were both leaders, givers, and caretakers, and the Core Sound communities of Down East knew that best. Their political connections were a vital part of keeping Down East "on the map" and keeping fishermen on the water. From the National Republican Conventions in Dallas and New Orleans to the inaugural ceremonies in Washington, D.C., to Senator Jesse Helms's inner circle and to Raleigh during the Jim Martin and Jim Holshouser administrations, Janice and Billy made sure that commercial fishing issues in North Carolina were not overlooked.

Their legacy to the waterfowl history and commercial fishing culture of Down East is honored at the Core Sound Waterfowl Museum and Heritage Center, which they helped found in the 1990s. The museum is a testament to community leadership and hard work. Billy Smith's vision and Janice Smith's touches are everywhere: the beautiful room dedicated to Billy, the stained glass artwork over the entryway dedicated to Janice's mother, the endless cooking and sharing of Down East food traditions, all of it gifts from the Smith Family.

a Republican, but his concerns for the working class have garnered him the "Rino" appellation, "Republican in Name Only." He knows the water, loves his community, and is a tireless advocate for carrying on the maritime trades of his people.

"My father built my boat the *Down East*," Robinson said proudly. The *Down East* is a traditional Core Sound–style wooden vessel. Father and son worked together on the boat, but Jonathan is quick to defer to the skills of his father, who had a long career building and fishing menhaden vessels. "That is an artisan and a craft. There's nothing built on the square so it takes some time and effort to learn the shipwright's skills." When asked why he named the boat *Down East*, he responded, "I named my boat out of my love."

Robinson, having a foot in the different worlds of local government and commercial fishing, makes an interesting observation about fishing. "I think there's a camaraderie in the fisheries that doesn't exist in some industries," he declared. "I've seen a lot of people throw down a day's work to give somebody a hand working on an engine or a net or towing somebody back in—I don't think they do that on Wall Street."

Atlantic is a jumping-off point to north Core Banks and Portsmouth Island. The small vehicle ferries *Donza Lee* and the *Green Grass* transport adventurers from Morris Marina, located at 1000 Morris Marina Road. The hour-long ride across Core Sound carries fishermen and vacationers to Long Point Cabins on Portsmouth Island, managed by the National Park Service. The cabins are rustic, equipped with bunk beds, kitchen table and chairs, cookstove, and bathroom. The cabins, like the ferry service, must be reserved in advance at www.recreation.gov. A small bar and grill operates out of Morris Marina as well.

"After several days of bugs, sunburns, and saltwater," wrote one visitor in an online review of the Morris Marina, "having your food order taken on the ferry ride home is a Godsend—all year I dream of that hard-earned shrimp burger awaiting me."

## CEDAR ISLAND

*I was born and raised on a sailboat, and that's the most beautiful going in all the world, is onto a sailboat. —Worth Harris, Cedar Island*

The trip to Cedar Island is marked by crossing the Monroe Gaskill Bridge, a high-rise that crosses "the Thoroughfare" canal. From the top of the bridge, travelers are treated to a spectacular view of the 14,000-acre Cedar Island National Wildlife Refuge stretching in every direction.

The Cedar Island National Wildlife Refuge was created in 1964 to protect habitat for a rare, mouse-sized bird known as the black rail. "Cedar Island has the largest concentration of black rail on the planet," refuge employee Kevin Keeler emphasized. The refuge's headquarters is located at 879 Lola Road, which turns off Highway 12 just inside the village boundaries. The modest visitor center provides information about the wildlife in the area, from diving ducks to otters and black bears. Primitive hiking opportunities abound, but exploring the wilds is best during the cold-weather months, when mosquitoes are at a minimum. On the way to the refuge office on Lola Road is the Pilgrims Rest Original Freewill Baptist Church, with a graveyard containing rare cedar markers in lieu of headstones.

Hog Island, located just northeast of Cedar Island, was once a small community known as Lupton, made up of about 200 people. Lupton had a school, a church, and a post office. Writer Bland Simpson describes the

Beautiful, pristine Cedar Island marsh, looking east toward Core Sound.
(Photo by Lillie Miller)

tragedy of the last postmistress of Hog Island in his book *The Inner Islands*. The young woman poisoned herself and her children when her cash drawer came up short. The post office closed shortly thereafter in 1920, and the community was eventually abandoned by the early 1930s. Many Hog Islanders simply moved to Cedar Island. Hog Island was home to a hunting club, still standing today. Nearby, Cedar Island's Harbor Island Hunt Club, built of seashells, sand, and mortar, is a mere relic of its former self, washing away in Cedar Island Bay.

Cedar Island, the northernmost village before travelers take the ferry to Ocracoke, is probably Down East's most viable fishing community. People are often seen mending fishing nets or cleaning crab pots in the yard. Some drive around in their funky "boom" trucks, which are salt-rusted pickups with a boom and wench welded onto the bed for lifting nets. People might gather at the community harbor to watch the latest boat unload its catch. Cedar Island fishermen have easy access to both Core Sound and the deeper Pamlico Sound, which contributes to their relative success.

Cedar Island was once made up of two distinct communities: Lola and Roe. Lola was located down Lola Road, where the wildlife refuge office is located. Roe was the village proper, on the main road going toward the ferry terminal. Locals still refer to Lola and Roe. In fact, white oval bumper stickers have appeared that proudly bear the old community names. Resi-

*Crossing North River*

Mid-twentieth-century Cedar Island Road, lined with workboats. (Photo courtesy of the State Archives of North Carolina)

dents eventually joined as Cedar Island, named so when a new post office came in the 1950s.

People are comfortable with the distance between themselves and the busier towns to the west. Some find gainful employment at the Cedar Island–Ocracoke ferry terminal, as ferry captains, crew members, or shore personnel. When off shift, however, many are quick to return to their oilskins and resume commercial fishing or net making. Others make a long daily trek to Beaufort, Morehead City, or even Cherry Point for work.

Two fish houses operate on the island today, Bradley Styron's Quality Seafood at 2890 Cedar Island Road and Big A and Little A's fish house, 2714 Cedar Island Road. Both fish houses are interesting stops for anyone who wants to know what fish are in season or the latest news in fish politics. Bradley was a longtime member of the state Marine Fisheries Commission

We grew up being taught they started the first colony on the shores of Roanoke Island in the late 1500s. I recently came across folks who are certain the 115 colonists from Sir Walter Raleigh's expedition were actually setting up housekeeping on Cedar Island, located in the northeast corner of Carteret County, N.C. My wife and I drove to Cedar Island when we were visiting the area several years ago, just to see the coastal highway.

I had no idea there was a 400-year-old controversy brewing there at the time. One of my distant cousins, who follows this blog, sent me an email about the story awhile back and I decided to look into it. Jean Day wrote a book called *Cedar Island Fisher Folk* in 1994 that tells the Lost Colony story that had been passed down in her family for generations.

In fact there have been scholarly reports that proposed the Lost Colony settlement location was really on Cedar Island going back to at least the 1940s. They based this on the journals that survived, measurements and descriptions of the island, the physical layout of the North Carolina Coast, and the currents and tidal action around Roanoke Island that would have not allowed the English ships to get close to it but match Cedar Island perfectly. There is also a Spanish explorer's report from 1606 about finding white men in the Cedar Island area.

So how do white settlers stay in an area so close to the later expeditions and remain hidden from view? The local account is they decided to live with the Indians, taking Indian wives and enjoying the land they had found. That is after all what their original purpose was in crossing the Ocean. They raised their families, planted crops, fished, and lived out their life, happy to be in a good place. If you want to read all the technical arguments, pick up Day's book or find a copy of *Riddle of the Lost Colony* by Melvin Robinson or read the many newspaper articles about the Cedar Island connection using Google news. There is also a recent news flash about an old map supposedly with invisible ink showing the secret location of the Lost Colony, not at Roanoke Island.

For me the interesting part is the strong belief that has carried down over the centuries from those who live on Cedar Island. They have documentation of place names and deeds going back to the 1700s in the names of Berry, Smith, and others who were part of the colony, and the same names are found there today. Many of these are related to my family via multiple marriage connections. That is what happens when they stay in the same place for centuries.

But for the folks who live on Cedar Island today, there is no question where their ancestors came from. They've always known they were from the Lost Colony settlement! They tell you, their folks were never lost, they always knew where they were, it was the English explorers and financiers back home who were lost.

Source: Mark Green, "Southern Greens," May 12, 2012 (online blog)

Big A (*with pole*) and Little A (*foreground*) Styron, still fishing the old way, setting pound nets, Cedar Island.

and is extremely knowledgeable about fisheries issues. Aron Styron (Big A) and his son (Little A) are passionate about fishing and clearly prefer the world of water to the land of regulations and paperwork.

Big A and Little A are among a handful of fishermen pioneering new marketing techniques. Flounder caught in their pound nets are transferred to holding ponds and sold to Asian buyers who arrive with trucks outfitted to keep the fish alive for market. Aron Styron and crew participate in Walking

Playing at the water's edge, Cedar Island beach. (Photo by Susan M. Mason)

Fish, a community-supported fishery based in Beaufort that sells "shares" of local seafood in advance to clients, helping consumers learn where and how—and by whom—their seafood is caught. Cedar Island fishermen are a lively and opinionated bunch, and they manage to keep a keen sense of humor despite all the challenges they face.

At the end of the road on the north end of Cedar Island is the North Carolina Cedar-Island-to-Ocracoke ferry terminal. The visitor center at the terminal provides the only public restrooms Down East, which is one reason it is a popular stop! Check the website for up-to-date schedules and prices (www.ncdot.gov/ferry/). Expect about a two-hour-and-fifteen-minute crossing on the vast and lovely Pamlico Sound. Reservations are highly recommended (1-800-by-ferry; 1-800-293-3779), especially between Easter and Labor Day.

While waiting for the ferry, check out the horses and cattle on the east side of the terminal, remnants of Cedar Island's "pony penning" past. A popular campground operates next to the ferry terminal as well. If the winds are right, the eastern beach where the livestock roam becomes a hotspot for kiteboarders, who ski the shallows, jump a wave, and soar several feet into the air.

Cedar Island beach, a white sandy strip of paradise on the west side of the ferry landing, is definitely worth the trip whether you are ferry-bound or not. It is the perfect place to relax at the water's edge and take in the beauty of Pamlico Sound.

*Crossing North River*

# Taking It Home

"Something you don't depend on," reflected Gene Ballance of Ocracoke, "you can't be as interested in taking care of it." The soft-spoken fisherman was talking about fisheries resources. If we aren't dependent on our oyster reefs, for example, we are less likely to invest in good water quality. But this same logic could be applied to the likes of him and other resource-dependent people. If we are less dependent on our food producers, are we not decreasing our support for them and their role in society?

People of the water have an enduring relationship with the sea, and if their connection to the environment gets severed, so does ours.

Mother Nature can't put into words what the sea has given us or taught us, or how it has shaped the worldview of those working, playing, and praying at its edges. But the people who have lived this "life of salt and scales" can give voice to such matters. They have seen many things wash up, wash out, and disappear altogether.

We hope that you, the reader, gain insight into "living on the edge" and take home with you a renewed respect for this place and the people—their resilience, their ingenuity, their determination, and most of all, their deep ties to this place that has shaped them for generations. And still does.

This guide is a beginning, designed to whet your desire to explore and spark your curiosity to know more. May you visit with the folks of Down East, Ocracoke, and Hatteras Island and swap tales along the way. There is much to be learned from one another.

The road at the water's edge is a two-way path. Caring about people and places helps sustain them and helps protect the sacred places we all love.

I have learned many things in the process of helping put this book together . . . people (past and present) whose names I had never known, places I had never been, dates and events I did not know. I have lived here forever and I am overwhelmed; this truly is an amazing place!

The great writer Wallace Stegner must have thought about our kind of people when he wrote, and I paraphrase, "Tell me where you're from and I'll tell you who you are." There is nowhere on the planet where this truth is more evident. This book only reaffirms what he knew then and we know now, and it is absolute proof that he was right, as we realize more and more the value of this sacred gift of inheritance.

The process of putting this guide together has been a deeply personal experience. For me, this is my dissertation, a glimpse of all that I have learned over the past twenty-five years of documenting the stories of my people and helping create a safe place where these traditions can be protected and shared. This is also my thesis defense, the reasons for my daily struggle to protect and defend my community of communities, my badge of courage, my sermon on the mount, my battle song. Josiah Bailey once told me, "Your writing means something if it makes YOU cry," so maybe it is right, because I have cried all along the way.

I have tried with all my heart, but I really cannot tell you what it means to have been here forever. Even before I was born, I believe I was here. With my roots deep below the water table, I was here. . . . Here with William Henry when he bought that sixty acres on Harkers Island, with Devine when he built the whaling boats on Shackleford, with Blind Joe, sailing across Back Sound to Wade's Shore, where he clammed for my daddy's supper. I was here on Harkers Island with Uncle Mac when they turned on the lights in 1939, a power grid that he engineered on notebook paper with only a high school education, and I can feel how proud he was (without saying a word) of the R-E-A, as it was known and loved on Harkers Island. This was Harkers Island's first step into the new world.

I was here when Granny picked crabmeat at the end of the road on Marshallberg and then walked home at the end of the day. As tired as she was, she salvaged the bent nails from the day's work and "beat them straight" so Uncle Curt could finish rebuilding this house after World War II when there was no money. It was her grandmother's house and is now my house. I can see Granny and Granddaddy standing on this same front porch that Christmas Eve Sunday morning when Uncle Wilbur got on the bus to go to war. In the war years that followed, she shared the pain and longing as she watched Miss Annie walk by every day to the post office, looking for that letter from her son in that same war, hoping for word from him that seldom came. "No letter today," she said as she waved and hanged her head. I was here.

I can see it in my heart, I don't know how, but I feel their struggle, and I hope that somehow I have given their strength and determination its rightful honor in my writing here as I continue *tending totems on my sacred ground.*

So with that, I apologize to all who will struggle through my pieces of this book because I am not really a writer. As much as I would like to be, I'm not. I'm a rambler, a defender, a preacher of sorts, carrying the message of why these sandbanks, with all their untouched beauty, overwhelming challenges, rich history, and our deepest fears and highest hopes — this *place* and these *people* — are so vital to those of us born here.

Most of all, as the pages of this book come together, I am more thankful than ever before, more indebted and grateful to my forebears for a heritage that cannot be bought or sold, a deep and lasting kinship to this place — the swaying marshes and those steadfast oaks, the hard, cold northeast winds that I love, those proud trawlers in the sunset. And the people, the men and women, past and present, stubborn, determined, talented, and giving, who will always define who I am, who we are, who we will be.

No matter what change comes or how these rising seas and shifting sands redefine this place, know this: We will hold on — to this place and one another — just like it has always been. And for that, I am even more blessed, and hopeful, for the place I leave my children, and theirs. It is a gift beyond words that cannot be measured, only felt, deep down inside ... when the roe mullets run and the geese honk off east'ard beach, and the wind blows. ...

# Readings, Sources, and Resources

## PUBLISHED WORKS

There are many great writings on the maritime history and culture of coastal North Carolina. Our work is especially informed, directly or indirectly, by the following books and authors.

David Stick's *The Outer Banks of North Carolina, 1584–1958* (University of North Carolina Press, 1958) is a benchmark history of maritime North Carolina. His *Graveyard of the Atlantic: Shipwrecks of the North Carolina Coast* (University of North Carolina Press, 1952) offers an in-depth look at shipwrecks. His 1998 anthology of writings in *An Outer Banks Reader* is equally outstanding (University of North Carolina Press).

Barbara Garrity-Blake's report *Ethnohistorical Description of the Eight Villages Adjoining Cape Hatteras National Seashore and Interpretive Themes of History and Heritage* informed this work (Impact Assessment Inc., U.S. Department of the Interior, 2005). Much of what she's learned about fisheries and fishing communities is found in her works *Fish House Opera*, with Susan West (Mystic Seaport Press, 2003), and *The Fish Factory* (University of Tennessee Press, 1994).

Karen Willis Amspacher and Joel Hancock edited *The Mailboat* journal, which informed our writing on Down East. Karen also edited the popular *Island Born and Bred: A Collection of Harkers Island Food, Fun, Fact, and Fiction* (Harkers Island United Methodist Women, Owen Dunn Co., 1987) and *Our Shared Past: Diamond City & Ca'e Bankers Reunion* (Core Sound Waterfowl Museum, 1999). Like *The Mailboat*, we relied on the local history and folklore essays of Cape Hatteras School's journal the *Sea Chest* (Buxton, 1973–85).

Cameron Binkley's study, *The Creation and Establishment of Cape Hatteras National Seashore* (National Park Service, 2007), is a thorough and fascinating history of how our nation's first seashore came to be. A fine companion to this is the report *Gateway to the Atlantic World: Cape Lookout National Seashore Historic Resource Study* (U.S. Department of the Interior, 2015), by David E. Whisnant and Ann Mitchell Whisnant.

David Cecelski has greatly deepened our understanding of African American history in maritime North Carolina. *The Waterman's Song: Slavery and Freedom in Maritime North Carolina* (University of North Carolina Press, 2001) is our go-to resource. Cecelski has researched the Davis Ridge African American Community in *A Historian's Coast: Adventures into the Tidewater Past* (John F. Blair, 2000); in the same volume he writes of the Hatteras porpoise fishery, midwifery, and other topics.

Bland Simpson is prolific in his University of North Carolina Press writings about the coast. His beloved hometown of Elizabeth City anchors the journey of *Into the Sound Country: A Carolinian's Coastal Plain* (1997). He collaborated with photographer Scott Taylor in *The Coasts of Carolina: Seaside to Sound Country* (2010) and with his wife, Ann Cary Simpson, who grew up in the Down East community of Sea Level, on several works, including *Little Rivers and Waterway Tales: A Carolinian's Eastern Streams* (2015). He has written about every inch of marsh and river and brought to life gripping stories, such as the mystery of the *Carroll A. Deering* in *Ghost Ship of Diamond Shoals* (2005) and the tragic life of a Hog Island postmistress depicted in *The Inner Islands: A Carolinian's Sound Country Chronicle* (2006).

Carmine Prioli, folklore professor at the University of North Carolina, has documented the saga of the Shackleford horses in his John F. Blair publication, *The Wild Horses of Shackleford Banks*, with Scott Taylor (2007). He and Candy Beal edited the Coastal Carolina Press book *Life at the Edge of the Sea* (2002), helping our understanding of coastal geology, ecology, and other topics. His Down Home Press publication, *Hope for a Good Season*, with Edwin Martin (1998) has become a timeless and treasured portrait of the fishermen of Harkers Island.

The writings of two schoolteachers will remain an important voice in the history of the Outer Banks. Nell Wise Wechter, from Stumpy Point, North Carolina, wrote the timeless classics *Taffy of Torpedo Junction* (University of North Carolina Press, 1996) and *The Mighty Midgetts of Chicamacomico* (Times Printing Company, 1974). Stanley E. Green wrote the delightful *Kinnakeet Adventure* (Vantage Press, 1971).

Down East and the southern banks are described in Bob Simpson's classic *When the Water Smokes* (Algonquin Books, 1990). Larry Earley's *The Workboats of Core Sound: Stories and Photographs of a Changing World* (University of North Carolina Press, 2013) describes the long-haul fishery of Down East. Local author Jean Day wrote *Cedar Island Fisher Folk* (Golden Age Press, 1994) and Melvin Robinson argued his case for Cedar Island in *Riddle of the Lost Colony* (Literary Licensing, 2013).

Marcus B. Simpson and Sallie W. Simpson wrote a detailed history of the Shackleford Banks whale fishery, *Whaling on the North Carolina Coast* (North Carolina Division of Archives, 1990). Marshallberg's own Sonny Williamson was a prolific writer of local history and tales, including his Grandma Publications *Sailing with Grandpa* (1987), *Unsung Heroes of the Surf* (1992), and *Jumpin' Mullets and Collard Greens* (1989). We miss him every day.

*Strengthened by the Storm* (Campbell and Campbell, 1998) is written by Harkers Island's native son Joel Hancock. He shares a fascinating account of life on Shackleford and Harkers Island at the turn of the twentieth century, drawing on the journals of Mormon elders who came to Shackleford in the late 1890s. His online journal "The Education of an Island Boy" is also a treasure (http://jghislandstories.blogspot.com).

Our friend and educator extraordinaire Alton Ballance wrote the classic *Ocracokers* (University of North Carolina Press, 1989), which enlightens us about the fishermen and everyday life of Ocracoke. Carl Goerch, a huge promoter of all things North Carolina and founder of *Our State* magazine, is author of the charming book *Ocracoke* (John F. Blair, 1956). Linguists Walt Wolfram and Natalie Schilling-Estes authored *Hoi Toide on the Outer Banks: The Story of the Ocracoke Brogue* (University of North Carolina Press, 1997).

Philip Howard's *Ocracoke Newsletter* gave us a gripping account of a shipwreck and countless other historical and cultural tidbits. Newsletters and Howard's daily journal can be accessed at the Village Craftsmen website, www.villagecraftsmen.com. Islander Jenny Scarborough wrote the historically informative *Ocracoke Walking Tour and Guide Book* (Narayana, 2009).

Several community histories have been recorded by Ocracoke native Ellen Cloud, including *Ocracoke Lighthouse* (Live Oak Publications, 1993), *Ocracoke Speaks* (Ocracoke Preservation Society, 1999), and *Portsmouth: The Way It Was* (Heritage Books, 2011). Dot Salter Willis and Ben Willis wrote *Portsmouth Island: Short Stories and History*, edited by Frances Eubanks and Lynn Salsi (Montville Publications, 2004).

Hatteras Island writings helped us understand important details unique to the region, including Jan DeBlieu's classic *Hatteras Journal* (John F. Blair, 1998). Tom Carlson fleshed out the iconic story of the *Albatross* fleet in *Hatteras Blues: A Story from the Edge of America* (University of North Carolina Press, 2010). Lynne Foster and Linda Nunn edited *A Hatteras Anthology* (Outer Banks Press, 2003), a wonderful collection of local writings. Writer Elizabeth Weigand explores traditional recipes and locally sourced food in *The Outer Banks Cookbook: Recipes and Traditions from North Carolina's Barrier Islands* (Rowman & Littlefield, 2013).

For a coastwide perspective, Roger Payne's *Place Names of the Outer Banks* (Thomas Williams, 1985) is an invaluable resource, as is Jay Barnes's *North Carolina's Hurricane History* (University of North Carolina Press, 2001). For an understanding of the dynamic geological and environmental processes of North Carolina's coast, we recommend the University of North Carolina Press works by Orrin Pilkey et al., *How to Read a North Carolina Beach: Bubble Holes, Barking Sands, and Rippled Runnels* (2004), and Stanley Riggs et al., *The Battle for North Carolina's Coast: Evolutionary History, Present Crisis, and Vision for the Future* (2011). For an overview of the history of boatbuilding in North Carolina, the Conoley family's *Carolina Flare* is a great resource (Carolina Flare, 2007). Doug Stover, retired cultural resources manager for the park service, has published a book full of photos of the region in *Outer Banks Scenic Byway* (Arcadia Press, 2016).

For those who want to drink from the source, *Lawson's History of North Carolina* (Garrett and Massie, 1952), by British explorer John Lawson, is indispensable, as is *A New Voyage to Carolina* (2010). Both books chronicle his observations and experiences in North Carolina in the early 1700s before he was killed by the Tuscarora in 1711.

## ONLINE RESOURCES

### Travel Information

*Cape Hatteras National Seashore*
www.nps.gov/caha

*Cape Lookout National Seashore*
www.nps.gov/calo

*Carteret County Visitor Center*
www.crystalcoastnc.org

*National Weather Service*
www.weather.gov

*North Carolina Ferry Service*
www.ncdot.gov/ferry

*Ocracoke Civic and Business Association*
www.ocracokevillage.com

*Outer Banks Heritage Trails*
www.outerbankstrails.org

*Outer Banks National Scenic Byway*
www.outerbanksbyway.org

*Outer Banks Visitor Center*
www.outerbanks.org

## Organizations and Partners

*Coastal Voices Oral Histories*
  www.carolinacoastalvoices.org
*Core Sound Decoy Carvers Guild*
  www.decoyguild.com
*Core Sound Waterfowl Museum*
*and Heritage Center*
  www.coresound.com
*Day at the Docks Festival on Hatteras*
  www.dayatthedocks.org
*Down East Community Online Tour*
  www.downeasttour.com
*Friends of Portsmouth Island*
  www.friendsofportsmouthisland.org
*Graveyard of the Atlantic Museum*
  www.graveyardoftheatlantic.com
*Hatteras Village Online Tour*
  www.hatterasonmymind.com
*NC Catch Local Seafood*
  www.nccatch.org

*North Carolina Coastal Federation*
  www.nccoast.org
*North Carolina Maritime Museum*
  www.ncmaritimemuseums.com
  /beaufort
*North Carolina Sea Grant College Program*
  www.ncseagrant.org
*Ocracoke Alive*
  www.ocracokealive.org
*Ocracoke Foundation*
  www.ocracokefoundation.org
*Outer Banks History Center*
  www.archives.ncdcr.gov/Public
  /Outer-Banks-History-Center
*Outer Banks Lighthouse Society*
  www.outerbankslighthousesociety.org
*Saltwater Connections*
  www.saltwaterconnections.org

## Community News

*Down East Community News*
  www.downeastcommunitynews.org
*Island Free Press*
  www.islandfreepress.org
*Ocracoke Current*
  www.ocracokecurrent.com

# Acknowledgments

We extend our sincere appreciation to the many people who helped us develop this heritage guide. First and foremost, we thank UNC Press's former editor David Perry for his invitation to embark upon this project years ago, and current editor Mark Simpson-Vos for his perseverance in seeing it through. Our heartfelt appreciation goes to Carmine Prioli and Bland Simpson, who reviewed our initial manuscript. Their thoughtful suggestions and understanding of our communities helped guide this work. We extend a personal thank you to authors David Cecelski and Alton Ballance for their faith and encouragement.

Connie Mason, Lauren Salter, and Jennifer Allen helped edit drafts of this work when we needed fresh eyes. Susan West, Alton Ballance, and Jonathan Robinson took time to write welcome messages for their regions. The staff at the Core Sound Waterfowl Museum and Heritage Center, particularly Pam Morris, helped in countless ways. The folks at the North Carolina Office of Archives and History, Outer Banks History Center, the University of North Carolina libraries, and Ocracoke Preservation Society were always helpful, as were the many local photographers, writers, and researchers who shared their work. We appreciate those who contributed family pictures and community memories. This publication has been a "friends and family effort" in many ways.

We'd like to recognize the vision and commitment of the Outer Banks Byway Advisory Committee members from Dare, Hyde, and Carteret Counties. Their years of hard work have been significant. Their commitment in attending meetings up and down the byway in all kinds of weather gives new meaning to the cultural connections between Outer Banks communities.

A portion of the research for this book was undertaken as part of two reports for the National Park Service that Barbara took part in: *Ethnohistorical Description of the Eight Villages Adjoining Cape Hatteras National Seashore* (Impact Assessment Inc.) and, with James Sabella, *Ethnohistorical Description of Four Communities Associated with Cape Lookout National Seashore* (University of North Carolina at Wilmington). We thank the National Park Service for assistance in these studies and continued dedication to preserving the cultural heritage and natural resources of the region.

Most of all, we thank our families for their love and patience, and our friends and neighbors of Hatteras, Ocracoke, and Down East for helping us get the story right. Through all of the research over the years by historians, researchers, and writers, it has been the willingness of the *people* of the banks communities to share their experiences that has helped us better understand this way of life, and for that, we are most grateful.

How fortunate and honored we are to call this place "home."

# Index

BARBARA GARRITY-BLAKE is a cultural anthropologist with a Ph.D. from the University of Virginia. She is author of *The Fish Factory*, a labor history of the Atlantic Coast menhaden fishmeal and oil industry, and *Fish House Opera* (with Susan West), about North Carolina fishermen. She has collected oral histories up and down the North Carolina coast and co-manages the oral history project *Coastal Voices*. She teaches marine fisheries policy at the Duke Marine Laboratory in Beaufort, introducing students to real-world fisheries issues on the docks and harbors and in fish houses along the coast. She served on the advisory board of the North Carolina Sea Grant College Program, Carteret Catch (a local seafood branding effort), and the National Working Waterfront Network. She and her husband, Bryan, live in the Down East community of Gloucester, where they organize two festivals (Gloucester Mardi Gras and Wild Caught Local Seafood and Music) and "let the good times roll" with their Cajun Zydeco band, the Unknown Tongues.

KAREN WILLIS AMSPACHER is a native of Harkers Island, where her family has been a part of the boatbuilding and fishing traditions for generations. She is a graduate of Appalachian State University and editor of several community publications, including *The Mailboat* and Harkers Island's beloved *Island Born & Bred*. As founding director of the Core Sound Waterfowl Museum and Heritage Center she has engaged community members in all facets of museum programming and has served as the community liaison for documentary projects with the Southern Oral History Collection at UNC–Chapel Hill, the NC Folklife Division of the Arts Council, Duke University's Center for Documentary Studies, and the Smithsonian. In her role as coordinator of Core Sound's regional outreach initiative, Saltwater Connections, she fosters community leadership, provides resources for community-led projects, and builds partnerships for long-term community sustainability. She raised her family in her maternal grandmother's house in Marshallberg, where she lives with her husband, Jimmy, a retired engineer who builds wooden boats and models in their backyard—the old way.